The Dell War Series

The Dell War Series takes you onto the battlefield, into the jungles, and beneath the oceans with unforgettable stories that offer a new look at the terrors and triumphs of America's war experience. Many of these books are eye-witness accounts of the duty-bound fighting man. From the intrepid foot soldiers, sailors, pilots, and commanders, to the elite warriors of the Special Forces, here are stories of men who fight because their lives depend on it.

"THE FIGURES WERE THERE:
IF YOU WERE A PILOT IN THE AIR CAV
AND YOU WERE KILLED,
YOU WERE PROBABLY A *SCOUT* PILOT."

LOW LEVEL HELL

A tremendous burst of ground fire came up on the front and left side of the aircraft. Not from just one weapon, but from AK-47s and .30- and .50-caliber machine guns.

I jerked a hard right turn and tried to dive for the treetops. Just as I turned, I caught new fire from across the valley coming up at me from twelve o'clock dead ahead. I was getting hit. I could feel the hits in the aircraft.

I instinctively pulled another hard right. Fortunately I still had forty to fifty knots of speed, but my last right turn headed us right back into another blanket of enemy fire.

I had to let go with a blast of the minigun and Farrar was still giving them hell, his 60 blazing. He was leaning out of the aircraft, down under the tail boom, and shooting 60 lead out behind us. . . .

"No volume better describes the feelings from the cockpit. Mills has captured the realities of a select group of aviators who shot craps with death on every mission. [But] this is a book for anyone, aviator or not." —R. S. Maxham, Director, U.S. Army Aviation Museum, Fort Ricker, AL

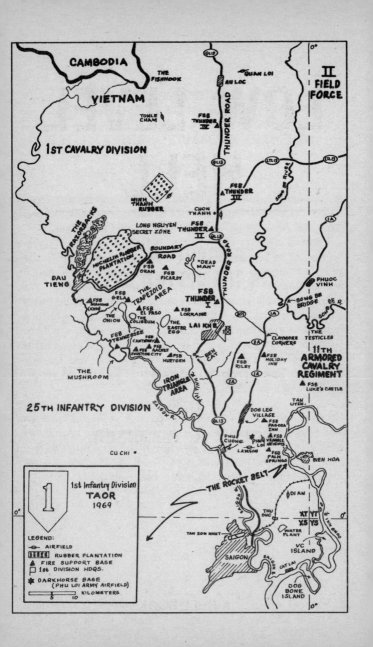

LOW LEVEL HELL

HELL

**A SCOUT PILOT
IN THE BIG RED ONE**

**Hugh L. Mills, Jr.
with
Robert A. Anderson**

A DELL BOOK

Published by
Dell Publishing
a division of
Bantam Doubleday Dell Publishing Group, Inc.
1540 Broadway
New York, New York 10036

ISBN: 0-440-21549-8

Reprinted by arrangement with Presidio Press

Printed in the United States of America

Published simultaneously in Canada

June 1993

10 9 8 7 6 5 4

OPM

This book is dedicated to the memory of the officers, non-commissioned officers, and troopers who died on the field of battle with Darkhorse in 1969. May they rest in peace.

WO1 James K. Ameigh, aeroscout pilot,
  24 June.
PFC William J. Brown, aerorifleman,
  17 November.
SGT Allen H. Caldwell, aerorifleman,
  17 November.
SP5 James L. Downing, aeroscout gunner,
  6 November.
1LT Bruce S. Gibson, aeroscout pilot,
  11 September.
SP4 August F. Hamilton, aerorifleman,
  28 July.
SP4 Eric T. Harshbarger, aerolift crew chief,
  1 November
PFC Michael H. Lawhon, aerorifleman,
  11 August.
SSG James R. Potter, aeroscout gunner,
  11 September.
SP4 James A. Slater, aeroscout gunner,
  24 June.
WO1 Henry J. Vad, aeroscout pilot,
  6 November.
SGT James R. Woods, aerorifleman,
  11 August.

CONTENTS

FOREWORD

Ever since man began to create military forces, the role of the military scout has been an extremely dangerous one. Working out in front of friendly forces, he has been exposed continually to the enemy—the first to make contact, and usually outgunned and outnumbered.

During the settlement of our country the scouts along the frontier laid their lives on the line daily. They played a major role in our development and are some of the true heroes of the times.

With the advent of the balloon in the middle of the last century, aerial reconnaissance was born. Scouts in the Civil War observed enemy activities from these lofty perches. Then came the manned airplane, and the drone airplane followed.

When the helicopter was introduced to the military inventory in the mid-twentieth century, the aeroscout technique was developed. It came into its own in the Vietnam War. Without taking anything away from the exploits of those brave men who gained fame in the early stages of our country's development, men such as Davy Crockett, Kit Carson, and Jim Bowie, the aeroscout achieved an effectiveness far superior to that of his forebears. Also, his exposure to the enemy was increased manyfold. Long hours of daily exposure to heavy ground fire, in often-marginal weather and over treacherous terrain, served to test the mettle of these brave young men.

This book is an account of one man's experiences in the Vietnam War as an aeroscout pilot. Hugh Mills is eminently qualified to write such a story. He served two tours in Vietnam as an aeroscout pilot and was instrumental in developing many of the tactics and techniques employed by the aeroscouts, as well as improving upon some of the original concepts. During that time he was shot down sixteen times, wounded three times, and earned numerous decorations for valor, including three Silver Stars, four Distinguished Flying Crosses, and three Bronze Stars with V devices. He knows whereof he speaks.

On my second tour in Vietnam it was my good fortune to be assigned as commander of the 1st Infantry Division, The Big Red One. Early on, the aeroscouts came to my attention. An extraordinary amount of enemy information being received at division headquarters came from this small unit. Naturally, I was somewhat skeptical. Compared with the volume and detail furnished by other intelligence-gathering agencies, it appeared that the aeroscouts might be overly imaginative. Accordingly, I set out to determine just who was doing what. I frequently overflew aeroscout operations and monitored their communications from my command-and-control helicopter. It was quickly evident that these hardy souls were reliable, expert, and, above all, very brave. They were furnishing the lion's share of intelligence information because they had the knowledge, the will, and the guts to go out and get it.

During the monsoon season they flew at times when even the native ducks were grounded. When they suspected enemy presence but could not observe any signs, they deliberately and routinely exposed themselves to hostile fire by dropping through "holes" in the jungle canopy to hover at ground level and look under the trees. They invited someone to shoot at them. Anyone who has heard the snap of bullets flying by his head, or has experienced the shattering sound of enemy fire slamming into the fuselage of an aircraft, can appreciate the kind of courage it takes to invite such action.

The point to be made here is that although this book may appear to be a novel with historical background, it is not. Neither is it a self-serving attempt on the part of Hugh Mills to appear as a hero. It is a factual account of a group of extraordinarily valiant young men who fought as aeroscouts in the Vietnam War. All who read it should be extremely grateful to them.

A. E. Milloy
Major General, U.S. Army, Retired

CHAPTER 1

THUNDER ROAD

South Vietnam, July 1969

"Phu Loi tower, this is Darkhorse One Six. I've got a hunter-killer team on the cav pad. North departure to Lai Khe."

"Roger, Darkhorse One Six flight of two. You're cleared to hover."

Cobra pilot Dean Sinor (Three One) and I were heading up to Thunder Road to provide aerial cover to a heavy northbound supply convoy. A scout and gun team ran ahead of convoys coming out of Lai Khe to run a low-level inspection of the entire road up to An Loc. Even though dismounted engineer and infantry swept the highway for mines every morning at first light, this stretch of road had proved highly susceptible to ambush attack.

With Sinor at altitude, I put my Loach down low and slow, to pick up anything out of place on or along the road. It was possible for the enemy to get in and plant a few mines between the time it was swept by the engineers and the arrival of the convoy. Early in the morning, once the highway had been swept by the engineers, civilian traffic was always bustling along Thunder Road—motorcycles, mopeds, carts, Cushman-type vehicles, little buses, and small trucks. But never before the U.S. Army had cleared the road for mines. It was far too dangerous.

Working about a mile ahead of the convoy, I headed straight down the highway, banked to the east, then back south to check the cleared area on the column's right flank. I cut west over the last vehicle and headed back north to check out the left side of the convoy, creating a boxlike search pattern.

On my first run back along the east side of the road, I saw evidence of recent heavy foot traffic, enough to make me feel very uneasy. I didn't see any enemy, so I headed across the tail end of the convoy to make my run back north on the west flank.

As I got about six hundred yards out ahead of the column, I picked up heavy foot trails again. There wasn't any good reason for people to have been out in the Rome-plowed area next to the highway, so I decided to follow one of the trails to see where it took me. It led to a drainage ditch that stretched for nearly a mile—right along the side of the highway! But, again, not a single person in sight.

Circling over the area, I keyed the intercom to my crew chief. "Parker, do you see anything? Something's damned screwy about this. What do you make of it?"

"Don't see anything but footprints, Lieutenant. Not a soul, sir!"

About that time I made a sharp turn over a thick clump of tall grass on the west side of the road near the drainage ditch, about ten feet from the side of the highway. Not more than four to five feet below me, I glimpsed a slight movement and something dark lying on the ground.

"Son of a bitch, Jim! Did you see that?" I hollered into the intercom.

I hauled the Loach around to hover right above the spot. Then Parker and I saw the two dark brown eyes staring up at us from a hole dug into the ground under an area of pushed-up dirt created by the Rome plow months before.

Without me saying a word, Jim Parker opened up. I winced at the explosion of the M-60 right behind my head. The enemy soldier jerked violently and slumped over in his hole.

I got on the radio to Sinor. "Three One, One Six. We got a dink. The gunner shot a dink dug into the grass up under a Rome plow mound, not more than ten feet off the west side of the highway. I think they're all over the place —up close, not in the jungle! They've dug in spider holes right on top of the convoy!"

The head of the convoy was just seconds away at this point, heading right into an ambush. Sinor immediately called the convoy commander on FM.

The minute the convoy commander got the word that the enemy was close to him, I knew he would order all convoy weapons to open up on both sides of the highway, and woe be to the Loach pilot who was out there when all that ordnance started to go off.

Three One knew it too. "Get the hell out of there, One Six," he yelled. "Get up to altitude, NOW!"

But which way can I go? I thought. No time to get any altitude. And I can't go parallel to the convoy, or I'll make myself a tailor-made flank shot for every gun—ours and theirs. So I pulled the hardest right turn I could, made a 180-degree arc, and headed back south again—right on top of the northbound convoy. I figured the safest place for a Loach at that moment was five feet off the tops of those trucks, where hot rounds would least likely be criss-crossing.

I barely made it on top of the convoy when all hell broke loose. The enemy, now fully alerted by Parker's shooting of the soldier in the spider hole, sprung its ambush. They pushed aside the overhead camouflage and rose up out of their holes, guns blazing. At point-blank range, they opened up into the convoy with everything they had: AK-47s, RPGs, grenades, SGMs. The column simultaneously let go with their machine guns, 90mm cannon firing canister rounds, and every other weapon carried on the vehicles in the convoy. It was like one giant, sustained explosion. Bullets flew everywhere. Deafening noise erupted. Smoke and flying debris engulfed the entire convoy. And there, in the midst of that sudden hell, were Parker and me flying at antenna level, straight down the back of the convoy, trying our best to stay out of the way of both enemy and friendly fire.

As the convoy charged north, we flew south, blistering along at well over one hundred knots, Parker working with his M-60 from the right side of the aircraft. His tracers were impacting on the spider holes as we ripped past, his targets not more than ten to twenty yards from his muzzle. We were so low that if someone had reached up out of a truck or tank turret, they probably could have caught our skid.

Suddenly, not more than a hundred yards to my front, a five-thousand-gallon tanker truck took a direct RPG hit, and the diesel fuel it was carrying exploded like a nuclear bomb. Sheets of flame, parts of the truck, smoke, and dust shot up, momentarily blinding me. The little OH-6 lurched violently with the shock of the explosion, as though a giant unseen fist had landed a smashing blow to the nose of the aircraft.

I jerked aft as hard as I could on the cyclic and yanked in a load of collective. The resulting g's nearly sent my buttocks through the armor plate in the bottom of my seat. I don't know how Parker was able to hang on.

As the fast-reacting Loach wrenched up over the eruption, I said silently, "God bless this helicopter!" then yelled to Sinor over UHF: "Three One, One Six. I'm coming up to altitude. We're OK, but that was close! You're cleared in. I'm out of the way. Hit the tree line to the west of the convoy."

The battle between Charlie and the convoy continued

with ferocity. Shortly after the tanker truck exploded, a five-ton rig near the middle of the convoy was hit. It was loaded with ammunition—enough to knock everything around it off the road. Then a tank went up, its turret flying into the air fifteen to twenty feet, turning a somersault, and crashing back down.

The convoy's intent was to continue moving north as fast as it could, and it managed to do just that. If a vehicle was hit, the driver made every attempt to get it off the road under its own power. If it was hit too badly to move itself out of the way, the driver behind rammed it and pushed it off. The key was to break free of the killing zone and accelerate out of the ambush area, while pumping all possible fire into the ambushers to gain fire superiority.

The enemy's RPGs did the most damage. Once a vehicle was disabled with rocket fire, the automatic weapons would open up. Charlie had prepared well; he was hitting hard from a position of advantage.

When the enemy had lost the element of surprise and the defenders began to gain the firepower advantage, the enemy troops usually would attempt to break contact and fade into the jungle before an organized pursuit could be launched. With this in mind, I keyed Sinor as he pulled out of his rocket and minigun run along the western line. "Three One, let's cut off the avenue of retreat. Work up some artillery and give us two brackets of artillery fire on both sides of the road running north and south. We'll pin them against the highway with no back door."

Moments later artillery began to pound down, blocking any enemy effort to disengage at the highway and make an escape to the jungle. Adding to the enemy's problems, fast movers (USAF close air support) were called in to put down bombs and napalm all along the tree line on both sides of the highway. Then the APCs that had stayed behind the convoy were poised to sweep the Rome-plowed area and mop up the ambush survivors.

Parker and I had to return to Lai Khe to rearm and

refuel; while we were on the ground it soon became evident that everybody out there—the armor, artillery, close air support, the Cobra—had the situation in hand. Working in close support on the flanks, they had knocked out virtually all resistance. The enemy was badly decimated and the survivors were trying to make it back to their base camps.

Several hours later the ambushed convoy made it to Quan Loi. We had six or eight vehicles destroyed and many more damaged in the brief, fierce battle.

With the convoy gone and the shooting over, our local security forces situated near the site of the ambush were preparing to sweep through the area to check on enemy dead. They needed me back on station to scout out ahead of the ACAVs and provide cover. Once back at the contact area, I radioed Sinor, who was still orbiting over the ambush point, and told him that I was going down out of altitude to make a pass over the Rome-plowed corridor on the west side of Thunder Road. Then I would work my way over to the tree line to see if any enemy might have made it to the jungle.

I made my first pass from south to north right down on the deck ten to fifteen yards out from the highway. After completing that pass, I keyed Sinor with a report. "OK, Thirty-one, this is One Six. I don't know how bad the convoy got hurt, but we really nailed their asses down here. I see forty to fifty bodies strewn around, many body parts, numerous blood trails and drag marks. Looks like the remnants of the enemy force moved off to the tree line on the west, dragging along as many of their KIA and wounded as possible. But they've left a lot of dead and a lot of equipment."

After several more passes up and down the Rome-plowed area, I moved over to the trees and began to look for trails of the enemy retreating into the jungle. I was about three hundred yards deep into the tree line, right at the area where our Thunder II base camp was located, when I heard what sounded like a quick, sharp explosion. Suddenly my aircraft became almost uncontrollable. The vibration was so extreme that I couldn't control the ship up or down. I knew I had been hit, undoubtedly in the rotor system.

I fought to control the Loach, which seemed on the verge of shaking itself right out of the sky. I tried to accelerate and found that made the ship all the harder to control. So I decelerated and immediately began looking for a spot to put the bird down.

There was a line of nipa palm trees just north of Thunder II and I could just see beyond it. With my eyes jerking from the violent vibrations of the aircraft, I could barely make out a fairly open rice paddy—the size of a small golf course—just over the nipa palm line.

I yelled into UHF, "One Six is hit, we're hit. We're going down!" I pointed the nose toward the rice paddy and prepared to enter autorotation just as soon as we cleared the trees. The engine sounded so awful that I thought the whole damned thing was either going to explode or shake itself apart before I could get the ship over the tree line.

Seeing our bird wallowing through the air, and having heard me screaming over the radio, the front-seater of Sinor's Cobra came up on VHF: "Twelve o'clock . . . twelve o'clock . . . the open field . . . the rice paddy. Go for it . . . go for it, One Six!" He had obviously spotted the same hole in the jungle.

With only about forty feet of altitude, I had decided to autorotate in because I wasn't sure I still had a functioning engine. This was no time to have it seize up and bind the transmission. I wanted to be able to control the aircraft as I hit the water in the flooded rice paddy.

Jim Parker hadn't said a word through all of this. I grabbed a quick glance over my right shoulder and saw him leaning half out of the aircraft, looking ahead as if he was trying to help me find a place to put down. I didn't have to tell him that we were in trouble, but, as superfluous as it was, I managed to key the intercom and say, "Hang on, Jimbo, we're going to hit hard!"

Autorotation was working. I had rolled off the throttle, reduced the collective to the bottom pitch setting, and come aft with the cyclic. The result was a deceleration with the nose up and the forward motion and mass of the aircraft building up RPMs in the rotor system. This allowed me to better control the aircraft as it settled into the rice paddy. The skids sliced through the water and sank to the mud floor of the paddy, and the bottom of the fuselage smacked into the water like a ton of bricks. Spray and mud flew everywhere.

I quickly followed the emergency procedures—pulled up the emergency fuel shutoff and flipped off the master battery switch. This shut down the fuel and electrical systems in case there was a post-crash fire. Then I wanted to get out of that cockpit ASAP. I tried to roll over to my right to jump out of the aircraft and into the water. But I couldn't move.

"You dumb shit!" I muttered, cursing my stupidity. I was still strapped into my seat. I reached down and hit the handle to release my seat belt and shoulder harness.

The rice paddy water was almost up to the door, so all I had to do was lift my left leg up over the cyclic stick and roll out. A quick inventory told me that I still had all my body parts and didn't seem to be hurting anywhere. Parker was still struggling with his seat belt, trying to get out of the aircraft, so I stood up to give him a hand.

Once in the water, Parker leaned back into the aircraft to retrieve his M-60 machine gun and a seven-foot belt of ammo. As he threw the ammo over his shoulder he looked at me and asked, "What in the hell happened, Lieutenant?"

"I don't know, but whatever it was sure raised hell with the rotor system."

We both looked up at the main rotor blades just as they

were slowing down to a stop. One of the blades came to a halt right over our heads.

"My God," I whispered. A .50-caliber machine-gun round had gone right through the leading edge, about four feet from the tip of the blade, shattering the spar. The only thing holding the blade together was the honeycomb structure in back of the blade's leading edge.

"My God," I repeated. "By all rights, that blade should have come off four feet from the end. And if that had happened, the aircraft would have come apart in midair." Then I noticed Parker's chin. It was bloody and looked like it had been laid open to the bone. He patted the front sight of his 60. When the Loach slammed down into the rice paddy, the impact had thrown Parker's head forward, into the machine gun. Parker was the kind of guy who would never say a word about it.

I reached back in the ship for the Prick Ten (PRC-10) emergency radio so I could report in to Sinor. The gunship was off to the east, circling at altitude. "Three One, this is One Six. We're down in the rice paddy. We're OK, except Parker nearly cut off his chin when we hit. Keep your speed up, Dino, it's a .50 just west of Thunder II."

"Roger that, One Six. I saw the tracers. That's affirmative on the .50 cal."

"Hey, Thirty-one, why don't you scramble the ARPs to come in and pick us up. Get Pipe Smoke to yank the bird, then you can get some more guns on station to go after that fifty."

"OK, One Six," Sinor rogered. "ARPs are on the way. Have advised Darkhorse Control that we have a Loach down. How are you fixed for Victor Charlies?"

"No sign of enemy," I answered. "What I'm going to do now is climb up and pull the hinge pins on the rotor blades so Pipe Smoke can zip in here and throw a harness around the rotor head and recover this bird."

I climbed up on the fuselage to reach the hinge pins. It was a simple procedure of just pulling up the four inverted

U-shaped retaining pins and dropping the blades. Parker stood beside me, trying to feel how badly his chin was cut.

Suddenly the silence around us was shattered by a sharp burst of readily identifiable AK-47 fire. The AK was immediately joined by another enemy weapon—probably a .30-caliber machine gun—firing much faster. Bullets were plunking into the water all around the ship, and I could hear rounds tearing through the aircraft. The enemy was still very much present in the area, and they obviously knew exactly where we were.

I instinctively ducked my head, then jumped backward off the fuselage into the rice paddy. I landed on my feet in about twelve inches of water, but immediately fell over on my backside—Parker would probably have been laughing at me if he hadn't been busy ducking, too.

As the enemy rounds let up for a second, Parker ran around the tail of the aircraft and threw himself, and his M-60 and ammo belt, down on top of a nearby paddy dike. Crawling out of the water, I reached back into the cockpit and grabbed my CAR-15 along with a bandolier of magazines, then rolled around the back of the ship and fell prone on the ground next to Parker. Bullets were kicking up all around us. No doubt the enemy had seen us move out from behind the aircraft and were determined to nail us.

I raised my head just enough to try to see where the fire was coming from. Then I got back on the PRC-10 and fairly well screamed to Sinor: "Three One, we're in deep trouble down here! We've got bad guys to the west of us, bad guys to the west. We're taking heavy fire on the ground from the wood line two seven zero degrees due west our location, at a range of about three hundred yards."

"Roger, I'm in," Sinor said as he rolled the Cobra and began his run right over the tree line. I heard the noise as he punched off several pairs of rockets. The first pair hit a little short; the second and third pairs looked as though they were pretty close to where I thought the fire was coming from.

As Sinor broke to come around again, I said, "Second and third pairs look like good rocks. Give 'em hell!"

On his next pass, all I heard was his minigun fire. Then Sinor came back up on the radio. "I didn't get any rocks off that time. I'm coming back in. I'm recycling rockets, so keep your heads down."

Sinor rolled in at about 140 to 160 knots, leveled out nose down, and ran the length of the tree line without firing a single rocket.

What the hell? I thought as Sinor sped off to the north. Then Sinor came back with the news. "I'm empty. Most of my ordnance was expended during the convoy ambush and I haven't reloaded. ARPs are on the way. I'll keep making dry runs on Charlie to try to keep their heads down. Stay cool."

So there we were. Down in a rice paddy, the enemy just three hundred yards away, and we had a defanged Cobra! Sinor continued to make runs, with horrendous fire coming up at him from the enemy. But after about three dry passes, Charlie quit shooting at the Cobra.

Two things became obvious to Parker and me as we lay there on the dike half in and half out of that foul rice paddy water: the enemy had wised up to the fact that the gunship was out of ammo, and it wasn't the gunship they wanted anyway. Those bastards wanted the Loach crew; they wanted *us!*

Just then Parker yelled, "Lieutenant!" and pointed toward the tree line. I immediately saw two men standing at the edge of the jungle not more than 175 yards to my right front. One man wore a blue shirt, the other dark green. Neither had headgear, but both were carrying AK-47s. They apparently hadn't seen Parker and me on the dike, and probably thought we were still in or behind the aircraft.

One of the VC pointed toward the bird and the other

one let go with a burst of AK fire. As he fired, more AKs from the tree line let go—shooting the hell out of the rice paddy where they thought we were.

Adding to the blanket of fire the AK-47s were sending in, an RPG-7 round suddenly exploded not more than fifteen to twenty yards from us, showering us with mud and foul-smelling water.

"These sons a bitches ain't kidding," I shouted into Parker's ear. "They're coming after us!"

Parker opened up with his machine gun, and I cut loose with my CAR-15. The two soldiers caught the full blast of our combined fire and were blown backward into the grass at the edge of the tree line.

Parker didn't let up. He kept spraying the jungle and yelling above the chatter of his M-60, "The bastards aren't gonna get me . . . the bastards aren't gonna get me!"

He soon shot his belt dry, and at the same time his gun jammed. I worked with his weapon trying to clear it, while he crawled back over to the ship to get another belt of ammo.

With a fresh six-foot belt, Parker let go again. I fired three more CAR-15 magazines into the jungle behind where we had dropped the two bad guys. Between bursts, I managed to tell Parker, "If they start coming at us, we're dropping this stuff and running for it, got me? We'll run eastbound, toward Thunder Road." He nodded and kept pumping rounds through the M-60.

One of our mech units over on Thunder Road was probably trying to get across the stream to help us. It made a lot more sense to head toward them, rather than try to hold off a bunch of enemy soldiers if they decided to rush us.

Just then, as if fate had suddenly looked down on us and smiled, a Huey came out of nowhere in a steep, descending spiral and hit a hover right across the corner of the rice paddy, not more than twenty feet from us. I grabbed

Parker by the back of the neck. "Come on, Jimbo, let's get the hell out of here!"

Clutching our weapons, we cut across the corner of the paddy and moved as fast as we could in the thigh-deep water toward the hovering UH-1. The Huey door gunner was shooting like crazy over our heads as I climbed out of the rice paddy and dove into the open right door. Parker was right behind me. I grabbed his M-60 as he struggled to get aboard. The Huey lifted off with me still yanking on his arm and half of his body still flailing outside the aircraft.

Finally, both of us were sitting on the Huey cabin floor, looking at each other, trying to smile. The ship climbed to altitude and headed back to Phu Loi.

We found out that we were in a command and control helicopter belonging to the commander, 3d Brigade, 1st Infantry Division. He had been in the general area and heard Sinor go up on the Guard push. Realizing that an aeroscout crew was on the ground, the CO had ordered in his C and C ship to snatch us up and zip us out of there. He and his crew had sure saved the bacon of a couple of wet, scared aeroscout crewmen that day.

Back at Phu Loi, I learned through operations that after Parker and I were out of there Sinor had called in close air support on the wooded area where the enemy was located. The whole sector from the edge of the Rome-plow to about a quarter mile into the jungle was boxed and worked with fast movers.

Parker's cut on the chin, though serious, wasn't as bad as it had looked the day before. He had gone over to the medic when we got back to base and had it stitched.

The next morning, we had a requirement to go back out and assist sweep-up units. A scout-gunship team was needed to help look for blood trails and search for the enemy force that had hit the convoy along Thunder Road.

Realizing that I was going out on the mission, Parker came to me that morning and asked to go. "Look, Lieutenant, I'm fine. I want to go back out there because I've got a score to settle with those bastards."

I understood his feelings, but I knew the regulations: "I can't let you fly today, it's not legal. You know as well as I do that stitches are a grounding condition."

"Come on, sir, I want to go," he pleaded.

I liked his spunk and I finally gave in. "Get in the aircraft, but if the Old Man finds out about this, it's my ass." He gave me a smile as big as his stitched-up chin would allow and headed off to the flight line with his M-60 cradled under his arm.

We flew directly to the ambush site. Coming up on the Rome-plowed area in front of the tree line, we saw that some of our tanks were still there. We could see the tracks where 113s had rolled through, policing up the enemy bodies and looking for any personal gear or documents that could be of help to division intelligence.

To get oriented again, we first made a north-south pass up the west side of the highway, running at about sixty knots and thirty to forty feet off the ground. As I made my turn at the far north end to start back, I saw a VC body lying on the ground. It was behind a large mound of dirt that had obviously been pushed up during the original Rome-plowing of the area. I hauled the Loach around and keyed Parker on the intercom. "Look there, they missed a body. I thought the friendlies picked all those guys up and buried them."

Holding in a small circle over the body at ten feet, I took a closer look. He had on long blue pants, a long dark green shirt, and Ho Chi Minh sandals. Then I noticed that there was something around his body. Looking closer I could see it was a map case.

I got up on Uniform to report to Sinor, who was my gun cover again that day. "Three One, One Six. I've got a dead guy down here with a map case on him. The grunts have missed him. I'm going to go down here and land—it's wide open, no problem. I'm going down and recover that map case."

"OK, One Six, roger that. But be careful, he could be booby-trapped."

I briefed Parker. "When I land, I want you to get out and get that map case. Get the hook out. I'll put down behind that mound of dirt from the body. You pull the hook over him and stay behind the mound when you pull the body over."

Parker jumped out with the grappling hook line over his shoulder and his drawn .45 in hand.

"Hey, wait a minute," I yelled to him over the sound of the idling engine. "Take this with you." I handed Parker the CAR-15 submachine gun. He reholstered his .45 and disappeared around the corner of the dirt mound, cradling the carbine under his arm.

Just as I lost sight of Parker, I heard the CAR-15 go off, all thirty rounds in a sustained burst. Parker came running around the mound for all he was worth and dove head first into the gunner's compartment. "Get out of here, sir, *NOW!* He's not dead!"

I pulled pitch and squeezed the gun trigger to the four thousand rounds per minute stop. The OH-6 shuddered as it spewed tracers and clawed for altitude. The tongue of fire raked over the soldier's body and blew dust and debris across my windscreen.

"What the hell happened back there?"

Parker was panting. "The bastard had an RPG round in his hand when I came around the corner. His eyes were closed, the bastard looked dead to me, but as I walked up close to him, he opened his eyes. His left arm was blown away, but he had this RPG round in his right hand. And when I got up close to him he picked the RPG round up and slammed it into the ground, picked it up, and did it again. The son of a bitch tried to blow me up!"

Ground troops from the security forces were arriving, now cautious at our recent outburst of fire. They came around their APC, weapons at the ready. Before getting too close to the body, one infantryman took a couple of insurance shots to make sure the VC was dead and wouldn't try to detonate the RPG round still tightly gripped in his hand.

Parker and I were watching from a nearby orbit as the grunts carefully removed the map case and took it back to the M-113. Then the officer in the personnel carrier called on FM. "Jackpot, One Six. Charlie was an officer type. We've got maps, and we've got operational overlays. Looks like good stuff for G-2. Thanks for finding this dude. Your crew chief OK?"

"OK, thanks," I came back. "Crew chief is OK, other than what I might do to him for shooting up all my CAR-15 ammo into Victor Charlie. You'll get the map case contents back to Brigade?"

"This is really good intel, One Six. From a quick look at these overlays, it looks like the dinks who ambushed the convoy are headed back to their sanctuaries in the Fish Hook. As far as the map case contents, we're tied up here for a little while. Can you get it down to Tango One [Thunder I Fire Base]? Then they'll get it on back to division."

"Roger, we'll get it back to Tango One," I answered.

That was Parker's cue to cut back in on the intercom. "Horse shit, Lieutenant," he said to me jokingly. "No disrespect intended, sir, but I don't care what you say, I'm *not* getting out of this damn aircraft one more time to screw around with some dink's map case!"

"Cool it, Jimbo," I chuckled. "Don't worry about the bad guy, he's dead."

"Well, no offense, Lieutenant, but I'd just as soon one of those grunts handle the map case while I stay to-hell inside this helicopter."

Smiling to myself, I set the ship down next to the M-113, and one of the infantrymen brought me the map case. I didn't even have to ask Parker to get it.

That day, 21 July 1969, ended up being a pretty short flying day for Parker and me. We ran the map case on down to Thunder I, turned it over to the brigade S-2, and headed back to Phu Loi. As I cruised leisurely back to base, I wondered again if my decision eighteen months before had been a good one.

CHAPTER 2

SILVER WINGS

Fort Knox, Kentucky, 1967

I pressed my way up to the Echo Company bulletin board to see what everybody was reading. Just pinned up, the notice said that the army was looking for more rotary-wing aviators and that interested officer candidates who qualified would be given the opportunity to go on to army flight school after completing officer candidate school (OCS).

I was interested enough to reread the last part. It said that any candidate wishing to pursue aviator training had to submit to an orientation flight in an army helicopter to be conducted from the Fort Knox airfield on a specified future date. I had never considered being a pilot, but taking an army helicopter ride didn't sound too bad.

The only problem was getting the time off to do it. We were about midcourse in OCS training at the armor school and our schedules were hectic. But between field problems, inspections, getting demerits, and working off demerits, I signed up.

I had never ridden in a helicopter. I hadn't even seen many of them down around Hot Springs, Arkansas, where I grew up. Before enlisting in the army, I had belonged to a sport parachuting club. We jumped, of course, from small, propeller-type airplanes, so the concept of being off the ground and flying wasn't all that new to me.

But flying helicopters? The prospect had never occurred to me. Yet becoming an armor officer candidate at Fort Knox, Kentucky, really hadn't been in my plans, either.

I had enlisted on 1 February 1967 after one semester of college, with the specific objective of becoming an army airborne infantryman. During basic training at Fort Polk, Louisiana, I decided to go on to OCS. I still wanted the infantry branch but got my second choice, armor, instead.

When the appointed day came to take the army helicopter ride, I and another candidate who had indicated interest got our proper permissions, and off we went down to Fort Knox airfield. Reporting at the flight line, we were greeted by a young army captain. He introduced himself as the pilot who would be taking us on our orientation flight, then pointed over his shoulder to the little helicopter sitting on the ramp.

"That, gentlemen," he said, "is the army Cayuse Model OH-6A observation helicopter. It is manufactured by Hughes Tool Company, Aircraft Division, and is basically an all-metal, single-engine, rotary-wing aircraft."

The helicopter looked brand new. Its fresh olive-drab (OD) finish glistened in the sunlight, and was accented by a yellow number painted at the top of the fuselage and a big United States Army painted across the tail boom. But what most caught my attention was the distinctive shape of the little fuselage. It looked like a teardrop, with the cockpit located in the big end of the drop and the back cabin tapering to the tail of the aircraft.

"This helicopter model," the captain continued, "is just now coming into the army's inventory. This one's just fresh out of the factory, in fact. And if you'll come with me, we'll get strapped in and take it for a little spin."

As we walked toward the aircraft, the captain continued his enthusiastic but almost textbook description of the OH-6A. "It's powered by an Allison T63-A-5A turbine engine," he recited, "that drives both the four-bladed main rotor and the antitorque tail rotor."

"What does the army use a helicopter like this for?" the other candidate asked.

The captain seemed glad for the question. "The OH-6A is primarily an observation helicopter—that's what the 'OH' stands for. It's mostly designed for doing reconnaissance work at very low level."

As we got to the ship, the captain opened both the cockpit and rear cabin doors so we could look inside. "The pilot sits in the right front seat," he explained, "and the copilot, or observer, as the case may be, sits in the left seat. That's a little different from most airplanes you might be familiar with, and though I haven't been to Nam, I understand that the reason has to do with the way the scout pilots fly their observation patterns in combat."

The captain pointed to my fellow candidate. "OK, why don't you sit up front with me in the copilot's seat . . . ," then, looking at me, "and, Candidate Mills, you can sit back here in the crew member's seat on the first leg, then swap into the front when we fly back home."

We eagerly climbed into the helicopter while the captain explained how to buckle up, and how the guy in the front seat should put on the flight helmet and plug his headset into the aircraft radios. I didn't have a helmet in the back, but I'd get my turn.

After securing myself in the seat, I looked around the inside of the ship and was surprised at how little room there was. The captain had said that I was sitting where the crew chief-door gunner would sit in combat. If any of those guys was a six-footer like me, they must have a heck of a time sandwiching in back with an M-60 machine gun!

I followed what was going on up front by watching through the little window in the bulkhead that separated me from the pilot's compartment. I couldn't see much of the magic that the captain was working to start the engine, but the turbine sound soon told me that we were getting ready to go.

The soft whine grew in intensity, and through the glass panel over my head I could see the four rotor blades begin to turn—slowly at first, then accelerating to a circular blur. The sound of the whirling rotors soon drowned out most of the earsplitting engine whine. Then, as if somebody had kicked us square in the seat of the pants, up we went.

Hot damn, I thought, this is *all* right!

We flew for fifteen to twenty minutes. In the front, the captain was explaining over the intercom what he was doing and what was going on.

It seemed as though we hadn't any more than gotten up when we landed again, in a small grassy field out in the country. After the captain shut down the engine, we unstrapped and walked over to a little airport building where we had a cup of coffee and talked. I was having fun asking questions and listening to the captain, but I couldn't wait to return to the OH-6 for the ride back to Knox, in the front seat this time.

I eagerly climbed into the front seat, hooked the harness, and slipped on the helmet. I felt a tremendous exhilaration, and a fascination with the machine.

I was lost in thought when the captain's voice popped into my earphones, startling me. He showed me the button on the cyclic stick that I could push to talk back to him, then briefly explained his preflight checklist and engine-starting procedures.

Up again and headed back toward Fort Knox, the captain demonstrated the basic helicopter controls: the collective pitch stick, which made the ship go up and down; the cyclic stick, which controlled the longitudinal pitch of the aircraft; and the foot pedals, which made the ship go right and left. He then explained the purpose of all the buttons on the top of the cyclic stick: the radio-intercom, cyclic trim, gun pod elevation-depression, armament two-position trigger, and two or three others just for spares.

After we reached an altitude of about three thousand feet, the captain came back on the intercom. "OK, Mills, take the controls for a while and see what she's like."

A little hesitantly, I put my feet on the pedals and wrapped my hand around the pistol grip on the cyclic stick. I was thrilled. I was flying an army helicopter!

"Now look at the black ball," he said, pointing to the instrument near the upper center of the instrument panel. "What you want to do is keep the black ball in the middle. When it slides out to the left, push a little left pedal until it comes back to the middle. Same to the right. Just step on the ball and keep flying toward the horizon."

It worked just the way he said it would, but I found out very quickly that I shouldn't try to monkey around with the controls. The less I did, the less the aircraft moved around.

All too soon we were back at Fort Knox airfield. Though I didn't think that I flew all that badly, my fellow candidate in the back cabin was violently airsick when we got down.

But not me. I was feeling good and was extremely excited by the entire experience. I decided on the spot that I wanted to go on to flight school after OCS and learn to really fly the army OH-6 helicopter.

My enthusiasm was duly noted by the captain but quickly forgotten by me. I still had about three months of OCS left, and that demanding schedule left me no time to think about helicopters or wonder whether my application would be approved.

During the last week of OCS, however, I learned that I had been accepted for army flight training. Somehow everything had fallen together. That excitement blended with the deep satisfaction I felt with graduating from OCS.

On 15 December 1967, members of Armor Officer Candidate Class 1-68 passed across the stage of Budinot Hall to receive their commissioning certificates.

It was a proud moment.

* * *

Though I had been approved for flight school, my orders hadn't been cut yet to get me into Fort Wolters for Primary. The lapse gave me time to get in a couple weeks of leave. It was the Christmas season and a great time to be home with my family.

When the orders did come, they were the most unusual I had ever seen. In a couple of short paragraphs, they covered everything I was to do in the army for the next full year—from Fort Knox, Kentucky, to the U.S. Army Primary Helicopter School at Fort Wolters, Texas; from there to Advanced Flight Training School at Fort Rucker, Alabama; then home for leave; and, finally, on to assignment in the Republic of Vietnam.

So, with brand-new second-lieutenant bars on my shoulders, off I went to helicopter school, where I discovered that there was more to flying an army helicopter than watching the little black ball.

I didn't waste any time after receiving my army aviator wings at the Rucker graduation ceremony. My gear was already packed in the back of my 390 GT, and I immediately headed back to Arkansas for forty-five days of leave at home. My Vietnam travel orders would be sent to me there.

Being home was a period of quiet anxiousness for me. Quiet because I didn't do much, just saw some friends and water-skied. Anxious because I was ready to go to Vietnam. It meant a chance to test my newly acquired skills in combat situations, and I was comfortable with that. I had faith in my equipment, in the people who had taught me, and in the caliber of the people I would be flying with. I was ready for the next chapter of my life.

While I was at home, neither Mother nor Dad even brought up the subject of Vietnam. They knew that's where my orders would send me, and there wasn't any more to be said about it. They were very much aware of what the war in Vietnam was all about. It was inescapable.

They had been watching it on the TV news for several years.

Mother did, however, ask me one day, "Hugh, how do you keep your head down in a helicopter?" I remember answering, "With a great deal of difficulty!" That kind of flippant response was pretty typical of me. I guess it satisfied Mother because she didn't mention it again.

My Vietnam orders finally arrived, instructing me to report to San Francisco on 30 December 1968 for transportation to USARV (United States Army Republic of Vietnam).

On New Year's Day, 1969, I was in Saigon, getting off the bus in front of the headquarters of the 90th Replacement Battalion. This was where we would be processed into the country and receive our tactical unit assignments. For the first time, I felt a twinge of apprehension. I knew where I *wanted* to be assigned: the 1st Cavalry Division (Airmobile), the outfit I had seen so much of in all the training films at flight school. I perceived 1st Cav as *the* premier unit making Vietnam combat history, and setting the pace on aviation tactics and technology. My second choice was the 11th Armored Cavalry Regiment. Known as the Blackhorse Regiment, this was an old regular army outfit that dated back to action in the Philippine Insurrection, Mexican Expedition, and World War II. It had been in Vietnam since '66, and had made a lot of headlines during 1968, when it was commanded by then Col. George S. Patton III.

But after three days of processing at the 90th, when my assignment was finally posted I was bitterly disappointed to read "1st Infantry Division." My first thought was, oh, my God, what kind of justice would send an armor officer to an infantry division? I was in sheer panic. I wanted desperately to fly scouts, and I didn't know how I could cope with being assigned to a Slick (troop-carrying utility missions) outfit . . . in an infantry division!

My appraisal of the whole situation worsened that afternoon. My friend John Field, who had also been assigned to the Big Red One, and I were told to be at the personnel loading area at 1400 for transportation to our unit. Sitting there expecting a Jeep and driver to pick us up, we were almost choked to death by a cloud of dust raised by a five-ton army cargo truck. When the dust settled, we saw that this five-ton was loaded to the gunnels with dirty, smelly army fatigues. By damn, this was a laundry truck!

Then a soldier in the back end hollered, "Are you the officers going to the 1st Division?" My "yes . . ." sounded more like a question than a statement. "Well, jump on," the soldier yelled. "We're your ride, just as soon as we dump this load of dirty clothes over at the laundry."

We finally rumbled out of Saigon city and headed north and east on Highway QL1 toward 1st Division forward headquarters at Di An (pronounced zee-on). "This sure isn't what I expected," I muttered to myself as Field and I jumped off the laundry truck at Di An. I was still smarting about a brand-new cavalry officer—breathing fire and itching to get into the war flying scouts—being assigned to an infantry division. Besides, this place didn't look much like a forward headquarters to me. I didn't see anything but rear area personnel/running around fighting paperwork.

But there were some encouraging signs. Di An was also home base for an air cav troop of the 3d Squadron, 17th Cavalry, 1st Aviation Brigade. Also, squadron headquarters for the 1st Squadron, 4th Cavalry, 1st Aviation Battalion. That meant there were aeroscouts in the squadron's air cavalry troop!

As I sat talking to the assignment officer at the Di An headquarters hootch, I must admit that my attention was divided. As he talked to me, I nodded my head, but in fact I was looking over his head at the information board on the wall behind him. An organizational chart was posted showing the air units assigned to the 1st Aviation Battalion at Phu Loi, the base where Field and I had been told we

were being sent. The chart showed Delta 1/4 Cav—D
Troop, 1st Squadron, 4th Cavalry Regiment. That meant a
platoon of aeroscouts *had* to be operating out of Phu Loi.
Things were looking up. Maybe the 1st Infantry Division
wouldn't be that bad after all.

As I stared at the wall chart, I realized I had heard
about the 4th U.S. Cavalry. At OCS some of its Vietnam
exploits had been used as study examples. I remembered
that this outfit had been in Vietnam since 1965 and had
chalked up quite an impressive combat record. It was one
of the first units to prove armor effectiveness in Vietnam's
II Corps tactical zone. No question, 4th Cav was actively
showing all the boldness, dash, and aggressiveness that
had marked every generation of cavalrymen since 1855,
when that regiment had come into being.

Bringing my attention back to the assignment officer, I
asked if he had any information on the 4th Cav at Phu Loi.

"That's the Darkhorse unit. They're the air cavalry
troop for the 1st Division," he responded.

"How about their scouts?" I shot back.

"Their scout platoon over there is called the Outcasts.
They fly the Loaches. The troop's also got those new Cobra gunships and a platoon of Hueys."

I heard only what he said about the Loaches—the light
observation helicopters, OH-6As. Maybe, just maybe, I
thought, I am still alive for flying scouts after all.

The next morning, John and I threw our gear into the
back of a Jeep that had been sent down from Phu Loi to
get us. We headed north out of Di An toward Highway 13.
That highway—really nothing more than a two-lane jungle
dirt road—was a well-known north–south artery that I
would come to know later as Thunder Road. It wound
north through the heart of 1st Division's assigned operational area.

We passed a lot of Vietnamese villages, nothing more
than little knots of dilapidated shacks—hootches, as I
would soon be calling them. They stuck up like

matchboxes all along the side of the road. Children, cows, and chickens roamed through their living areas. Little kids were everywhere, waving and yelling to us as we passed. Most of them were wearing at least one or two articles of somehow-garnered American GI clothing—a bush hat, jungle boots, or maybe a khaki T-shirt. After about half an hour's ride, we pulled into the main gate at Phu Loi. An MP with an M-16 rifle looked up from the long line of Vietnamese civilians he was checking. Then he nodded to our driver and waved us on.

Field and I looked at each other, puzzled by what the MP was doing. Our driver explained: "ID card check. They're hootch maids and other civilian workers that work here on post. They arrive in the morning and then leave right at the stroke of 1600. You'd think they belonged to a labor union or something the way they clear out of here right at four o'clock."

The Jeep squealed to a stop at the headquarters building, 1st Aviation Battalion, and the driver ushered us in to the executive officer. "Two new pilots for you, sir," said the driver. Then he got back in his Jeep and sped off.

"You men have a seat," the XO said. "The Old Man is tied up right now, but he'll see you in a minute."

Four or five clerks were sitting around pounding typewriters, and somewhere down at the other end of the room we heard a radio playing rock music. We were amazed—it sure didn't seem as though we were in the middle of a war.

Obviously amused at the just-in-country, newbie look on our faces, one of the clerks finally volunteered, "That's AFVN, Armed Forces Vietnam Radio, down in Saigon. Pretty good stuff, huh?"

Before either one of us could mumble an acknowledgment, the executive officer reappeared at the door of the battalion commander's office and waved us in.

Once inside, we snapped to attention, came to smart salutes, and, in our best military manner, said, "Sir, Lieutenants Mills and Field reporting to the commander for duty."

The lieutenant colonel returned our salutes and walked around his desk to shake hands and offer us a seat. "On behalf of the 1st Division," he said, "welcome to Vietnam."

"Thank you, sir," we replied, almost in unison.

He sat back down at his desk, picked up our personnel jackets, and gave them a quick look. "You men have come to a good outfit. You both fly Hueys, I see."

We both nodded, but I was still hoping he would pick up on my prior request for scouts and OH-6s.

He asked us some general background questions and quickly scribbled something in his notebook. "Lieutenant Field, you're an infantry officer, so I'm going to assign you to the 1st Aviation Battalion. You'll go to A Company and fly in our lift unit, the Bulldogs. It supports the entire division." I could tell that John was happy with his assignment.

"Lieutenant Mills," he said after a moment, "because you're an armor officer, I'm going to send you across the runway to D Troop, 1st Squadron, 4th Cavalry."

I couldn't hide the smile that cut across my face as he continued. "D Troop operates as part of the division cavalry squadron, but it is actually detached from the squadron and attached to the 1st Aviation Battalion over here for support and administration.

"Being an armor officer," he went on, "you really belong in an air cavalry reconnaissance outfit . . . and I understand they have some pilot vacancies over there where you can put your qualifications to work right away."

Damn, I thought. Things are falling into place! I fairly well floated out of the battalion commander's office, thinking that I had just beaten the odds. Going to the 1st Infantry Division was going to be OK after all!

John and I said our good-byes and headed off on our own. A Jeep from the "Quarter Cav" picked me up, and on the way over to the troop the driver gave me a little background on the airfield. "This basic north–south runway here at Phu Loi was actually built by the Japanese. They used it as a fighter strip during World War II. Ain't that somethin', sir?" He grinned. "Way back in World War II."

As soon as we were on the air cav side of the runway, I noticed a big change in the way things looked. At least the drab paint color changed. Back on the battalion side, the numeral 1 was painted big and red everywhere; it represented the division's shoulder patch insignia. Here everything was painted red and white, U.S. Cavalry flag colors. I mean everything—the signs, the hootches, even the rocks on the ground that outlined the walkways. I said to myself, here's the good old cavalry pride and spirit; I'm really going to like this place!

In front of the flight operations building, a large concrete sign announced Troop D (Air), 1st Squadron, 4th U.S. Cavalry—Darkhorse. I liked the name Darkhorse. It had pizzazz and said something about the flair and fighting spirit of the troop.

On the runway I saw a lineup of sleek, new AH-1G Cobras and OH-6A scout ships. These were the first Cobras I had seen up close, but I knew that the armament they carried was awesome. They had the firepower to ruin the day of anyone on the receiving end. Their 7.62mm miniguns could pump out four thousand rounds a minute. Then there was the 40mm grenade launcher, and the arsenal of 2.75-inch rockets under each stubby little wing. That aircraft was like a flying tank!

The troop first sergeant, Martin Laurent, met me at the door of the orderly room and relieved me of my duffel bag. The troop commander—Major Cummings—was right there also to shake my hand and introduce himself, then he pointed me into his office. Offering me a seat, he settled himself behind his desk. After studying me for a moment, he broke the silence. "Where you from, Mills?"

"Arkansas, sir . . . Hot Springs."

He nodded and picked up my file that First Sergeant Laurent had laid on his desk. "I see you're an armor officer and right out of flight school. Do you have any special qualifications we should know about?" he asked, leaning back in his chair.

"No," I responded, "I'm basically qualified in utility aircraft with training as a gunship pilot. I'm not qualified in the Cobra, but I certainly would like to fly scouts. I've wanted to be a scout pilot ever since I first saw the OH-6A."

The major pushed even farther back in his chair, stroked his chin a couple of times, and then wrung his hands together. I could tell that this was not what he had in mind. "I appreciate knowing your feelings, Lieutenant," he frowned, "but I don't have any vacancies in the scouts right now. What I do need is a lieutenant in the slick platoon."

Damn, I thought.

"However," he continued, "the platoon leader over in scouts is Lieutenant Herchert, and he might be moving over to flight operations one of these days soon. If that happens, I'll see to it that you get first crack at scouts."

After a bit more small talk, the major wound things up. "Mills, I'm assigning you to our lift platoon. Their mission is to airlift our aerorifle platoon using the Hueys. Any questions?"

"No, sir," I said, "I guess I'm the new guy, and I'd better learn what's going on in the lift section." Then, lying through my teeth, I added, "Yes, sir, the lift platoon will be just fine." All I could do was hope that the major picked up on my disappointment, and would remember my request for scouts as soon as there was an opening.

As I left the Old Man's office, I met another lieutenant who was standing in the orderly room. He turned to me. "Hi, you the new guy?"

"Yes, my name's Mills and I'm going to the lift section."

"Great," he said. "I'm Wayne McAdoo, assistant platoon leader for the slicks. We're called the Clowns, or the Flying Circus. Come on, I'll walk you over to the hootches and help you find a bunk."

McAdoo took me across a small drainage ditch to the troop officers' hootches. As I entered, I noticed that connecting the hootch to the next building in line was a large built-up bunker with no exterior entrance. Sandbags covered the whole thing from top to ground level. I was told that in case of incoming rocket and artillery fire, we could dive into the bunker without having to go outside the hootch. The entrance hole was located right at the foot of my bunk.

McAdoo helped me move my clothes into the wall locker, then suggested that we meet some of the other guys. Bunking across from me was a warrant officer dressed only in ragged cutoff khaki shorts and a pair of shower shoes. He was comfortably propped up on his bunk, listening to the rock music that flooded the room from the stereo player. Warrant Officer Bob Davis was from Barberton, Ohio, and a scout pilot. He had been in Vietnam for only two to three weeks. The more I looked at him, the more I was convinced that I had seen him someplace before. As it turned out, Davis had been in flight school at Fort Rucker at the same time I was.

Everybody in the hootch was friendly, but nobody came rushing up to greet me. They just nodded approvingly, and invariably asked the same question: "Where are you assigned . . . slicks, guns, or scouts?" Continuing around the hootch with McAdoo, I next met Barney Stevens, a slick pilot and a warrant officer first class. Then there was 1st Lt. Dean Sinor, CW2. Benny Parker, and, finally, Capt. Don Trent. Sinor, Parker, and Trent were Cobra pilots in the gun platoon.

It became obvious that the pilots didn't live together in their respective platoon hootches. Every hootch had a mixture of gun, scout, and slick pilots. There was no caste system; every man had the same basic living area, consisting of an army standard metal folding bunk with a book-thin mattress, covered with what looked to be a nylon camouflage poncho liner. Every man had a foot locker at the end of his bed, as well as an individual wall locker. And everybody—to a man—had a portable, pedestal fan. In each of the hootches was a small bar space with a hot plate, refrigerator, small storage area, and generally a television and a stereo set with tape deck. Not a bad setup for the middle of a war zone.

The next person I met was Bob Harris, the aerorifle (ARP) platoon leader. He filled me in on the platoon's job and how his twenty-eight-man unit of select infantrymen fit into overall troop operations.

Next stop was supply, where the first thing I was given was an APH-5 flight helmet. "It's *supposed* to be bullet-resistant," the supply sergeant told me. Next, I went to the arms room for the issue of a personal weapon. The armorer handed me the pilot's standard side arm, a .38-caliber model number 10 Smith & Wesson revolver. While he was shoving the .38 across the counter to me, I was studying the rack behind him, filled with .45 automatic pistols, 1911A1s, and M-16 and CAR-15 rifles. I was particularly intrigued by the CAR-15; it was a shortened version of the M-16 that had been developed for commando use.

I pushed the .38 back across the counter. "I really don't want a revolver. How about one of those .45s?"

He looked a little surprised. "But, sir, not one of the pilots carries a .45."

I grinned at him. "But I'm just not one of the pilots, and I would rather have a .45."

"Lieutenant, you can have whatever side arm you want," and he reached behind him for a .45 automatic and a couple of magazines of ammo.

"And I would also like one of those CAR-15s."

"Sorry, sir, the CAR-15s are reserved for the Cobra and scout pilots."

"OK, then, how about an M-16?"

I knew that the armorer was beginning to wonder just what kind of a first lieutenant he had run into. But he reached behind him, pulled out an M-16, and signed it out to me along with the .45. Most pilots coming into Vietnam for the first time probably didn't have a real preference as to what firearms they were issued. But I had been around guns all my life—my Uncle Billy had introduced me to guns as soon as I was old enough to hold one. I just felt more secure with a hard-hitting .45 strapped on.

The other equipment issued included flight suits, jungle boots, aircraft crewman's body armor, and a flare gun. Also a strobe light, survival kit, flight gloves, mosquito net, blankets . . . plus an item I'd never seen before—a blood chit—a large silk document with a big U.S. flag on it and paragraphs of information in several languages. As the supply sergeant handed it to me, he said, "If you get shot down and have to approach a Vietnamese for assistance, he'll be able to read one of these dialects and know that you're a downed American pilot in need of friendly help." Oh, sure, I thought.

The rest of that first afternoon was free and I used it to look around the field. Fortunately, I met one of the troop pilots who was about to fly an OH-6A down to the Saigon PX. He asked if I wanted to ride along. I couldn't jump in fast enough for my first in-country flight, and in a scout ship at that. I strapped myself in the left seat and immediately began surveying the instrument panel. It was much simpler than the Huey, which carried all kinds of navigational avionics.

I noticed that the pilot and I were sitting in armored seats, which brought home the fact that I was now in a combat zone. There were tungston carbide plates beneath the seats, in the seat backs, and in a wraparound shield that provided partial armor protection to the pilot's right side and the co-pilot's left side. "Chicken plate" was also worn to protect against rounds coming into the aircraft from the front. Of course, that still left your head, arms, and legs as targets of opportunity, but it was a lot better than nothing. Besides the armor protecting the pilot and observer, this combat-equipped OH-6 also had armored engine components, such as the fuel control and compressor unit.

I was surprised by the short amount of time it took the pilot to get the little OH-6 into the air. The pilot's hands raced through the preflight checks and engine start procedures. We were cranked, checking the tower for takeoff, and in the air before I would have even gotten around to putting my finger on the starter-ignition button.

It was just a 20-minute flight down to Ben Hoa, which was the Air Force's big base at Saigon, located right next to Tan Son Nhut airport, where I had come into country just six days ago. The Ben Hoa base was huge. You could probably see one of every kind of aircraft that the United States had in Vietnam at the time.

We landed at a place called Hotel Alpha, a big, open area with a chain-link fence around it. Our approach was to the large blacktop pad inside the fence, followed by a short hover into one of the available parking spots.

We checked our weapons with the security guard at the gate and walked across the street to the PX. (In later trips to the PX in Saigon, we would avoid checking our side arms by sticking them under our clothes and telling the gate guard that we weren't carrying any. Or we would check them with the guard, but have "spares" conveniently stowed away. The command considered Saigon secure and didn't want soldiers wandering around with guns and no adult supervision, but we always felt more comfortable having our personal weapons on us.)

We were back to the troop by about 1830, and I had logged my first in-country flight. One point three hours of copilot flying time. Not exactly airlifting troops to a hot

LZ in a slick, but a thoroughly enjoyable trip in an OH-6 scout bird!

My first breakfast in Delta Troop ended up being no breakfast at all. Instead, as I was walking up to the mess hall, all hell broke loose. In the stillness of that early morning, there was the heavy thud of an explosion from the direction of the ARP–crew chief hootch area. I froze.

It was still very dark, at 5:30 A.M. that first morning after I was assigned into the unit. Though officers took their evening meal at the O club, everybody went to the troop mess hall for breakfast and lunch. I had just headed up the troop sidewalk from my hootch, and was adjacent to the orderly room.

It sounded as though the explosion wasn't more than forty to fifty feet away. Then I heard screaming and cries of pain, telling even this fresh in-country newbie that somebody was badly hurt. My first instinct was to drop into a crouch beside the orderly room, pull out my .45, and chamber a round.

Moments later a man ran around the corner of the building and suddenly appeared in the dark right in front of me. He looked Vietnamese—probably an enemy sapper who had infiltrated the base area and thrown the grenade I just heard.

My .45 was up and on him. Shoot, I told myself, and my finger tightened on the trigger. But in that split second I somehow noticed that he was wearing U.S. camouflage fatigue pants, and boots—shined boots. No black pajamas or sandals!

I released the trigger, and the man stumbled toward me and collapsed into my arms. He was barechested and had small, bleeding pepper marks all over his upper body where he had evidently been hit by shrapnel. He was not dead, but his eyes were closed and he was obviously in shock and in a great deal of pain.

He was Vietnamese all right, now that I could see his

face close up. But why was he wearing our pants and boots?

As I was trying to pull him over to the orderly room and prop him up against the wall, Bob Harris came running up from his hootch just around the corner, his CAR-15 at the ready. "What the hell's going on?" he demanded.

"I don't know, but an explosion just went off back in there." I pointed toward the ARP hootch area.

Harris leaned down close to the man's face. "You OK, Toi? What happened?"

"Holy shit! Is this one of *your* guys?"

"Yes, he's one of my Kit Carson scouts."

"Thank God," I groaned. "I nearly put a .45 round right between this guy's eyes. What do you want me to do now?"

"You stay right here, and I'll go around this way and see what happened," Harris snapped as he disappeared around the corner.

A few minutes later, I learned that about six of our men had been hurt by what was thought to be an indiscriminate round that the enemy had lobbed into the ARP–crew chief hootch area. It had landed between the hootches where the men shaved and got cleaned up in the morning. Toi was one of them, and when he was hit by the enemy grenade shrapnel, he ran. Right into my arms.

In just over one day at Phu Loi, I had already seen evidence of my first enemy fire, and had almost shot one of the ARP platoon leader's prized Kit Carson scouts— former Viet Cong who became indispensable members of our fighting units and were always in short supply.

For the next four days Wayne McAdoo served as my mentor, showing me things that flight school didn't teach —such as how to land with your tail rotor shot out, combatlike autorotations, tricks of flying under in-country conditions—techniques that were not yet in the books. I flew more than seven hours in the command pilot's seat of Wayne's UH-1D while he sharpened me up for the in-country check flight. I wasn't too rusty, but it had still been about two months since I had actually been at the controls of a Huey.

Shortly thereafter, I was checked out and declared ready for immediate piloting duty in the lift platoon. As it happened, however, there wasn't yet room for me there. Not for a week or ten days, until a couple of the guys were rotated back home. Without a permanent slick piloting job, I got my only flying duty in C and C. The usual purpose of these flights was to transport squadron and troop commanders to base camps, fire bases, and night defensive positions (NDPs) for conferences with ground commanders. I flew maybe four C and C missions before a regular piloting opportunity opened up for me to airlift the ARPs.

As much as I grew to admire the work done by those guys in the aerorifle platoon, I never did like being a slick driver for them. Every day during that stint, I watched the early morning hunter-killer visual reconnaissance (VR) teams take off, heading out to find and engage the enemy. I desperately wanted to go.

The plight of the slick pilot was to sit on the ground and wait. Wait until the scout uncovered some sort of enemy activity that warranted the Cobra relaying the pulse-pounding call back to the base: "Scramble the ARPs!" Sometimes we took the ARPs directly into an LZ, but sometimes the order would be to just move the aerorifle platoon out of Phu Loi to another base closer to the point of action. After getting them to the new location, we'd just shut down the aircraft and wait for the possibility of a later call to move them into the action zone.

So, again, we'd wait. We'd read, sleep, maybe crawl up on the doghouse of the Huey to get a little suntan. And wait.

CHAPTER 3

SCOUTS

By the middle of March '69, being a slick driver looked as though it might become my life's profession. Not a day passed that I didn't wonder if Major Cummings had forgotten all about moving me to scouts. But while I was flying slicks, and wishing for scouts, I was learning. I was getting some in-country experience that helped me dry out a bit behind the ears.

I was becoming familiar with the 1st Division's tactical area of operational responsibility (TAOR). Vietnam's III Corps geography (war zones C and D) was getting pretty familiar to me: from the city of Saigon, the Dog Bone, and VC Island in the south to, roughly, Phuoc Vinh on the east, the Cambodian Parrot's Beak and Fishhook to the west on up to the Cambodian border on the north.

And I learned about going into hot LZs with enemy AK rounds tearing through the airframe, staying "in trail" while all hell broke loose around you. Though I desperately wanted out of Hueys and into OH-6s, I knew that I'd never sell slick pilots short on raw determination and basic courage. Slicks were not gunships. They weren't equipped with the firepower to deal with an enemy trying to shoot you out of the sky. The mission was to breach the enemy ground fire, stay in trail formation, touch down in that LZ long enough for the ARPs to jump out of the ship (usually no longer than about three seconds), and then get the hell out of Dodge. At fifteen hundred feet or more, where ground fire wasn't a hazard, most Huey pilots kept their seats adjusted high enough to see well out of the cockpit. But as their ships hit final into the landing zone, the pilots would pop the vertical adjustment so that the seat dropped down inside the seat armor plate. When the seat was all the way down, the top of the armor shield was just about at eye level—eyeball defilade, we called it. Then, when enemy rounds cracked through the aircraft, only your legs, part of your arms, and the top of your head were outside the armor plate. The front of your body was protected by the "chicken plate," and the .45 holster, tucked neatly between your legs, protected your masculinity.

In addition, I learned how to plot and call artillery strikes on a hostile target to neutralize the area before taking a flight of Hueys into the landing zone. And, on the ground, I also gained fame as the greatest rat-killer in the history of hootch number 28, having some legendary face-offs with the very large Vietnamese rodent.

But there was one thing I never did learn while I was flying slicks. That was how to be patient when I saw the hunter-killer teams taking off to scout out and lay destruction on the enemy. I didn't want to just react to the enemy. I wanted to be out there *finding* the enemy and laying the point of the bayonet to him.

During the days that I was flying Hueys, John Herchert was in and out of my hootch every once in a while. Herchert was commanding officer of the scout platoon, the Outcasts.

One day Herchert stopped by my bunk to tell me that one of his scout pilots had been hurt and there would be an opening in the platoon. "I need a section leader," he told me. "If you still want to fly scouts, we've got a job for you."

My transfer from slicks to the scout platoon was made on 23 March 1969. I had finally made it to the Outcasts!

The instructor pilot for the OH-6, CW2. Bill Hayes, was off on R and R for a few days when I was transferred, so I started my OH-6 orientation with scout pilots Bill Jones (One Eight) and Jim Morrison (One Four). I had a lot to learn.

The OH-6 had a personality all her own. She was light, nimble, and extremely responsive to every control input. While the Huey was stable, dependable, kind of like the faithful family sedan, the OH-6 was like getting a brand-new MGA Roadster. She was sexy!

The ship was unusually quiet in flight, giving her the added advantage of being practically on top of a potential enemy before anyone on the ground even knew a helicopter was around.

By design, the OH-6 was small and cramped. Her mission gross weight was just over 2,160 pounds. With the main rotor extended, she was only 30 feet, 3¾ inches long, and at the pilot's cabin just a fraction over 4½ feet wide. Not much space for two pilot seats side by side, with an instrument console in between.

There was room inside for just three people—the crew chief–door gunner on the right side of the rear cabin, the pilot in the right front seat, and the copilot-observer in the left front seat.

In combat configuration, the crew chief's jump seat in the back was rigged so that the gunner sat sideways facing the open right rear cabin door. His M-60 hung in front of him from a bungee cord. Having no seat belt harness per se, the crew chief had a "monkey strap" that secured him to the aircraft but allowed him to move around the cabin.

Vulnerable as he was to ground fire from the bottom and into both sides of the aircraft, the crew chief sat in a canvas jump seat, the underside of which was fitted with a tungsten carbide armor plate. He also wore two chicken plate body armor units, one shielding his chest and the other covering his back. The chicken plate body armor for aircrewmen consisted of a curved ceramic fiberglass shell over a tungsten carbide inner liner. This ballistic barrier was capable of defeating up to 7.62mm small-arms fire (such as AK-47 enemy rounds), but nothing as large as .50-caliber projectiles.

Under Herchert's system of flying three-man scout crews, each crew member had his own area of responsibility. The pilot basically flew the airplane. The crew chief, in the backseat right behind the pilot, was the door gunner and the crewman responsible for releasing grenades out the door. The various types of grenades were lined up on a wire strung across the back of the pilot's armor plate. These usually included several colors of smoke, Willie Pete (white phosphorus), and concussion and fragmentation grenades. Besides his M-60, the crew chief might also have other ordnance stowed around and under his seat, such as an M-79 grenade launcher, a shotgun, and an M-16 rifle. The experienced crew chief also helped with the scouting work on the right side of the aircraft in support of the pilot, who had to split his scouting mission between watching forward and sideways to the right while at the same time flying the aircraft.

The observer had the visual responsibility for the left side of the aircraft, from about twelve o'clock to his front to eight or eight-thirty behind. Strapped into the copilot's seat, it was difficult for him to see very far over his left shoulder toward the rear of the ship, but there was an excellent view to the immediate left and left forward. Scout ships flew without doors, so there was an uninterrupted field of vision.

The observer carried a weapon that he could fire out the left side. This was in lieu of minigun units, which were not mounted on Herchert's OH-6s. Some left-seaters had a standard M-60, but that weapon was less than satisfactory because of its weight and the fact that it would jam easily when fired with its casing ejector pointed against the airstream. So most observers used M-16s or CAR-15s. The CAR-15 was shorter and easier to handle. Both the M-16 and CAR-15 resisted jamming because they were magazine-fed from the bottom of the weapon and not affected by the force of the airstream.

The observer would also st. ing smoke, gas, and incendiary grenades on wires all over the front of the cockpit. Wires were hooked anyplace they could be on the side of the ship, and then connected to the ship's instrument panel. That provided room for extra grenades to be attached by their spoons to various places on the aircraft. Sometimes they were even stuck in holes in the instrument panel if instruments had been removed for repair.

The weight of the three crew members left no room for a minigun and ammunition. Scouting policy, as established by Major Cummings and John Herchert, was that a scout was to scout—nothing else. The scout half of the Loach-Cobra team was to find the enemy and, if fired upon, drop smoke and call in the Cobra to shoot up the place. The scout usually didn't even go back into the area to recon it after the gun made its passes.

I was aware that probably nine or ten sets of the XM27E1 minigun kits for the OH-6 were sitting in storage over at aircraft maintenance. But they had never been installed on the ships. The reasoning was that, with a minigun on the aircraft, the Loach pilot would be concentrating on shooting and not focusing on the scouting requirements at hand. It was not a scout's job, according to Herchert, to try to kill the enemy—just to find him for the Cobras.

It always seemed to me that the enemy, under those rules, had more control of his situation than we did. All Charlie had to do when a Loach got too close was to rip off a burst or two in the scout's general direction, and the OH-6 was gone, probably for good.

My first scout orientation flight was with Bill Jones, Darkhorse One Eight. On that first flight, I flew as the observer, in the left front seat. I was to be the third set of eyeballs on the mission, my initial VR-1 (visual reconnaissance team 1) operation. The date was 24 March 1969, and we were scheduled to depart at 0530.

We flew in the company of our "snake" (Cobra gunship) and headed for a recon of the Michelin rubber plantation, located about forty-five kilometers northwest of our base at Phu Loi. One scout and one Cobra usually comprised the hunter-killer team, and VR-1 was always the first regularly scheduled helicopter flight to go out in the early morning for normal reconnaissance of enemy activity.

The Michelin was known to contain large concentrations of enemy troops—a perfect place for me to start learning how to scout.

Dawn was still fifteen minutes away when Jones and I climbed aboard the OH-6 and strapped in. The crew chief was always the last one to get into the ship. It was his job to unsnap the fire extinguisher that was stowed at the pilot's right foot and stand fire guard at the rear of the ship while the pilot was cranking. He watched the engine section and, in case of a fire on start-up, he would alert the crew and allow them to exit the aircraft while applying the extinguisher.

While One Eight was running up the engine, he asked me to get on the radio and check artillery. Our flight was to take us from Phu Loi up to the vicinity of Dau Tieng, then on over the Michelin. The point in checking artillery activity was, as Jones subtly put it, "My whole day would be ruined if we fly into our own artillery rounds on the way up there."

When Jones had the aircraft at full running RPMs, he called the Phu Loi tower for clearance. The crew chief had replaced the fire extinguisher in the aircraft and climbed back aboard to secure his seat belt and monkey strap harness.

As we departed and cleared the perimeter fence outbound, the door gunner armed his M-60. He pulled the

bolt to the rear, locking it in place, then lifted the feed tray
cover, pulled on the safety, and inserted a belt of ammunition. The belt was tied directly to the fifteen hundred to
three thousand rounds of linked ammo in the wooden box
at his feet. He was then ready to fire with just the flick-off
of the gun's safety.

En route, Jones lined up on the usual forty-five-degree
angle off his Cobra's left wing and maintained altitude at
fifteen hundred feet. This altitude kept us out of the range
of enemy small-arms ground fire.

I kept a close eye on One Eight and paid careful attention to everything he was doing. There really wasn't much
for the observer to do until the mission area was reached.
I also noticed the team coordination between the scout
pilot, the scout gunner, and the observer. It was evident
that the scout pilot was the cement that held the team
together.

We were nearing Dau Tieng. Off at about two o'clock I
could see the tall, straight, tightly interwoven rubber trees
of the Michelin plantation. They looked lush and beautiful.

One Eight had told me that the area below us was
loaded with enemy soldiers, who felt secure there for a
couple of reasons. First of all, the thick foliage made it
nearly impossible to detect movement or military activity.
Second, the bad guys were aware that the United States
was reluctant to create an international incident and
would avoid going into the plantation after them, and possibly shooting up the invaluable rubber trees!

Jones was now on the radio talking to his gunship, asking about the rules of engagement for this mission. This
was always done before a scout ship descended into the
area to be worked. In some mission areas, the Cobra
would instruct the scout to maintain a "weapons tight"
condition, which meant that the scout was permitted to
fire only in self-defense. In other areas the scout had
"weapons free" authorization—he could shoot anything

that appeared hostile. Weapons free was the order for that day. One Eight was quick to tell me, however, that there was a modifier to both of those weapons conditions, that being the Darkhorse rules of engagement. It was troop law that nobody shot noncombatants or women or children, unless they were shooting at you.

Jones kicked the bird out of altitude and down to treetop level, where we would begin our scouting patterns. Until I had actually taken that helicopter fall from fifteen hundred feet to treetop level, I had no idea how dramatic and violent, how exhilarating and terrifying, that maneuver was. You were moving along comfortably in your aircraft on a horizontal axis. Then suddenly the ship was kicked over into a near-vertical descent, and your stomach felt as though it had just been pitched into the roof of your mouth.

Then, just as suddenly, that movement was followed by a recovery back into a horizontal axis for entry into the search area. The next thing you noticed was how close you were to the trees—how they suddenly were rushing by your feet at what seemed like hundreds of miles an hour, although you were flying somewhere in the vicinity of only sixty knots. But to a fledgling scout pilot, that seemed too damned fast!

All I could see was a sea of green—a blurred rush of foliage beneath the ship's bubble that was totally indistinguishable. The sensation actually made me airsick. The only way I could even briefly relieve my nausea was to concentrate on something in the cockpit that was not moving.

I wondered how in the hell a scout pilot was supposed to see anything on the ground flying like this. I had flown low level before, but always concentrating on my piloting, not on what was passing beneath me.

"Always," Jones said after we were down, "come out of altitude in an irregular manner." In his own quiet, almost philosophical way, Jones continued to instruct me over the intercom. "Remember back at Rucker how they taught you to come down in a standard flight school spiral . . . how to do those broad, regular, descending orbits that were just as predictable as going down a spiral staircase? Well, *don't ever do that* when you're scouting. It's not all that difficult for an enemy to determine your descent pattern and angle. He'll fix where you're going to come out over the ground, orient all his weapons in that specific area, and put his rounds right into your gut." That made sense to me.

"What you want to do," he went on, "is get out of altitude quickly. Come down a good distance away from the area you intend to work, then slide in low and fast so the bad guys have less chance of picking you up. Then as soon as you're down and start your sweeps of the area, begin looking for anything that jumps out at you, anything that looks different from everything else."

Jones radioed that he was breaking to go low level and start his pattern. His gun replied, "Roger that, One Eight . . . and why don't you take a look at that clearing off your right nose for any signs of bunkers in the tree line?"

Jones had come out of our descent at treetop level a mile or so away from the search area; now he made for the clearing pointed out by the gun.

After a few seconds running along the tree line, One Eight barked at me over the intercom. "Did you see that?"

"See what?" I yelled back as I scoured the ground.

"I'll come around again, and when I say 'now,' you look hard three o'clock right over my helmet visor and tell me what you see." I still didn't see anything but a clearing in the jungle; absolutely nothing seemed out of place.

Finally, in desperation, Jones said, "Look where I'm pointing. See the square shape there on the ground just beyond the tree line? That's a ten-by-ten enemy bunker. The entrances are the dark holes on either side." He continued in his schoolteacher manner. "The reason the bunker pops out to the scout is that square shape amidst a shapeless bunch of trees. It's out of place. It doesn't belong there."

Circling the area, Jones went on with his observations. "You can see also that the bunker hasn't been used recently—no beat-down trails in the grass around it, and the color of the camouflage foliage on top of the bunker is browner, deader-looking, than the surroundings." Jones turned to me. "If you're going to be a scout, you've just got to be alert to *anything*—"

At that moment, One Eight abruptly broke off his comment. I looked ahead to see the top of a dead tree looming in front of the ship. Jones jerked the cyclic stick back into his gut and hauled up the collective nearly out of the floor. The agile little OH-6 literally jumped over the top of the tree. We heard branches brush against the Plexiglas bubble and underside of the fuselage as we blew by.

"Holy shit!" I gasped.

Jones calmly went on talking. "You've just got to be alert to anything that jumps out at you, including the tops of old, dead trees."

It became obvious that learning to scout from a helicopter would be a continuing process of on-the-job training. There were no army manuals to consult, no special training classes to attend. There was, in fact, no in-place source for helicopter scouting information at all in the army, except the experienced aeroscout pilots who flew every day. Only they could tell and show you what signs to look for, and how to read, report, and react to those signs once you found them in the field.

The aeroscout's job, I learned, fell generally into four basic types of work (though all four might occur in a single scouting mission):

1. **Conducting Visual Recons (VRs).** Scouting for enemy base camps, fighting positions, supply caches, trails, and any and all signs of enemy movement and activity.

2. **Making Bomb Damage Assessments (BDAs).** Scouting areas hit by our B-52 strikes to evaluate bomb damage to the terrain, enemy structures, and personnel. This was generally done immediately following the strike.
3. **Evaluating Landing Zones (LZ Recon).** Scouting out potential landing areas for the lift platoon's Hueys. Making a careful aerial check of physical characteristics of the LZ, asking yourself the question, if I were flying with the slicks, would I like to land in that area?
4. **Screening for Ground Units (for example, the ARPs).** Flying on all sides of the friendly unit on the ground as aerial eyes to help them reach their objective, to give them information to guide their direction of movement, to help them choose the most advantageous terrain, and to keep the unit informed as to the area and situation to its front and flanks.

From 24 to 29 March, I continued to fly as copilot-observer with scout pilots Bill Jones and Jim Morrison. With my new scout call sign, Darkhorse One Seven, I logged 14.4 hours of combat flying, mostly in the Trapezoid area, which included the "Iron T," and the Michelin rubber plantation.

Both Jones and Morrison were excellent scouts and good teachers. They had been in Vietnam about the same length of time and had flown together, learning their scouting techniques from each other. Their basic methods were pretty much alike, but Morrison emphasized airspeed. "Don't get under sixty knots. If you do, you're going to get hit," he would say.

After much flying experience, I came to agree that Morrison was statistically correct. The more often a scout flew less than sixty knots, the more often he would take hits—no question about it. The Vietnamese ground gunners had a habit of firing right at you without applying any lead. By moving across the ground at sixty to seventy knots, their rounds would often hit three to four feet behind the ship.

With Bill Jones, scouting meant paying attention to every detail while still seeing the whole. Concentrating on shapes, colors, and hues, Jones made scouting an art. He understood, and introduced me to, the five basic principles of scouting from a helicopter: strict attention to contrast, color, glint, angles, and movement.

In time, I was able to lend my own degree of perception to these basics. I would discover, and rediscover many times over, just how fundamental these concepts were in finding, fixing, and destroying the enemy—especially an adversary who was so cunning in disguising his activities, and who was at home in his own environment.

Returning to base from those first scouting flights, I was physically drained but emotionally high—excited to get back into the air and do better next time. In self-evaluation, I recognized my problem: I was trying to see everything there was to see on the ground. Therefore I saw only masses of terrain swirling by. I did what every beginner scout pilot did—focused on the macro, not the micro. It flooded my senses, overloaded my sensory capabilities.

By 31 March, Bill Hayes was back from leave. That signaled the opportunity for me to start OH-6 transition, with Hayes as instructor pilot (IP) and me as first pilot.

Bill Hayes was a powerful, good-natured black man who must have weighed more than 220 pounds, stood at least six feet two, and had hands as big as tennis rackets. The scout bird was a small helicopter, and Bill Hayes didn't simply get *into* an OH-6—he put it on. Everybody who knew Bill well enough to get away with it called him Buff, which stood for big ugly fat fucker!

The first time I climbed aboard the OH-6 with Hayes, I couldn't help but notice how that scout bird settled down onto the ground with his weight. The landing gear on the OH-6 had shock dampers on the struts that supported the aircraft, to provide a hydraulic cushion to the skids during takeoffs and landings. As each crew member stepped up into the airplane, you could see the skids settle and spread out. When one of those people was Buff Hayes, you could almost hear the landing gear groan.

I had studied my dash 10 operator's manual, as well as the maintenance dash 20 and 30, and had been all over the Loach dozens of times, both by myself and with the crew chief. And I had spent literally hours in the airplane cold, in the pilot's seat with my eyes closed, mentally establishing where all the cockpit switches and instruments were.

On our first flight, Hayes instructed me to "get the ship out here in the area and hover it." This was the first thing a helicopter pilot did when transitioning into a new aircraft—hover the ship about three feet off the ground, then taxi forward and back, to the left and right. The exercise told you a lot very quickly about the idiosyncrasies of a particular aircraft.

Doing this basic maneuver in the OH-6, I learned something right away about this ship—left pedal pressure. On the OH-6, there is so much torque in the tail rotor that the left pedal had built-in pressure applied to it. You could actually feel that pressure in your feet.

In the Huey I was used to the foot pedals being somewhat unresponsive, almost mushy. If you took your feet off the pedals, there was no telling which pedal might gain movement over the other. In the OH-6, you *knew* what would happen. When you took your feet off the pedals, the left pedal jumped right back at you, invariably causing the nose to spin to the right. To turn the Loach left, I pushed the left pedal; to turn right, all I had to do was let off the left pedal.

After I got used to the ground handling characteristics, Hayes told me to take the OH-6 up in the pattern where I could get a feel for the bird's general control touch and how the ship flew and responded. By that time, I was beginning to fall in love with that machine. I tried not to display all the excitement I was feeling to Hayes. He just sat there in the left seat, very relaxed, watching my moves.

Hayes was known in the troop as one of those guys with

absolutely great PT (pilot technique). The old heads in the platoon had their own methods of rating their pilots. They would say, "He's a good stick man," or, "He's a good stick and rudder guy," or possibly, worse, "He's mechanical . . . he's behind the aircraft." But Hayes had overall pilot finesse that was rivaled by very few other fliers in the unit. Though he looked like a fullback in the pros, he flew a Loach the way Mikhail Baryshnikov danced. I felt fortunate that he was the guy teaching me to fly the OH-6.

I notified the tower, then took off and climbed straight out the runway heading to about eight hundred feet, then turned right into the crosswind, gaining altitude as I headed for fifteen hundred feet. Hayes would occasionally say something to me about a system or procedure, but he was generally quiet, carefully watching how I was reacting to the helicopter.

A good instructor pilot, such as Hayes, usually had his hands on the controls, lightly following the collective and cyclic sticks as the student flew the airplane. The smart transitioning pilot, which I hoped I was, always tried to watch the IP's left hand on the collective. With just a quick flick of his wrist, Hayes could suddenly twist off the throttle and shut down engine power, throwing me into an autorotation mode. I was then faced with getting the aircraft to a safe landing on the ground without the help of engine power.

If you were cruising along at an altitude of fifteen hundred feet, you'd have time to execute a standard autorotation procedure. But if you were at ninety knots and only twenty to thirty feet off the ground, you had to initiate a low-level, high-speed autorotation procedure designed to give you some more altitude before heading back down for a powerless landing. Either way, fast pilot reaction was necessary to get to the ground in one piece. Down collective, immediately, took the pitch out of the main rotor blades and set up air resistance against the flattened blades to keep you from falling out of the sky like a rock.

At the same time, you pulled the cyclic stick back into your gut. This action tilted back the rotor head, keeping the bird's nose up when what it really wanted to do was drop down to the ground.

Hayes warned me, however, about an imprudent move of the cyclic when in a low-level, high-speed situation. Such a movement held the potential of abnormally flexing the OH-6's main rotor blades and cutting off the tail boom of the helicopter.

The more I flew the Loach, and the more Hayes tested me, the more I fell in love with the OH-6. It handled beautifully. It was lively, responsive, and as light to the touch and maneuverable as any hot sports car. I logged 12.6 hours transitioning into the OH-6, most of that time with Hayes in the left seat, the rest with me alone in the ship.

Before Hayes signed off on my check ride slip, fully qualifying me in the OH-6, he took me on one more ride —down to the Saigon River to shoot the Loach minigun. Since our scout ships were ordinarily not armed with miniguns, Hayes had had an XM27E1 system especially mounted on one of the OH-6s just for transitioning pilots. He wanted me to fire the minigun to get a feel for aiming and to see what it was like to pull the trigger to the first indent, letting go with two thousand rounds per minute, then to the second indent, letting four thousand rounds a minute blaze into the target.

The armament system consisted of several components but was basically a 7.62mm, six-barreled machine-gun assembly, an electric gun drive assembly and ammunition feed and eject mechanisms, and a reflex sight. The sight, I learned, was never used or even carried. It wasn't too accurate and, worse than that, was totally in the way of the pilot in the cockpit.

Flying out and back from the firing site gave me a chance to talk to Hayes about my feeling that the scout ships should be armed with miniguns. I still felt strongly that aeroscouts should have the ability to shoot back at an enemy.

Hayes didn't agree. He, like John Herchert, Jim Morrison, and Bill Jones, felt that having guns routinely mounted on OH-6s could get scouts into trouble. It could cause them to think so much about shooting that they'd forget that their real mission was scouting.

I finished transitioning with Hayes on 3 April, and for the next couple of days went back to flying copilot-observer with Bill Jones. He was a master at spotting anything that contrasted with the natural environment. He might catch a slightly different color in the vegetation, maybe the glint of something shiny. Or possibly a movement would grab his attention, or an angular shape that appeared out of place in an otherwise shapeless jungle.

Bill continued to give me tips. He advised me to focus my eyes farther away from the ship, which would slow down the movement of the terrain and give me the chance to see individual objects instead of just a sickening blur. He told me, also, to "penetrate" my vision as the ship came in low and slow, to look through the top layer of jungle and concentrate on seeing right down to the ground.

One day Jones swooped down extra low. "Did you see those VC down there?" he asked me over the intercom.

All I saw were treetops. He brought the ship around again, decelerated, and told me to look down. Focusing my eyes past the tops of the trees, I looked through the foliage and there they were! Five angry-looking, brown VC faces staring up at us from the ground. Maybe I was beginning to get the hang of this.

In addition to being able to spot things on the ground, the scout pilot had to know how to coordinate with his Cobra orbiting above him. Being down on the deck most of the time, there were limits to what a scout could do. Flying the aircraft and having his eyes almost constantly focused on the ground, a scout seldom had time to glance at his instrument panel, let alone look at maps or talk on the radio. Therefore, his Cobra crew did all that for him. The gunship orbited a good distance above, watching every move the scout made. The copilot-gunner in the Cobra read the map, marked coordinates, and transmitted radio messages. He also aimed and fired the turret ordnance when the scout dropped smoke and called for a strike on a ground target. The pilot, the back-seater in this tandem crew AH-1 aircraft, flew the aircraft, always circling in the opposite direction of the OH-6, so that the Loach was always inside the gunship. The pilot kept a constant eye on the scout, so he'd know immediately if his little brother was getting into any trouble.

This was the hunter-killer team concept. The teamwork between these two elements grew to the point where the Cobra and scout actually anticipated each other's actions. Just a voice inflection over the radio could tell exactly what was happening, or about to happen.

So the scout had to learn to talk over the radio to keep his gunship informed. All of the scout's radio messages to the Cobra went out over the OH-6's UHF frequency. All of the Cobra's messages back to the scout were transmitted over VHF. Using both UHF and VHF ensured that a radio transmission between scout and Cobra was never garbled because both were talking at the same time over the same frequency. The scout usually talked all the time when he was working down low, conversationally reporting what he was seeing on the ground as the aircraft flew its search pattern. The Cobra crew was normally quiet, breaking silence only once in a while with two quick movements on the radio transmit button. This staticlike sound told the scout that the Cobra was receiving and understood. Radio conversation took place only when the gun pilot wanted the scout to do something.

Riding with Jones as copilot-observer, I carefully listened to his ongoing radio talk to the Cobra as he worked his pattern, while I tracked what he was seeing on the ground. As Bill pushed his search circles farther out over the area, he studied the ground below for a sign of traffic, reporting to the Cobra. Foot traffic could be picked up by coming across a trail or a marshy area where the enemy had moved through, leaving footprints, bent elephant grass, or some other sign of passage. From the appearance of the trail, Jones could estimate the approximate number of troops, as well as how old the trail was.

Footprints that could be seen distinctly indicated light traffic—only a few people. If the trail appeared indistinct and generally messed up, you'd know that heavy traffic had moved along it, walking over each other's foot impressions.

Bill went on to teach me that the direction of the traffic movement could also be determined by studying the footprint characteristics. Many VC wore what were called Ho Chi Minh sandals—nothing more than a couple of flat pieces of rubber cut from an old tire and strapped to the wearer's foot. The toe and heel parts were of the same shape, but when walking along, more weight was concentrated on the heel, resulting in a deeper impression. In addition, the toe pushed up a little ridge of dirt. By carefully checking out the heel and toe impressions left on the dusty ground, you could tell which way the people on the trail were traveling.

Suddenly coming across a sign of foot traffic below, Jones radioed the gun: "I've got a trail." Call signs between scout and gun were usually dropped when there was only one team of aircraft in the area. "It runs off to the northeast, heading zero three zero degrees, to the southwest at two one zero degrees. Indications of light recent traffic—two or three people within the last twelve hours, northeast bound. I'm going to move up the trail and check it out." Our phones hissed, "C-h-h-h-e-s-h-h . . . c-h-h-h-e-s-h-h," indicating that the Cobra had copied.

Bill started moving the OH-6 toward the northeast by using the trail as a guide and pushing his coverage circles out a little farther with each orbit, all the time studying the footprints, and any other signs along the way, to make sure that the enemy party hadn't left the trail.

"OK, I've got a place off the trail here to the right. Looks like they had supper here last night. I've got the remains of a small cooking fire. It's not smoldering . . . it's out."

The footprints took off again to the northeast, and Jones moved the Loach up the trail. "There's a bunker . . . about fifty feet off to the left of the trail. Looks like a twelve by twelve . . . maybe a storage bunker . . . a foot and a half, maybe three feet of overhead cover, well made, freshly camouflaged."

"Typically," Jones briefed me, "the bunkers we find fall into pretty uniform sizes: five by seven, eight by ten, twelve by twelve, fifteen by ten, with a twenty by forty being about the largest.

"When you report a bunker to the gun, give him the overall outside dimension and the estimated degree of the overhead cover. He'll record all that information on his charts for G-2 back at the base."

The scout identified a bunker by its shape, the condition of the camouflage on top of it, and the entrance holes either at the corners or on the flat sides. Those entrances showed up as dark splotches on the ground, and were usually dug in an L shape so Charlie could fire at you from the hole and then get back under cover. The L blunted any rounds fired into the entranceway after him. The smaller bunkers were generally to provide cover for VC moving along the trail. The larger ones were usually storage bunkers for supplies used to sustain Charlie while he was passing through or fighting in the area. Some were used as command posts.

Those additional days I flew as copilot-observer with Bill Jones were invaluable. I hung on his every word. Jones seemed able to sense trouble ahead. He would know in advance that he might be taking fire from an unseen enemy. I hoped that I would develop some of that warning light instinct.

CHAPTER 4

DARKHORSE ONE SEVEN

It was 8 April 1969, my twenty-first birthday.

Now, I smiled to myself, I could take a drink legally. I could also vote. I could even get, maybe, a slight reduction in my car insurance rates, if I were back home. It all sounded pretty silly in Vietnam.

First light was breaking over the Phu Loi runway, and the fact that it was my birthday was the least thing in my mind as I walked out of operations toward the revetment line where the OH-6As were parked.

Today I'd be on my own for the first time. I would be flying my own ship as the scout half of VR-1 hunter-killer team. Operations had just briefed us that gun pilot Phil Carriss (Three Eight) and I (One Seven) would be making a visual reconnaissance of the banks of the Thi Tinh and Saigon rivers. We'd be starting near Phu Cuong, making our way north along the Saigon River to the intersection of the Big Blue (Song Saigon) and the Little Blue (Song Thi Tinh). Then we'd scout north following the Saigon, winding our way up along the west side of the Iron T to see what Charlie might be up to along the rivers.

For my first solo scout mission, I would be flying a brand-new OH-6, tail number 249, belonging to crew chief Joe Crockett. I say "belonging to" Joe Crockett because I didn't have a specific airplane assigned to me. Platoon Sergeant Tim "Toon Daddy" McDivitt was the scout platoon sergeant for Troop D (Air), 1st Squadron, 4th Cavalry. He told the pilots what airplane they would be flying on a certain day, but the crew chief assigned to an airframe automatically flew with that ship.

I checked into 249's revetment, which was just across from the operations hootch, and Joe Crockett was waiting for me. I had met him before around the troop while I was flying observer with Jones and Morrison.

Crockett was a little fellow, about five foot six, and maybe 135 to 140 pounds. He had blond hair and was deeply tanned. I remember him saying that he was from somewhere in California, so maybe he'd had a good start on that tan.

Crockett was one of the most senior scout crew chief–observers in the troop. He really knew what he was doing when it came to scouting, and handling a green scout pilot. That, of course, was why McDivitt assigned me to Crockett's ship. It was traditional to put a brand-new scout pilot with a very experienced crew chief. That way both men had a better chance of staying alive.

Crew chiefs were all enlisted ranks. Pilots were either warrants or commissioned officers. But in an OH-6 flying a scouting mission, we were a team. Our lives quite literally depended on how well each of us did our job.

Crockett and I began walking around the ship, conducting the preflight exterior check. Without even looking at the plane's logbook, I could see that 249 was right out of the stateside factory. The OD paint was fresh and shiny. The Quarter Cav red and white insignia practically jumped off the fuselage. The black horse and blue blanket that was the Darkhorse emblem shimmered on the engine cowling doors. Crockett was as proud as a mother hen with a new chick.

As Crockett and I worked around the ship, I stopped on the right side of the fuselage to stick my finger in the fuel tank filler neck. This was my preferred way of checking the JP-4 level. For some reason, I never completely trusted fuel gauges.

There was another thing new about number 249. At my request, a new XM27E1 armament subsystem was mounted on the aircraft's left side. This was the rotating six-barrel, 7.62mm minigun that, on slow fire, expended two thousand rounds per minute, and four thousand per minute on fast fire.

Though I had little support among the experienced scout pilots in the platoon, I wanted a minigun on my ship. I had taken fire on several occasions flying with Jones and Morrison, and I had made up my mind that I wanted to be able to throw a little stuff back when the situation required. Even though Herchert's policy didn't authorize scouts to fly with miniguns, he didn't seem too bent out of shape when I asked for one. Of course, I wasn't sure he knew that I had actually had one installed.

Finishing up our preflight outside, I climbed aboard and strapped in. Crockett grabbed the fire extinguisher from its rack on the right side of my seat and posted himself as fire guard. I fingered the starter switch with my right index finger and started cranking the turbine.

In a little more than a minute, the ship was running and ready to back out of the revetment. Crockett secured the fire extinguisher, made a quick walk around to the left side of the ship to remove the bullet trap assembly from the minigun barrels, then slid into his seat behind me.

With Crockett strapped in, I pulled the collective up enough to get the ship light on her skids. Then I did my health indicator and trend test (HIT) check to make sure that engine power was responding as it should, and I was ready to go. I keyed my intercom mike. "OK, Crockett, are we clear to the rear?"

Crockett leaned forward from his seat so that he could see out the door. "OK, sir, you're clear . . . up and rear." He quickly followed with, "Your tail is clear right," letting me know that I could swing into a climbing left turn out of the revetment area without running 249's tail into anything.

I keyed my mike again: "Phu Loi tower, this is Darkhorse One Seven. I've got a hunter-killer team on the cav pad . . . north departure Phu Cuong along the Saigon . . . Lai Khe."

"Roger, Darkhorse One Seven flight of two, you're cleared to taxi to and hold short of runway three three. Winds are three five zero at eight knots, gusting to twelve knots. Altimeter setting three zero zero six. You'll be number two for takeoff following the Beaver on takeoff run now."

I responded to the tower by reading back the altimeter setting, while I actually cranked in the setting on my instrument. This was always necessary in order to calibrate my altimeter to current barometric pressure.

Pulling up short of runway three three, I waited for the Cobra. It took them longer to get cranked since their engine and systems were more complicated than those of the OH-6. Once the aircraft was beside me, I looked over at Carriss and gave him a thumbs-up and keyed my mike on troop VHF: "Three Eight, this is One Seven. Are you ready?"

Carriss triggered his transmit switch twice, indicating that he was set to go.

We both picked up and moved out to three three, where Carriss led the takeoff. The Cobra was always in the lead on takeoff, with the scout pulling over to his side very carefully.

One of the critical things in this two-ship takeoff was to watch the Cobra's rotor downwash. The Cobra was a much bigger aircraft than the OH-6, and both aircraft were at maximum gross weight because of the full fuel and ammo load. If the OH-6 pulled in just below and in trail with the Cobra, he would be right in the gun's rotor wash. The scout could easily lose his lift and bounce off the runway a couple of times before he got out of the Cobra's disturbed air.

As both aircraft cleared the perimeter fence, I could see the Cobra's minigun turret flexing as Carriss's front-seater began checking out his gun system. In our ship, Crockett did the same. Passing the perimeter fence was his signal to pull his M-60 back into his lap, draw the bolt back, load, and take the gun from safe to fire.

It was my signal, too. I stuck my left knee under the collective stick to maintain rate of climb and reached over to the console circuit breaker to power-up the armament subsystem. Then I went to the instrument panel with my freed-up left hand to flip on the master arms switch and turn the selector switch to "fire norm."

At that point, all the weapons in the team were hot and ready for any situation we might encounter. Any area outside the base could hold an enemy capable of firing on our aircraft. So when we crossed the fence, we had to be ready.

At fifteen hundred feet, out of the range of small-arms fire, I pulled the ship up on the Cobra's wing and into an echelon left for the flight over to Phu Cuong. The Cobra maintained about ninety to one hundred knots so the scout could keep up.

Crockett and I practiced a few signals over the intercom so we'd know exactly how the other would react when we got down low. Then we relaxed and smoked a cigarette. As we cruised along toward Phu Cuong, we engaged in a little small talk about the weather and the terrain below, and just kidded around to relax a bit before reaching the search area and possible contact with the enemy.

Snapping me back to reality, Carriss came up on VHF: "One Seven, you see the intersection of the Thi Tinh and the Saigon right off your nose?"

"Yes, I've got it."

"Due east of the intersection about three hundred

yards, there's a big green open space. Let's put you down in that area and work from there."

"Roger that." I could feel my exhilaration building. Finally, here I was in control of my own scout ship. I wasn't on an orientation or transition flight with someone sitting in the cockpit checking me out. There was just me and the crew chief. Crockett was completely dependent on me to fly that aircraft.

I began a visual search of the grassy area below. One of the many things I had learned from Jones and Morrison was that you just don't go down from altitude into a search area. You look it over first, while you are still high enough to change your mind if the enemy is waiting for you. I was looking for people, some sign of foot trails, or for anything else that seemed out of the ordinary.

Sensing that the letdown area looked OK, Carriss came up on my VHF: "OK, One Seven, we're going to do a VR up the Saigon River. We've got a free-fire five hundred meters on both sides of the Big Blue. No river traffic is authorized until after 8 A.M., so anything you see this early is enemy. You'll be clear to fire once you're down. When you're down, come around on a heading of three three zero degrees until you hit the river and I'll give you another heading from there."

I hit the right pedal, moved the cyclic stick right forward, and dropped the collective. This was a maneuver that Jones had taught me: The aircraft went out of trim on the right side and quickly skidded into a right-hand descending turn. I lost altitude fast this way and was on the deck in seconds. Carriss put the Cobra into a left-hand orbit so he could keep me in sight.

As the ground approached, I leveled the ship by moving the cyclic to left forward and pulling in power with the collective. This rolled me out straight ahead with a cardinal direction, which I needed to change immediately. Steering a straight-line course directly into the search area could be fatal if enemy ground troops happened to be around.

So the minute I rolled out, I turned. Turned again. Then again, finally going into a couple of orbits around the grassy area to make sure I was OK. I didn't see anything, and nobody was shooting at me.

I keyed my mike to Carriss: "OK, Three Eight, we're OK. How about a heading?"

"Roger, One Seven. Turn right heading three three zero degrees to the Little Blue."

Carriss was still up at fifteen hundred feet and had me in sight all the time. At his altitude, he had the macro view. Being right down on the deck, mine was the micro.

Seeing me pick up three three zero, Carriss came back: "OK, there you go. The river that goes off to the north-northeast is the Thi Tinh. The Big Blue is the Saigon off to the northwest. Follow the Saigon."

Acknowledging, I came up on the left bank of the Saigon and began working. For the best coverage of the terrain, I settled in on the left bank and then took up a long orbiting maneuver that circled me back and forth across the river. With the pilot's seat on the right side of the aircraft, homing in on the west bank allowed me to see right down on that bank and straight across to the east bank.

I began my search pattern by flying northbound up the river about a hundred yards, crossing the water to my right, coming back down the right bank about the same hundred yards, then completing the circle by returning left across the river in a series of wide, overlapping orbits. The forward working orbits gave me a clear view of everything fifty yards or so in from each riverbank, plus the ability to look down into the water.

On one of these orbits, I picked up a five-foot by five-foot inactive bunker on the west bank, and a series of fish traps in one of the several little tributaries emptying into the Saigon.

I kept up a steady stream of UHF reporting on what I was seeing, and Carriss's front-seater, I knew, was marking them on his map. At the end of the mission, he would use that marked-up map in his debriefing with division G-2 and G-3.

After about fifteen minutes down low in the search pattern, I was making my orbit back toward the left bank when something like a black pencil line in the sky caught my attention. About three or four klicks (kilometers) away on my right horizon, pale gray smoke was rising.

I keyed my mike and told Carriss excitedly: "Hey, Three Eight, I've got smoke! A cooking fire out there at about three four zero degrees, maybe three klicks off to my right. Do you see? Is it on the river?"

"Naw, I can't see it. Why don't you head that way direct and let's see what we've got." I gave Crockett a "Hang on," pulled a fast right turn, and took off straight for the smoke.

As I left the river, heading across a large open rice paddy, Carriss came up on the radio. "You're going right for a bend in the river. It's probably a cooking fire. Make a first pass but keep it fast; don't take any chances. Don't slow it down."

Intelligence reports we had received made me think that anybody in this neck of the woods with a cooking fire going at this hour of the morning had to be an enemy. But they could be civilians. How could I know before I came up on top of them at sixty to seventy knots?

In those split seconds of breaking away from the river, I suddenly thought of something Uncle Billy had taught me back in the Arkansas mountains. A squirrel up a tree trunk will always stay on the opposite side of whatever he thinks is an adversary. He will back around the tree away from a noise, keeping the tree trunk between him and any possible danger. Uncle Billy had told me to throw a rock around to the other side of the tree; when the squirrel backed around the tree, you would have a clear shot.

Coming in behind that cooking fire began to seem like a good idea.

I veered off sharply to my right about a klick away from the smoke, making a broad arc. By dropping down very low, and weaving my way below treetop level where I could, I figured I might be able to circle right in over the cooking fire on a heading of about two two zero. If they did hear us, at least we might confuse them by coming in on their backs from the north, instead of doing the expected and popping in on their front from the south.

Hitting about fifty knots, I suddenly broke in over a small tributary. Smoke from the cooking fire curled up right in front of my bubble. Reacting faster than I knew I could at this point, I dropped the collective, kicked right pedal, and yanked in enough right rear cyclic to abruptly skid into a right-hand decelerating turn. I looked straight down from fifteen to twenty feet of altitude, right into the faces of six people squatting around the cooking fire.

I could see weapons lying around, mostly AK-47s. There was one SKS semiautomatic rifle lying on a log across a backpack. The people were wearing shorts, some blue, some green, and the rest black. Nobody was wearing a shirt. One man had on a vest that carried AK-47 magazines. They all had on Ho Chi Minh sandals but none wore headgear. They obviously hadn't heard me coming. I don't know if I keyed my mike or not. All I remember is thinking, Holy SHIT! What do I do now?

As the soldiers dove in all directions for cover, Crockett ended my indecision. Without a word from me, he cut loose from the back of the cabin with his M-60. By now I had the OH-6 in a right-hand turning maneuver over the area, with my turns becoming tighter and tighter. Crockett blazed away with the M-60.

As one man lurched up and ran toward the underbrush, Crockett fired at him; his rounds cut across the dirt in front of him, then down his back.

Tah-tah-tah-tah-tah-tah . . . tah-tah-tah-tah-tah.

Crockett stitched two more men as they broke and tried to run. I was still in tight right-hand turns, finding myself almost mesmerized as I stared with tunnel vision at what was happening right under the ship.

Suddenly I became conscious of Phil Carriss's voice firmly commanding: "Get out of there, One Seven, and let me shoot. Get the hell out of there, Mills!"

Breaking my concentration, I pulled on power and headed up and out of the killing zone. Seeing me roll out to the southeast, Carriss said, more calmly now, "I'm in hot!"

As I headed out, the Cobra rolled in right behind me. Carriss bored in with his front-seater's pipper right on the spot we had just vacated. I could hear the s-w-o-o-s-h-h . . . s-w-o-o-s-h-h . . . s-w-o-o-s-h-h as pairs of 2.75 rockets left his tubes.

He pulled out of his run for recovery with the minigun smoking. W-h-e-r-r-r . . . w-h-e-r-r-r it spat as the Cobra front-seater flexed his M-28 turret on the target, following the rockets with a devastating blast of 7.62 minigun fire. Smoke and debris boiled up out of the target area. As I watched from my orbiting position out to the southeast, I couldn't help thinking about the words on the sign hanging on the wall of the troop operations room:

AND LO, I BEHELD
A PALE RIDER ASTRIDE
A DARK HORSE, AND THE
RIDER'S NAME WAS
DEATH

Carriss came back up on VHF. "One Seven, I'm going to roll back in for another pass. Are you OK?"

"I'm OK, Three Eight, and holding down here on the southeast."

With that, Carriss pulled a one-eighty, rolled back into the target from south to north, and placed more "good rocks" right into the cooking fire area. The devastation was a terrifying and sobering sight.

Once back up to altitude, Carriss asked me if I wanted to make a recon of the target area. I pulled on power and started back inbound, this time headed from southwest to northeast. The cooking fire, though I hadn't noticed before, was on the south bank of this little tributary off the Saigon.

The gun's rockets had blown away most of the vegetation and overhanging growth. There were craters where the rockets had impacted, and the entire area looked as though it had been sprayed with fine dust, dirt, and mud. In spite of all that ordnance coming into this little spot in the jungle, the enemy's backpack was still in its original place on the log, with the SKS rifle lying across it.

I had made a couple of orbits, looking over the scene, when Crockett, obviously very excited, came up on the intercom. "I got three dead VC . . . three dead VC . . . I got 'em in sight, sir. You see 'em . . . do you see 'em?"

My vision tunneled right into that area below the ship, where the three bodies were sprawled. On my third orbit, it finally occurred to me to look over toward the water. "Holy shit!" I practically screamed. Coming up right on my nose were two sampans, side by side, lying parallel to the bank. My scouting inexperience was showing. I was still focusing on individual things—the pack, the bodies, the devastation. I had failed to sweep the whole target area to see what else might be around.

One of the sampans had military equipment piled in it. The other one had a VC lying in the bottom of it face up, with an AK-47 pointed right up at me. I jerked my head around over my right shoulder and yelled at Crockett: "See the guy . . . you see the guy?" I didn't think to tell Crockett it was the guy in the sampan.

Crockett came back. "No, I don't see him. Where is he?"

My minigun! I thought. I'll use the minigun, since

Crockett can't see him. But, again, my inexperience reared its ugly head. I was coming up too fast and close for a minigun shot. In that instant, however, I somehow managed to dump the nose and pull on power. I was suddenly almost standing on end, looking straight down at the ground through the bubble, the ship's tail sticking up in the air almost perpendicular to the ground.

I jerked the minigun trigger and in my excitement pulled right through the first trigger stop into a full four-thousand-round blast. I had the cyclic pushed full forward, tail in the air and losing more airspeed every second.

Fighting to regain control of the helicopter, I jerked back the cyclic, armpitted the collective, and nearly crashed into the top of a nipa palm. I could hear Crockett screaming into the intercom: "Son of a bitch . . . SON OF A BITCH, sir! You cut that son of a bitch right in half!"

Coming around again, we could see the results of the minigun, at four thousand rounds full fire: The sampan and VC were literally cut in half and sinking into the foul river water.

Crockett was back with his M-60, reconning with occasional bursts of fire. As he put some rounds into the second sampan, he asked, "Do you want me to shoot the pack?"

"No. We'll put the ARPs down to sweep the area . . . don't shoot the pack. How many people is that?"

"There's one in the water, three on the bank . . . that's four . . . and a couple more I can't see. Don't know about them, sir."

Trying to control my excitement, I keyed my mike for the gun. "Hey, Three Eight, we've got a lot of stuff down here. We've got four bad guys dead, two sampans . . . we've got a pack . . . a bunch of weapons. We need to get the ARPs up here."

"OK, One Seven, why don't you head out to the southeast, build up some airspeed, and come up to altitude.

Let's hold you at altitude until we can get the ARPs on the way up here, then we'll scout an LZ for them."

I rogered that, then monitored Carriss's FM call to Darkhorse Three (operations officer) back at the troop. "OK, Darkhorse, we've got a hot target with some body count. Let's get the ARPs out here and put them on the ground . . . grid X-Ray Tango 677263. You might want to start Scramble 1. Tell him that we've got about twenty-five minutes on station . . . and start another team up here."

The Hueys—shut down on the "hot line"—were about to get the word to crank. Harris's ARPs, with their equipment laid out, were always on scramble alert. Everybody would run full bore for the Hueys, and the flight would be off the ground in three minutes or less.

I needed to quickly scout out a landing zone. They would require a spot close to, but not directly on, the target area. I found a suitable place in a nearby dry rice paddy and radioed the location to the gun for transmitting to the slicks. I didn't put a smoke down at the spot for fear of it being seen by the enemy. No reason to tell the VC just where our men would be setting down. The smoke would go in just before the slicks landed, to give them wind direction and the exact location of the LZ.

Having reported our fuel situation, it wasn't long before another hunter-killer (H-K) team came up on station to relieve us. Hootch mate Bob Davis was my scout replacement. As soon as he joined up, we went back down to about five hundred feet over the sampan area and I began filling Davis in on the action.

"OK, One Three, see where the rockets worked out up that little tributary off the Blue? The rocks hit on the south side of the bank and right under me now—mark, mark—we got three bodies, a pack with an SKS lying across it, some AK-47s. Right at the edge of the water are two sampans—cut one in half . . . a guy was in it . . . it sank. And there's another one behind it. Took no fire after our initial runs. Follow me for the proposed LZ."

With Davis on my tail, I came around to the southwest of the sampan area and keyed One Three again. "Right under me now—mark, mark—is the dry rice paddy recommended as an LZ for the ARPs. I'm low on fuel . . . you got everything?"

Davis gave me two clicks from his transmitter and I headed back to altitude to join up with the Cobras. Having received our briefing, One Three and his gun were now in control of the area and would wait for the slicks to show up with the ARPs. I got on Carriss's wing and we headed back to Phu Loi to refuel and rearm. On the way back to base, we passed the Hueys carrying the aerorifle platoon. They gave us a wave and a thumbs-up. Not having touched base with Crockett for a while, I hit the intercom switch and asked him if everything was OK in back.

"Yup," he said, "I'm rigging a smoke."

Looking back over my right shoulder, I saw him wiring a red smoke grenade to the muzzle cover of his M-60. I knew it was traditional for red smoke to be trailed when an H-K team returned to base after having scored a kill. It was a visual symbol to everyone at the installation, like the submarines during World War II lashing a broom to the bridge, signifying a clean sweep.

Coming in on the downwind, Crockett's M-60 poked out the door, trailing red smoke for all the world to see. I was coming back from my first scout mission, in command of my own ship, and trailing red smoke marking our kills— including my first from the air.

The emotion was one of excitement mixed with horror. My hands were trembling and there were no words. There was no need for them. I had engaged the enemy in combat, face to face. I had made mistakes, but I had accomplished a mission and survived. And I had drawn my first blood.

Happy twenty-first birthday.

CHAPTER 5

IMPACT AWARD

During March and April 1969, the 1st Infantry Division mounted three in-strength offensives to flush out Charlie and try to make him fight in the open on a larger unit scale.

The first operation, Atlas Wedge (18 March to 2 April), was designed to hit elements of the 7th NVA Division in a pincer movement in the Michelin rubber plantation. The second was Atlas Power (10 April to 15 April), calculated to go back again after the 7th NVA in the Michelin.

Intelligence reports had pinpointed the enemy's propensity to reoccupy an area once U.S. units had been withdrawn. Taking G-2's lead, Atlas Wedge troops were pulled out of the Michelin to see if the enemy would filter back in. They did. Then we did—hitting them with Operation Atlas Power.

Plainsfield Warrior was launched on 18 April against VC-NVA main forces in the Trapezoid.

Sandwiched between flying Atlas Wedge and Plainsfield Warrior cover missions, I flew a regular early morning VR mission, assisting the movement of a mechanized unit northeast of the "Testicles" (named for the two distinctive bends in the Song Be River at that point). An armor column, with M-48A3 Patton tanks in the lead, was busting jungle for M113 armored personnel carriers. The column was moving in on an enemy base camp that had been discovered on one of the hilltops. We were to scout ahead of the column to keep them on the best course to the camp and to alert them to any trouble we might spot out in front of them or to their flanks.

My gun pilot on 17 April was Pat Ronan (Three Three). All the scouts enjoyed flying with Pat. He was an aggressive and flamboyant Cobra driver, yet, outside the cockpit, he was quiet and reserved. He had the most impressive and distinctive mustache in the entire troop—a blond, bushy "Yosemite Sam."

At first light, Pat and I lifted out of Phu Loi and pulled around to a heading of zero three five. It didn't take us long to reach the target area and pick up the column, which was already en route toward the NVA base camp.

Pat put me down in front of the column to check out the area and sweep the base camp a time or two to see if I would draw any fire. We didn't know if the camp was still occupied.

The call sign for the mechanized team leader on the ground was Strider One One. Working to his front and flanks, I saw nothing that caused me any concern for his column, so I told him to keep rolling toward his objective grid coordinates.

Flying over the base camp location, I didn't draw any fire, though there was evidence of recent foot traffic around some of the bunker entrances. I also noted that fresh camouflage had been placed here and there.

On my next sweep over the camp, my crew chief, Al Farrar, suddenly hit the intercom: "Sir, I smell dinks. They're in here, I know it. I smell 'em! Don't get too slow, Lieutenant. They're in here, I can smell the fuckers!"

Relatively new to the outfit, Al Farrar was a good-looking nineteen-year-old from Rhode Island. I had flown with Farrar before and knew I could trust his hunches. You actually *could* smell concentrations of the enemy from the air. I don't know if it was a lack of basic personal hygiene, their mostly fish diet, or a grim combination of the two. But you could catch a very distinctive odor when enough VC were together in one place—a pungent, putrid odor, heavy and musklike.

I switched my radio to FM transmit. "Strider One One, this is Darkhorse One Seven. My chief smells bad guys. Keep moving heading zero three five, straight for the base area."

The column commander came back: "Darkhorse One Seven, Strider One One. Roger that. Moving on zero three five."

Turning out of the base camp area, I came back over the armor column. I checked out Strider's flanks and then began a slow orbit over the column, watching it work.

Even as an armor officer, I had never seen anything like this. The two main battle tanks in front literally knocked down trees and burst through jungle undergrowth, making a path for the lighter, more vulnerable M113 personnel carriers.

Then I headed back for another look at the column's front and the base camp just beyond. Damn! As I swept back in over the base camp, there was an enemy soldier—big as life—standing on top of one of the bunkers. I could see his face clearly. No question, he was as surprised as I was.

In the split second it took me to pass over him, I could see that he was wearing a pair of tiger-striped fatigues and was holding an RPD light machine gun. The weapon had a wooden stock, pistol grip, drum magazine, and a bipod hanging from the end of the barrel—not yet pointed at me!

Just as I went over the soldier, he jumped down into the bunker and I could hear Farrar scream, "I've got a gomer!" The crew chief didn't even have time to key his mike. He let go with a yell that I could hear through my helmet and over the noise of the turbine and rotor blades.

Farrar triggered his M-60 and sent a hail of lead at the VC as he dove into the bunker entranceway. I banked a hard, quick right and decelerated to give Farrar a better shooting angle, then got on Uniform to Ronan: "Hey, Three Three, we've got enemy on the ground here and taking them under fire."

Watching what was happening below like a mother hen, Ronan came back instantly: "OK, One Seven, come on out of there and let me work the area with rockets."

I had been chided the last time for mixing it up too long with the sampans, so I rolled straight out of the area and got on FM to the mechanized team commander. "Strider One One, this is Darkhorse One Seven. You've got people in the bunkers ahead of you. I'm going to pull out of here and go up to altitude . . . the gun is going to work a little bit. Continue your movement and I'll be back with you as soon as we put some rockets on the ground."

Strider came back: "OK, Darkhorse, I roger that. We'll be clear to do a little fire to the front, and we've got the Cobra in sight."

Ronan made a run into the area, shooting rockets. Just as he was beginning to pull out of his run, green tracers arced up out of the base camp, directly toward the Cobra. Ronan broke over the radio, yelling, "Three Three's taking fire . . . TAKING FIRE!"

My eyes were glued to the Cobra. As Ronan broke off his run and peeled to the left, I could see his turret depressing underneath him, spraying the area with 7.62 minigun fire.

Hearing Ronan yell and seeing green tracers reaching up for his ship, I snapped. Without another thought, I rolled the little OH-6 practically on her back and aimed the ship right straight back into the bunker complex with my minigun trigger depressed.

"One Seven's in hot!" I managed to shout. It never occurred to me that, up to this point in time, no scout pilot had ever rolled in on a target in an effort to protect a gunship. I shot a descending run right in on top of the bunker, firing the minigun all the way. Coming up off the guns, I moved out a distance over the trees and then climbed back up to altitude.

By this time Ronan was back up to altitude and ready to let fly again. Peeling over to his left, he asked, "Are you out of there, One Seven?"

"Yes," I answered, "I'm coming out to the right."

"Three Three will be in hot from the north." With that, the Cobra rolled in shooting a second time, and again I could hear his pairs of rockets leave the tubes and trail smoke toward the base camp bunkers below. And, again, green tracers arced up toward him. "Three Three is taking fire . . . taking fire again."

Watching the base camp carefully for the source of the fire, I called Ronan. "One Seven's in hot from the south. Three Three, make your break to the left so I won't shoot into you."

In I went with minigun blasting, chewing up the terrain where I had seen the green tracers coming from. Between the rockets and minigun fire, the VC must have been taking casualties, or else they were burrowed awfully deep into the tunnel complex beneath the bunkers. We were causing a hell of a commotion topside.

We made one or two more hot passes, then Ronan went in cold a couple of times to see if he drew any fire. He didn't, so I went down for a fast scouting pass to confirm Charlie's demise.

While I was making a low, quick check of the damage done by Ronan's rockets, I caught a glimpse of another enemy soldier out the corner of my eye. This one was dressed in dark navy blue clothing and was hunkered down in a stretch of trench line that ran between two bunkers.

I instantly slid the OH-6 around into a decelerating right turn and looked the soldier square in the face. Probably thinking that he had me cold—which he did—the VC

raised his AK-47. His weapon seemed aimed right between my eyes. As I stared, my crew chief let go with his
M-60. The soldier lurched backward, practically cut in half
by machine-gun fire.

Holy shit, I thought. HOLY SHIT! Beads of sweat
pricked my forehead as I realized the situation that Farrar
had just pulled me—*us*—out of.

Just then Ronan radioed that another hunter-killer
team had come up on station to relieve us. The scout pilot
taking my place was Jim Ameigh (One Five), one of my
hootch mates. I briefed him on the situation, flying him
through the base camp area and back over Strider One
One, then joined Ronan for the flight back to Phu Loi. On
the way back, I really didn't think too much about the
action. It didn't seem like any big deal. But I had forgotten
about ops officer Capt. John Herchert.

He was smoking! I went into the operations hootch just
behind Ronan, and Herchert was waiting for me. He stuck
his face right into mine and stared me in the eye. Then, as
if to punctuate his words, he poked me in the chest with
his finger while he raked me over the coals. "You are not a
gunship. I didn't teach you to be a gunship, and you had
no business running in there hot like that. The gun on that
scout ship is going to get you killed."

I didn't intend to be insubordinate, but anger showed in
my voice when I shot back, "What in the hell did you
expect me to do? Nothing? Do nothing while Ronan is
down there getting shot at?"

Luckily for both of us, Ronan stepped in at that moment. "You know, John, if Mills hadn't fired when he did
to take the enemy pressure off me, they might have had
me cold."

Herchert turned to Ronan as if to ask what the hell he
was doing in this conversation, but Pat finished his comment: "I don't think what he did is a bad idea. He fired
from altitude in a diving pass and, frankly, I just don't
think it was a bad tactic at all."

Herchert's jaw went slack. Ronan turned and walked out of the room and off toward his hootch. So did I. Herchert never mentioned the subject to me again. Pat Ronan, however, did not forget the incident. Unknown to me at the time, he recommended me to receive the Distinguished Flying Cross.

It was not something I was consciously trying to do, but I was developing a reputation—especially among the gun and slick pilots—as a "hot dog."

I was flying scouts the only way I knew to fly scouts. I wanted the firepower of that minigun on my ship. I wanted to stay in there and duke it out with the enemy as long as I could, not just simply haul ass and take cover every time my scout ship took a round from the ground. I felt strongly that the accepted scouting tactic of making enemy contact and then backing off for the gun to come in and blast was bullshit.

Charlie wasn't dumb. He knew that a few AK-47 rounds thrown at a scout ship was a sure way to get the scout off his back. It was definitely to the enemy's advantage to shoot at a scout ship every time he had a chance. But when the scout stayed and slugged it out, the rules of the game changed in the scout's favor.

The enemy, once discovered, had a decision to make: Am I going to throw a few rounds at the scout to try to get him to back off, or am I seriously going to try and shoot down the scout? If I decide to shoot down the scout, can I? If I do knock him down, what the hell is that Cobra going to do to me?

That's the way I wanted to play with Charlie's mind. But I had definite limits on staying and playing with the enemy. I knew when to get myself out of Charlie's airspace in a hurry. When I saw that I had lost fire superiority and had failed to influence the action, it then became foolhardy to continue engaging the enemy. But until that time in a firefight, I saw no reason for the scout to break off.

If I was, indeed, becoming the hot dog in the troop, the younger, more aggressive scout pilots seemed to support it. However, my good friend and mentor, Bill Jones, told me in no uncertain terms that he thought I was crazy. "If you keep up that kind of stuff," he said to me one day, "you're going to get your ass loaded with lead. You're just plain going to get yourself killed!"

For the duration of Operation Plainsfield Warrior, we were flying four, five, six, or more hours a day. I was learning more about the OH-6 with every flight. With the added experience of every mission, I was becoming a better scout pilot. I was beginning to realize that the essence of scouting really hadn't changed over the years. From the cavalry scout of the Indian wars to the aeroscout of the Vietnam War, the essential quality for being a good scout remained the same: the ability to read sign.

I discovered that I was developing something of an instinct—a little warning bell that went off when danger was near. It was a feeling in my gut, coupled with a tingling on the back of my neck, almost as though it was electrified. When I got that feeling, my senses automatically doubled guard. I could trust my senses, too. When the internal alarm went off, I generally found trouble.

On 26 April 1969, I was just four days away from wrapping up my first full month of flying scouts. That day I was lined up with Cobra pilot Bruce Foster (Three Two) to fly another routine reconnaissance mission up north of the Iron Triangle in the western Trapezoid area.

As VR-2 that morning, we left Phu Loi at about eight o'clock and headed up north into the Thi Tinh River valley. The G-2 had instructed us to look for enemy traffic along trails, VC base camps, new construction, signs of occupation—anything that might show us the location or the movement of enemy troops. Charlie had been making himself fairly scarce these days.

We came on station up in the Trapezoid, roughly on an

east–west line running from fire support base (FSB) El
Paso to FSB Lorraine.

Foster put me down over an area we called the Easter
Egg and I began working along the trees. I twisted and
turned, trying to get a look down through the jungle vegetation. We took no fire, saw no enemy.

Suddenly Foster came up on VHF: "One Seven, turn
left to a heading of one eight zero degrees, southbound.
I'll give you steering corrections. We've got infantry troops
in contact down to our south. I just got a frag order to
move us down there to look at the area." I rogered the
transmission and pulled a hard left turn to come up on a
reverse heading of one eight zero.

Getting the order to make a move wasn't that much of a
surprise to us. We had heard Sidewinder come up on the
Guard frequency a minute or two earlier, asking for any
aircraft in the vicinity of grid X Ray Tango 677367 to give
assistance to an enemy-engaged ground unit. Guard was
the universal distress frequency. Sidewinder was the radio
call sign for the air force FACs (forward air controllers)
who operated in this area supporting the 1st Infantry Division. The FACs had the basic mission of directing artillery,
rescue, and calling in fighter-bomber strikes. They flew
USAF OV-10 Bronco twin-engine, twin-boom reconnaissance aircraft.

Sidewinder was also unique in that it had a number of
exchange pilots from the Australian Air Force. On this
day, the accent coming up on Guard told us immediately
that this Bronco driver was from down under: "This is
Sidewinder Two Two. I've got infantry just inserted on the
ground and not even out of the landing zone. They've
been hit . . . their column is cut . . . got troops missing,
and the company is bloody well pinned down."

Before I even heard the grid, I knew that the contact
point could not be far away from where I was working up
in the Trapezoid. I knew that because Foster left me down
when he gave me the one-eighty heading. If the action had

been quite a distance away, he would have brought me back up to altitude and put me on his wing for the trip.

I stayed on the deck, heading south along a small, nearly dried-up tributary. After a while, it led into the upper Thi Tinh valley and to the main body of the Thi Tinh River. Actually, the Thi Tinh is little more than a stream.

I couldn't see a hell of a lot, down as low as I was. But Foster was guiding me from altitude and was also briefing me on the tactical situation: "One Seven, follow the Thi Tinh south. Where the tributary turns back to the north-west, there's an LZ. We put Alpha of 2/16 Infantry in there . . . they moved up northeast into the woods. The lead element walked into a VC base area and has been cut off from the trail element. They've got four to six people down and they're split off from the main group. Can't make contact to locate missing parties or provide information on what's out in front of them."

Sidewinder had given us the call sign and FM frequency for the infantry unit on the ground in landing zone Toast, so I came up on fox mike 46.45 and keyed the ground unit commander. "Gangplank Six, this is Darkhorse One Seven. We are a hunter-killer team arriving from the north. Should be at your location in about thirty seconds. What have you got?"

With sporadic bursts of small-arms fire audible in the background, the ground unit commander sharply reported back on FM. "Roger, Darkhorse, this is Gangplank Six. We've got a platoon in the woods northeast of my position. As soon as they cleared the LZ we picked up heavy fire from light weapons. I've got one platoon pinned down . . . they're attempting to maneuver now against the bunkers. Got five or six people in the lead element who are cut off. We need to locate enemy position and find out what's happened to our people."

"Roger that," I responded. "I should be there about now. Can you give me a smoke to mark your lead element?"

"Smoke's coming."

Closing rapidly from the north, the LZ area popped out right ahead. Watching me like a hawk and monitoring all the radio transmissions, Foster asked me how I felt about starting a search pattern. "Ready!" I answered.

Foster immediately keyed Gangplank. "OK, I'm going to bring the scout in. Stop firing. I say again, stop firing so you don't hit him when he makes his pass to get an idea of how you're situated."

Then, to me, Foster instructed, "OK, One Seven, come in far enough south from the contact point that Charlie can't identify. Make your first pass fast from the southwest to the northeast. I'll guide you onto the LZ."

Looking over my right shoulder at my crew chief, I keyed the intercom. "Farrar, are you ready?"

I could see his boyish grin. "Ready, sir. Let's get 'em!"

In an instantaneous response to my control movements, the little OH-6 pulled into a hard right turn and came around directly over the trees. Foster gave me a fast, "Right ten degrees, back left five degrees."

I broke in over the jungle onto the southern end of the LZ just as I spotted the ground unit's yellow smoke billowing up—just into the tree line at the far end of the landing zone.

To let the ground commander know that both the gun and scout were aware of the lead element's location, Foster transmitted, "Gangplank, the gun's got your smoke, and identified."

I came roaring in low at a fast eighty to ninety knots, right over the heads of our troops in the landing zone area. I could see them deployed on each side of the LZ, guarding against the prospect of the VC making any movements against their flanks.

Then, as I approached the far end of the LZ, the company commander's position flashed underneath me. He was about fifty meters back from the tree line in the middle of the landing zone, with his RTO beside him, and he was motioning me in a northeasterly direction toward the location of his lead element.

I circled the tree line but didn't see anything. I came around again, circling at the yellow smoke. But I still didn't see anything or take any fire.

The area I was circling was approximately an acre in size with triple-canopy jungle. Trees were 100 to 150 feet in height, and at the speed I was going I couldn't see down into the jungle. I couldn't locate any sign of the friendly lead element or the enemy bunker area. I slowed down and tightened the circles I was making. I got slower and slower . . . still no ground fire. Still couldn't see anything.

The OH-6 began to talk back to me. As I got close to a hover, I had to begin to use the left rudder authority to hold the aircraft in trim. And I knew I was a perfect target for enemy ground fire.

But screw that. I kept the OH-6 lying over on her right side while I circled so I could see straight down into the trees. While I strained for a glimpse of the platoon's lead element, I kept keying the intercom to ask Farrar if he had seen anything. Al had his head poked as far out the door as he could get it. I could hear the air rushing by the aircraft when he answered, "No, sir, I don't have anything . . . nothing yet."

As I circled around for a third time, I cued the infantry ground commander. "Do you have any radio contact with your people out front?"

"No, Darkhorse, we haven't been able to talk to them, and every time we try to move forward we get fired on by AKs and SGM light machine guns. We haven't been fired on in the last few minutes, but every time we move they take a crack at us. We think that our people are fifteen to twenty meters ahead of us. They are our point team."

On the third pass, I spotted the lead element of the infantry company, half in and half out of the woods. Just at the tree line, one of the lead soldiers was lying on his back, waving to me and pointing to his front.

I needed to know who this soldier was. "Gangplank, I've got your lead element. A man is waving at me and pointing toward his front. Can you identify him?"

"Roger, Darkhorse. That's Three Six, Gangplank Three Six. He's the leader of our northernmost element, and it's the people from his outfit who are cut off."

"OK, Gangplank," I came back. "Now that I've got your lead element, let me go to work." I immediately pulled the ship into a tighter orbit—almost to a hover—then moved over top of the lead soldiers to a position where I could look down into the trees just beyond our friendlies. I still didn't see any sign of their point men.

Then, suddenly, Farrar yelled into my phones. "Hold on . . . hold on, sir, I see a leg . . . you see the leg?"

By the time Al shouted, I had gone past his point of reference. I hauled a sharp one-eighty and came to a hover just as Farrar yelled again, "Here, sir, right under us. Mark, mark right under us. Do you see the guy's leg?"

Sure enough! As I strained to see through the trees to the ground, I saw the leg of a soldier lying dead still on the jungle floor. I recognized the jungle fatigues—U.S. type—with an American jungle boot on the right foot. But that was all I could see—the point man's right leg and foot.

I keyed the mike. "OK, Gangplank, I've got your people located. They're out in front of you about forty meters and I'm going to—Damn! I'm taking fire . . . taking fire!"

I instantly pushed the OH-6's nose full forward on the cyclic and pulled an armpit full of collective. This jerked us up and away from the AK-47 that had opened up from directly below. It was definitely an AK-47. I had flown scouts long enough to recognize its loud, sharp, ripping staccato. Everybody remembered that weapon. It was a sound you never forgot.

Neither Farrar nor I saw where the rounds had come from. I could tell only that they were close beneath us, probably not more than twenty to thirty meters on either side.

I guessed, also, that our enemy below was probably NVA rather than VC. It was fairly well known that the Viet Cong, when discovered from the air, were less controlled and quicker to shoot at their target. Regular North Vietnamese Army troops were more disciplined. They would let a target come right up on them before revealing themselves by firing.

Cobra pilot Foster probably didn't need my "taking fire" radio outburst to know that I had undoubtedly run into a bunch of trouble. When he saw my nose drop down and my tail flip up, he knew I was trying to get my ass out of there in a hurry.

The maneuver had rolled me out straight ahead, putting some speed and distance between me and the AK-47. As I pushed the OH-6 for all she had, I keyed my mike to talk to Foster. "Three Two, One Seven is taking AK fire down here. I'm coming back around to the right."

I knew there wasn't anything the gun could do. He couldn't shoot because the friendlies were right underneath me. Speeding up to about sixty knots, I made a right turn and headed back over the landing zone again. In the few seconds that it took me, my mind was whirling. I kept asking myself, what in the hell am I going to do? I can't shoot, the gun can't shoot. I'm not sure where the cutoff friendlies are. The enemy can shoot at me, but we can't shoot back because we don't have a defined target. What can I do?

While I was trying to figure this out, I switched to FM and reported to Gangplank. "I took heavy fire from an AK-47 right underneath me, maybe from a trench line. The jungle is too thick for me to see who was firing. I did see one of your point men . . . at least one leg, that was all I could see. Couldn't tell if he was dead or alive."

Gangplank rogered as I tried to decide what tack to take. We had to think of something. The more I thought about it, the more I believed that the only way I could do any good was to define what was on the ground.

"Gangplank," I radioed, "I'm going to hover back into that last contact area on a heading of zero four zero, then widen up my orbit to see if I can draw their fire. When I do, you have Three Six begin crawling forward on zero four zero to see if he can link up and get his people the hell out of there."

Then I keyed the intercom to fill in Farrar. "Stand by, Al. The only thing I can figure out to locate the bad guys is for us to go in there low and slow and let them shoot at us, then hope that the infantry on the ground can see where the enemy fire is coming from and try to suppress it long enough to move forward and get their people out. How do you feel about that?"

There wasn't a sign of unwillingness or hesitation in his voice. "Whatever you say, sir. Let's do it now!"

I went in right on top of the trees at thirty to forty knots. I knew I was going to get shot at again, so I squirmed down inside my seat armor plate and waited for the rounds to come.

Realizing that OH-6 crew chiefs had no back or side armor on their jump seats, I snatched another fast look over my shoulder to see how Farrar was situated. He wasn't even *on* his jump seat! He had propped his left buttock against the leading edge of the little seat, anchored his right foot on the edge of the door, and swung his entire upper body outside the airplane. He had his M-60 pointed straight ahead with his finger on the trigger so he could shoot back the minute we were fired on.

"Shit," I muttered to myself. Here I was all hunkered down in the protected pilot's seat, and there was Farrar hanging outside the aircraft!

It doesn't make any difference if you are expecting it or not; the instant you take fire, it is a razor-sharp shock to your whole body.

R-R-R-R-R-R-I-P-P! The sudden AK bursts came back up again from the jungle floor.

"Taking fire . . . taking fire!" I shouted into the radio again. My voice had gone up a few octaves. "Mark. Mark! Right underneath us. AKs . . . AKs . . . again!"

I broke a hard right, then a hard left to zig me out of the line of fire. All the Cobra could say was, "Roger . . . roger . . . we mark." Foster was still in the unenviable position of only being able to locate on his map where all this was happening, rather than rolling in with all ordnance blazing.

Coming in from different directions, I repeated the decoy action several times during the next thirty minutes, each time marking the location we thought the fire was coming from.

As busy as I had been flying, trying to dodge fire, and searching the jungle floor below, I hadn't looked much at my flight instruments until Foster finally asked, "How are you doing on fuel?"

A quick glance at the gauge and I answered, "Wow! I've got to come up, Three Two. I've gotta go get some gas. How are you doin'?"

Foster came back. "I'm OK, I've got plenty for now. You think we better get another hunter-killer unit up here?"

I thought about that for a second. "OK, Three Two, roger that. But you better have the scout go on over to Lai Khe and shut down. No sense putting another scout down here and having him go through the same thing I've done. But we should probably keep the guns up full time over the contact area in case something develops."

Foster agreed and I switched back to FM. "Gangplank, this is Darkhorse One Seven. I've gotta get out of here for some fuel. Two more guns are on their way up here now. If you need ordnance on the target, contact Darkhorse Three Two on this push. We're not putting down a new

scout to stomp around in this mine field. As soon as I can
gas up, I'll be back. Hang in there, Gangplank."

"OK, roger that." Gangplank had a calm but urgent
tone in his voice. "We appreciate what you're doing, Darkhorse. We've made some progress, but Charlie is in a
bunker line and our people who are down are on the far
side of their trench line, so we've got gooks between us
and our point men, and they've got us cross-fired. So get
back to us, One Seven, as soon as you can, OK?"

Rogering that, I pulled the ship around to head southwest down the LZ, so I could build up some speed for an
altitude climb. When I reached 100 to 105 knots, I leaned
hard aft on the cyclic and pulled a cyclic climb up through
about eight hundred feet, then leveled off at a thousand
feet and made a direct course for Lai Khe.

Now that we were up and out of the contact area, I took
another look at Farrar. "How ya' doin' back there?"

He was back on his jump seat. "I'm fine. You OK, sir?"

"I'd be a hell of a lot better, Al, if you'd light me a
cigarette."

"I don't know if I can," he laughed, "my hands are shaking so goddamned bad!"

I grinned back at him. "I'm sure glad to hear you say
that, because my hands have been shaking ever since that
first pass." Then we both started laughing, which broke
the tension of the last hour.

I switched my radio to Lai Khe artillery and told them
that a single OH-6 was en route to their fueling pad to
take on a little gas and ammo. No artillery was coming out
of Lai Khe at the time so they cleared me direct.

The refueling pad was nothing more than a pinta-
primed assault pad with JP-4 lines running up and down
the sides and nozzles about every forty feet. There were no
support people there to help you. The crew of the aircraft
needing fuel was expected to do that.

I hovered into the pad area and set down near a nozzle
that was on the right side of the airplane. The fuel intake

port on the OH-6 was just under and slightly behind the crew chief's position.

We were refueling hot (not shutting down the airplane's engine), so Farrar stepped down out of the ship, lowered the visor on his helmet (a refueling safety precaution), picked up a nozzle, and started pumping JP-4. I stayed in the aircraft at the controls (I have a good, strong four-hour bladder) and kept the OH-6 at flight idle RPMs.

When Farrar finished fueling, he jumped back in the ship. I picked up to a hover and moved about a hundred yards down the strip to the rearm point.

We hadn't expended any rounds up till now, but Farrar wanted to throw in a handful of extra belts just in case. As he was laying in the fresh ammo, he plugged himself into the intercom. "Hang tight here for a minute, Lieutenant, and let me look over the ship."

Unplugging himself, Farrar began walking around the helicopter, looking at the blades, nose, underside, skids, and tail rotor. He came back to the cabin, shaking his head and with a grin on his face. "Lieutenant, you know the battery vent back there?"

"Yes, so?" There was a single vent on the bottom of the aircraft; while the engine was running, you could see battery fumes puff out of it every once in a while.

"Well, sir, we've got three of them now—the one the factory installed as original equipment, plus two modifications that were just put in during the last flight."

Two rounds of AK-47 fire had hit the bottom of the airplane, passed up through the self-sealing section of the fuel cell, and come out the top of the ship, putting holes in the transmission cowling in the doghouse area.

Thinking that some vital engine parts may have been hit, Farrar asked me to inspect my instruments. I carefully checked out the gauges that monitored engine functions. The turbine gas temperature (TGT) was OK, and everything else checked out within normal limits. "Everything seems OK," I reported to Farrar. "How big are the holes?"

"Pretty big, sir, about .30-caliber size. Wait a minute and let me check some more." He crawled back and opened the engine cowling doors. "Nothing seems to have fallen out. Looks OK to me. How do you feel about it, sir?"

"If you hadn't told me, Al, I'd never have known we had three battery vents. Let's fly."

For more than ten grueling hours, we continued that method of engaging, drawing fire, disengaging, refueling, and coming back in again. At no time during that period did we ever see the enemy who was shooting at us. Nor were we able to see more than one leg and foot of the people down on the point.

To top that off, the progress of the lead element in moving forward to retrieve their people was practically nil. In spite of our repeated passes, Charlie was still able to keep our infantry pinned to the jungle floor in a vicious cross fire.

To add to our frustrations, it was now about 8 P.M. and beginning to get dark. Farrar and I had been flying since eight that morning, and we still weren't sure how much we had been able to help Alpha Company.

I contacted the ground unit on FM: "OK, Gangplank, it's getting dark and pretty soon I'm going to have to break station because I can't see. What do you want to do?" I didn't tell him that the OH-6 had no night navigation capability, and that I had to find my way back to Phu Loi before dark.

"I hear you, Darkhorse," Gangplank responded, "but we've got to get our people out before dark. If it gets completely dark on us, I don't know if we'll ever get them back."

That message made my mind up instantly. "OK, Gangplank, here's what we're going to do. We've got a pretty good idea where your point men and Three Six's lead element are. There's probably not more than forty meters between them."

"Roger that," he responded.

"All right, then, we're going to do some shooting . . . I say again . . . we're going to shoot as best we can. Can't guarantee that we won't hit your friendlies. But if our fire can pin down Charlie, your guys can move up there and get your people out, providing they're all down in one area. You roger?"

"I roger. OK, Darkhorse, let's try it. Three Six will move out on your fire."

With another glance over my shoulder, I told Farrar, "I'm going to come around again, Al, and go in very slow. I know you probably feel like we're hanging it out pretty far, but they can't see us any better than we can see them."

Farrar nodded an OK as I continued. "They'll be shooting at sound—they can hear the airplane but they can't see us very well. If you see any fire coming up, shoot back immediately at the point of their fire. Don't spray a wide area; shoot directly at their muzzle flashes."

We made three more passes, and each time came the rips of AKs and light machine guns. Farrar, being ever careful to avoid hitting our ground troops, shot back in short, well-aimed bursts. He was leaning half out of the airplane, responding to enemy tracers that were streaking up at us.

Gangplank came back on the radio. "All right, One Seven, you're shooting about sixty meters directly ahead of Three Six. You roger? Sixty meters directly to Three Six's front."

"OK," I responded, "I think your lead element is just behind me now. . . . they're right behind me . . . I'm coming around again."

This time I cranked the OH-6 up to about fifty knots and came in from another direction. I could hear Farrar's M-60 pecking away in the same short, controlled bursts as Charlie's fire came up from below.

Suddenly, as I was looking down and to my right out of the airplane, I caught the blur of an image out the corner of my left eye. I jerked my head around just in time to see the top of a large dead tree looming up right in front of me. The twisted, blackened limbs looked like a giant claw, poised to snatch the little OH-6 right out of the sky.

"Holy shit!" I yelled and pulled all the power the bird had. Instantly responding to the controls, the tail flew up, automatically dropping the nose just enough to catch the top of those straggly limbs. With a shocking thump and scraping noise, the tree limbs burst through the front of the ship, sending debris flying into a dirty cloud that momentarily obscured the front section of the OH-6.

My headset crackled immediately as the gun above me barked, "What's going on down there, One Seven? What was that explosion?"

Realizing that the Cobra must have seen that sudden gust of dirt and crud flying from my nose, I answered, "Hell, that wasn't any explosion. I just hit a tree!"

The terrible rush of wind through the cabin made it obvious that the whole front end of the OH-6 had been knocked out. Both Plexiglas bubbles were smashed to smithereens and the wind was whistling through as though I was flying in an open cockpit.

Amazingly, the aircraft was still flying OK. The rotor system had apparently not been hit and the ship was still responding to my control movements.

After telling Farrar what had happened, I rang up Gangplank. "I hit the top of a tree up here, but we're OK. I'm going to hover again. How close is Three Six?"

Taking a few moments to check before answering me, Gangplank came back, "Three Six thinks he knows where the guys are. He can hear one of them moaning. Can you get in there again for one last try?"

"OK, one more pass. Only this time I'm going to put myself right in the middle of where I think the enemy base camp is, come to a hover, and shoot the shit out of that area with everything I've got. Now, when the door gunner lets go with his M-60, get your people up there and try to get those point guys out. It's the best chance we've got, and it's the last chance we've got. Roger?"

With Gangplank's acknowledgment, I headed in from the north over what I believed was the dead center of the enemy base camp. Just like every time before, Charlie opened up—AKs on my right side, a heavier light machine gun to my front, and at least two AKs behind me. Because I was at a hover, I could hear and feel the hits. They were ripping through the ship from every direction.

Farrar had leaned completely out of the OH-6 and was shooting underneath the tail boom at the two AKs behind us. Right in the middle of one of his long bursts, I saw Al fall out of the airplane. My God, I thought. He's hit!

Looking back, I saw that Al's foot had landed on the skid and broken his fall. His monkey strap had steadied him, and the bungee cord had kept the M-60 from going out with him. I tilted the ship to the left to make it easier for him to crawl back into the cabin. "Where are you hit, Al?" I yelled.

I could almost hear the chuckle in his voice. "Ah, shit, Lieutenant, I just slipped. I'm OK." Then he let go with another long M-60 blast!

Just as I was starting to tell Farrar to cool it, that we couldn't take any more hits and were going to pull the hell out and go home, Gangplank burst on the air. "OK, Dark-horse, get out of there . . . GET OUT OF THERE! WE GOT 'EM! WE GOT 'EM!"

I pulled power and was bringing the nose around in a sweeping right turn when Gangplank came back, "We got everybody out, One Seven. Everybody's alive. Say again, everybody's out and alive. One of the guys is hurt bad— shot through both legs. But they're going to make it."

With that happy message, Bruce Foster in the Cobra came up on UHF. "OK, One Seven. Sidewinder has got layers of fighters stacked up overhead waiting for ground

to get their people out so they can come in and put Charlie to sleep. You back it out of there and get over to the
LZ. When you tell us that all the friendlies are clear, we'll
put the fighters down on the base camp area."

As the infantry was moving out of the tree line and back
into the LZ, I passed the word on to Gangplank. "Get
your folks down and out of the way. We've got TAC fighters coming in with heavy ordnance to neutralize the base
camp area." Then I keyed Farrar, "Get me a Willie Pete
and a red smoke, one in each hand, and get ready to mark
the target."

As I moved toward the base area, Al primed the grenades and held both of them out the door, ready to drop
them on my command. I asked Foster to tell the FAC to
watch for the Willie Pete and the red smoke.

When we passed directly over what I thought was the
base camp location, I hollered, "Now!" and Farrar threw
both grenades straight down. From the jungle floor came a
solid white explosion, with fingers of burning white phosphorus boiling and shooting out of it. I knew we were right
on the button because the AK fire started again.

Just as I was about to pull power, the Cobra came back,
"OK, One Seven, FAC has got your smoke. Get out of
there. Get out of there now and come on up to altitude."

As I rolled out, Farrar got my attention. "Hey, Lieutenant, take a look at that." Off to the right, out of the lower-
ing cloud level, came two North American F-100 Super
Sabres, one behind the other, drilling in on the white
smoke that was still billowing up at the enemy base camp.

Screaming in fast, the first Sabre ticked off two napalm
canisters that landed smack-dab on top of the white smoke
and erupted into balls of flame. As the first F-100 peeled
off the target, the second one rolled in right behind him
and pickled off two more napalm canisters. The long axis
of the base camp was completely enveloped by a fierce
wall of fire.

The jets dropped two more canisters each, then

streaked around one more time as the Cobra warned, "All right, everybody stay clear." In they came, one behind the other, with 20mms blasting up and down the long axis of the base camp. As I watched their maneuvers, I thought to myself, there is no way any living thing could have survived all the ordnance those F-100s had dumped in there. The FAC came up: "The Sabres are Winchester," which meant they had expended all their napalm and internal guns.

One last time, I got on the radio to Gangplank. "Gangplank, this is Darkhorse One Seven. I'm going home. The guns are going to stay with you for a little while in case you need them. We've got Dustoff inbound to pick up your wounded. Take care."

"Hey, man," he came back, "we really appreciate it. Darkhorse sure saved our ass!"

When Farrar and I touched down at Phu Loi, I could hardly get out of the aircraft. After thirteen hours in the seat of that OH-6, my legs were numb, my buttocks were numb, even the bottom part of my thighs had no feeling in them. My entire body was so exhausted that I even had trouble working the pedals to hover the ship onto the strip.

Bruce Foster had shut down his Cobra at the same time, and we walked in from the parking area together. He put his arm around my shoulder. "One Seven, you are one crazy son of a bitch!"

I grinned back at him. "Man, I didn't envy you one goddamned bit, because there you were hanging up there in orbit and couldn't do one single thing all day to help me."

After a meal at the O club, I mustered enough energy to get back to the flight line and the little OH-6 that I had flown the hell out of all that day. By the time I arrived at the ship, Farrar was there, as was the scout platoon sergeant, Tim McDivitt. Sergeant McDivitt had some of the maintenance people going over the aircraft to assess the damage. All the crew chiefs called McDivitt "Toon

Daddy," short for "platoon daddy," the patriarch of the unit.

As I reached the ship, I called out to him, "What kind of shape is 249 in, Toon Daddy?"

He looked at me, and I quote his exact words. "Lieutenant . . ." He had a way of accenting that first syllable so it came out, L-E-W-W-tenant. "You have screwed up one U.S. Army helicopter . . . to the max!" He shook his head in disbelief. "Not only is all the goddamned nose Plexiglas blown out of this ship, but you've got thirty to forty holes in her, spread out from the rotor system to the belly and tail boom. It'll sure as hell take some major surgery to get her back in shape!"

But what had both of us scratching our heads was the fact that this OH-6 aircraft had hung together through thirteen hours of beating, with nothing vital hit, and was still totally flyable. What an aircraft!

As Toon Daddy was finishing his lecture to me, I noticed that Farrar was still walking around the ship, studying the damage. (As I said before, the crew chief considers the airplane *his.*) He was especially noticing the two AK holes through the cabin where he had been sitting. I knew he was wondering how in the hell we ever got us and that airplane back to Phu Loi in one piece.

Suddenly realizing that I was scheduled to fly VR-1 the next morning, I asked Al to help me move my personal gear from 249 over to the bird slated for first up VR. We walked together toward our hootches, then sat down for a minute near the orderly room and lit up cigarettes. As tired as we both were, it was good to "decompress" over a smoke and think back over what we had been through that day.

Farrar looked at me and hissed out a stream of inhaled smoke. "Shit, sir . . . holy shit!"

I grinned back at him. "You know, Al, we flew thirteen hours today. Would you believe that we could ever be in the saddle that long in one operation?"

"All I know, sir, is that my ass is numb. No, not numb . . . my ass is dead!"

"Mine, too," I mumbled, "but I want you to know that you did pretty goddamned good work today, for a Yankee." Coming from Cumberland, Rhode Island, Al was used to the Yankee kidding.

With that, I walked on down to my hootch and hit the rack. I didn't talk to anybody . . . didn't see anybody . . . didn't even take off my boots or flight suit. I just stretched out with my feet resting on top of the metal bar at the end of the bunk. I was asleep in moments.

An hour later the flip-flop noise of shower shoes tracking across the hootch floor awakened me. It was Bob Davis. He shook me by the shoulder until I finally growled, "Huh, what is it?"

"Hey, Hubie . . . you asleep?"

"I'm sure as hell not now," I groaned, my eyes still riveted shut.

"You know you got first up VR tomorrow," he whispered. "Do you want me to take it for you?"

I answered through my fogginess, "Nah, that's all right. I'll take it."

"Well," he said, "you better go back to sleep. You need the sleep because you look like shit."

"Thanks a lot," I snarled, and drifted off again.

It didn't seem like more than five minutes when I felt my shoulder being shaken again. This time it was the assistant operations charge of quarters (CQ). "Lieutenant, it's four o'clock. You're first up . . . it's time for you to get up."

I struggled up to a sitting position on the side of the bunk. It was almost like being in a drunken stupor. As I held my head in my hands, I looked down and saw I was still dressed in the same flight suit and boots I had worn the day before.

My feet were like two blocks of ice. I couldn't move them, and they tingled with prickly pain. I remembered

that I had fallen asleep with my feet hung over the rail of
the bunk. My limbs were dead from the knees down. I
couldn't even walk!

When the feeling in my feet finally returned, I picked up
my CAR-15 and chicken plate and stumbled out to the
flight line. I started to run up the aircraft, but decided to
wait until I was ready to leave. Maybe by then I'd be more
awake and alert.

I walked over to operations and talked with the gun
crew to find out what we were supposed to do that day.
The mission called for some VR in the Quan Loi area,
looking for base camps and trail activity.

We got off about 5 A.M. It was a cool, crisp morning,
which did its best to snap me back to reality. Our instructions called for us to fly up Highway 13 to An Loc, shut
down, and get a briefing from brigade before moving on
over to Quan Loi to scout for the 11th Armored Cavalry
Regiment (ACR).

We hadn't been in An Loc more than twenty minutes
before another OH-6 bearing Bob Davis's tail number
roared in from the south. He set down and came running
over to my ship.

"Hey, Hubie," he panted, "you need to get your ass
back to the troop pronto. You have obviously pissed off
somebody somethin' terrible and they want to see you at
division. Has something to do with yesterday's action.
That's all I know!"

"OK, but what in the hell have I done?"

"I told you all I know," Davis responded, "but you better get a move on."

I quickly filled Bob in on the briefing, then jumped back
into the airplane with crew chief Jim Slater and headed
back to Phu Loi.

It was not unusual when on a nontactical mission for the
crew chief to ride up front in the left seat. That's where
Slater jumped in, and as soon as we were up and on a
direct to Phu Loi, I told him, "Hey, Jimbo, you're going to

fly. I'm dead, man." He grabbed the controls. "Yes, sir! I *want* to fly, Lieutenant."

I pulled my legs up and tried to relax, but my leg muscles still cramped up every time I moved them. I lit a cigarette and thought to myself that I wouldn't last long in this damned war with many more days like yesterday. I wondered what I had done to get called off a mission and back to division.

Back down in Phu Loi, the operations CQ informed me that I was to go on to division headquarters at Lai Khe and see the G-2. "You are to brief intelligence on what you saw yesterday," he said, "and Mr. Ameigh will be going with you."

Ameigh was my hootch mate. He was a scout pilot and was also the troop historian. But why would he be going back to division with me? By now I was beginning to get pretty worried.

Ameigh climbed in the left seat with his camera in hand. "What are you carrying a camera for, Jim?" I asked him.

"You never know when there's a good picture waiting to be taken, ol' buddy."

The comment went right over the top of my head. But leaving it at that, we flew off to division headquarters, where we were met by a major who was the coordinator of the division commander's staff. He looked at my name tag and the Darkhorse patch on my flight suit. "Lieutenant Mills, the people you actually need to see are not here. I want you to go on up to fire support base Lorraine. There are some people there who want to talk to you."

Ameigh and I got back into the OH-6. I began to wonder if I had hit some friendlies on that last smokin' pass over the enemy base camp. FSB Lorraine was home base for Alpha Company, 2d Battalion, 16th Infantry—the same outfit that was pinned down yesterday at LZ Toast. My mind was conjuring up all the kinds of trouble I could be in.

As I came in on short final over Lorraine, I noticed that

all the troops at the base were standing formation out near the helicopter landing area. I landed, shut down the bird, and began walking over toward the formation. Nobody paid any attention to either Ameigh or me until a bedraggled captain came walking up and stuck out his hand. "Are you Darkhorse One Seven . . . Lieutenant Hugh Mills?" he asked.

I answered, "Yes, sir."

He grinned. "I'm Gangplank Six, the guy on the ground who you spent most of the day talking to yesterday."

"Hey . . . howya doin'?" We looked at each other for a moment. I laughed and said, "Sir, you look like shit!"

"You don't look a damned bit better yourself, One Seven!" He told me that he and his troops had been in the action area all night. Their lift into the base had dropped them off just an hour ago.

I asked him quietly, "What am I doing here? Did I hit one of your friendlies on that last pass at dusk?"

"No. Just hang on, there are some people coming out here to the fire base who want to talk to you."

About that time a Huey landed near my OH-6, and out stepped a general grade officer, a lieutenant who was obviously the general's aide, and a colonel wearing sunglasses. He looked like the stereotypical Hollywood press agent.

The lieutenant walked up to me and announced, "Lieutenant Mills, Brigadier General Herbert Smith is here to present you with a decoration, along with the division public affairs officer to get official pictures. If you will just kindly stand over there beside the assembled troops, the presentation will get under way."

I was flabbergasted. Seeing my jaw drop in surprise, the lieutenant continued in a patient tone. "Just stand over there, Lieutenant Mills. That's right, all you have to do is stand there. The general will handle the rest."

I went over to the ranks and stood at the indicated position. The brigade adjutant stepped forward and, speaking into a small public address system, began reading from a blue three-by-five card:

> On 26 April 1969, First Lieutenant Hugh L. Mills, flying a scout aircraft as part of a Delta 1/4 Cav hunter-killer team, flew in support of A Company, 2d Battalion, 16th Infantry. When elements of A Company attacked a bunker complex, two members were wounded in a position that kept other persons from recovering the wounded. Lieutenant Mills circled the contact area for more than ten hours, guiding the remainder of the company to the point of contact. Although he received enemy fire on every pass, he continued to return to the unit in contact. He did not leave the area until A Company had consolidated and withdrawn its wounded personnel. First Lieutenant Mills's heroic actions and extraordinary flying skill enabled A Company to clear the enemy from heavily fortified positions, resulting in eleven VC KIA. Lieutenant Mills's actions are in keeping with the finest traditions of military service and reflect great credit upon himself and the United States Army.

With that, the assistant division commander walked forward with his aide. The lieutenant removed the Distinguished Flying Cross medal from its presentation case and handed it to the general, who in turn pinned it on the left breast of my flight suit.

I was humbled beyond belief. Fortunately I had the presence of mind to salute. The general returned my salute and shook my hand. "Lieutenant, you should know that it's a very unusual situation when we present an impact award—an award that is made immediately following the action it honors."

He continued while still grasping my hand. "I found out last night at ten o'clock that both the company and battalion commanders of this unit wanted me to find the scout pilot who flew for them yesterday. They wanted me to give you a medal, which is, in itself, quite impressive. But what is really impressive to me is that it was the unanimous decision of *the men* of this company that you should be given a medal for what you did for them. And that you were to come here, to *their* fire support base, to get it!

"Lieutenant Mills, I am now going to step back and let every man in this unit have the opportunity to step forward and shake your hand."

CHAPTER 6

FSB GELA

On 1 May, a billet opened up in our troop for an R and R to Bangkok. I hadn't had any time off since arriving in Vietnam, so I took the opportunity to get a little rest and see the capital city of Thailand.

I had a week's leave, but ended up taking only four days because I really didn't like Bangkok. I enjoyed seeing the imperial temples and doing a little shopping in the market area, but I was sick the whole time I was there. My digestive system just couldn't tolerate the highly seasoned Thai food. So cutting short my leave, I got back to the troop on the fifth and was marked up to fly Scramble 1 the next morning.

The VR teams were sent out to fly regularly scheduled reconnaissance missions. The scramble teams, numbers 1 and 2, usually stayed at Phu Loi until they were needed to support either a particular tactical situation or an enemy contact made during a routine VR mission. It was top priority at the base to get the scramble team in the air the moment the call came. Controllers even stopped all normal traffic on the strip until they got off the scramble team.

As I went about my usual routine on the morning of the sixth, the troop loudspeaker suddenly hissed, telling the troop that an alert announcement was probably coming. I listened carefully.

"Attention. Hunter-killer team on the hot spot. Scramble north."

I grabbed my chicken plate and survival vest and shot out of the hootch door, sprinting to my parked OH-6. As I ran for the ship, my survival knife, hanging from my vest, bounced around wildly. I always wore my sheath knife on my vest, handle down, so if I were ever shot down, I'd have easy access to the knife to help cut or pry my way out of the cockpit. As it bounced, my handle-down knife apparently jarred out of its scabbard on the vest and fell to the ground. Only it didn't fall handle down.

Somehow in the drop, it flipped and landed, point down, directly on my right foot. It pierced my boot and entered the flesh, right behind my toes. I flew the scramble mission anyway, with blood oozing out of my boot and my foot hurting so damned bad I could hardly work the right pedal.

Not only did the incident teach me never to wear my knife handle down, it kept me from flying for several days. If my foot hadn't hurt so much, I would have kicked myself for doing such a dumb thing.

The world got better on 8 May, however. I got a call to see Major Cummings, the troop commander. His news was that scout platoon leader Capt. John Herchert was short on time left in country and was transferring to operations for the balance of his tour. I was to become the new One Six.

My appointment wasn't really a big surprise. Everyone had known for some time that Herchert was getting short, and as time wore down to DEROS, his natural reaction was to try to keep himself in one piece to go home. Besides, I was the only commissioned officer in the outfit. All the rest of the scout pilots were warrants. So Major Cummings really didn't have much difficulty in deciding who would fill Herchert's shoes. But that didn't lessen my excitement about the new job.

One of the first things I did was call the scout pilots together in my hootch. Huddled around my bunk were Bob Davis (One Three), Jim Ameigh (One Five), Joe Vad (Nine), Ed Eneboe (One Nine), Jim Morrison (One Four), Bill Jones (One Eight), and Mike Melo (One One). Darkhorse Five (troop XO) Joe Perkins came too, probably to hear what the new One Six might have to say to his scout pilots.

I hadn't planned a big pep talk. These guys knew me, had flown with me, and some of them had even lived with me in the same hootch. I felt I was one of them. But I couldn't resist preaching a little about the spirit of the cavalry. "It's important to remember," I told them, "that our air cavalry today is a descendent of the old horse cavalry that opened our nation's frontiers—that aggressiveness, flexibility, economy of force, and shock action are all watchwords of the cavalry. As aeroscout pilots, we have that heritage to live up to."

They all knew what I meant. Over the past month, every one of them had heard my opinion about scout pilots being more aggressive in carrying out their mission. I didn't want anybody taking any foolish chances, but I urged the scouts to stay on the target, take the fight to the enemy, and not get out until firepower advantage was lost. Once command of the situation was gone and the scout could no longer influence the action, at that point, and only then, was the scout clear to run and let the snake driver take over. After the target had been worked over by the Cobras, I wanted the scout pilot back into the area to check out the enemy situation. If the area was still too hot, get it worked over again, but keep going back!

At this point I told the pilots I was arming all the scout ships with miniguns. It would now be our intent to close with the enemy and lay cold steel on him every chance we got.

Ever mindful that the aeroscouts was strictly a volunteer unit, I left the men with the thought that they could "un-volunteer" at any time. Whenever a scout pilot was no longer willing to fly and fight, he could go over to slicks and never a discrediting word would be spoken about his decision.

"But in the meantime," I concluded, slapping my hand down on my bunk, "the mission of this unit is to fly and fight, and don't you ever forget it!"

Not long after that a sign bearing those exact words appeared in the operations hootch. Joe Perkins must have felt they had application beyond my little scout pilot get-together.

All the scout ships were outfitted immediately with miniguns, and the pilots learned to use them from the manuals and on-the-job training (OJT). We tried the cabin-mounted minigun sight, but ended up not using it. The sight was a rod with oval glass that stuck out in front of you in the cockpit, and it got in the way. It also could have been lethal in a crash. Instead, we devised an OJT way of aiming the guns. Through a little seat-of-the-pants experimentation and expenditure of a few rounds of ammo, we discovered the secret of hitting the target.

The gun was elevated and depressed by using a button on the cyclic stick. When the gun was raised to the point where the pilot in the right seat could look across and see the tip of the minigun barrel sticking up just above the left seat bottom, the gun would then shoot one hand's width above the cross tube on the front of the canopy.

Having learned that, we flew out to a rice paddy, where we pulled off a few bursts and observed exactly where the rounds were hitting. We started shooting at about two hundred yards out, then used a grease pencil to mark a big X on the canopy where the rounds were seen to impact. That hand-drawn X on the front Plexiglas bubble was used as the sight.

The newer aeroscouts, those with fire in their eyes and

fewer combat hours, welcomed the addition of miniguns to their Loaches. They didn't seem to have any trouble, either, with my order that scout pilots stay on the target as long as they were able to control the situation.

Experienced scouts, however, such as Hayes, Jones, and Morrison, cautioned against the new tactics. I respected their feelings that the risks overshadowed the advantages. Certainly, their experiences during the days of the '68 Tet Offensive had shown them that flying scouts—even with an armed observer aboard—was damned well risky enough.

Even the Cobra pilots minced no words in saying that the scouts were hanging it out too far when they started mixing it up with the enemy. "That's what the snake is up there for," they argued. They thought a scout was nuts to try to do anything more than locate a target for the gunship.

As the new One Six, I found out quickly that there was plenty to keep me busy in addition to flying my regular VR and scramble rotation. There was the administrative side of running the scout platoon. It wasn't that I couldn't handle paperwork, it was more that I didn't like handling paperwork.

Fortunately, I had two extremely capable noncommissioned officers who did their jobs so well that I could continue flying my rotation, confident that things on the ground were being capably looked after. First Sergeant Martin L. Laurent kept the platoon's regular administrative matters going like a well-oiled machine. Platoon Sergeant Tim ("Toon Daddy") McDivitt, among a host of other things, kept a careful eye on aircraft maintenance and our scout crew chiefs.

The crew chiefs were a particular concern of mine. They were the other half of the scout team and, in my book, were some of the finest soldiers to ever come down the chute. When a Loach took off, the crew chief's life was in the hands of the scout pilot. And vice versa. The crew chief's sharp eyes and well-aimed M-60 saved a Loach pilot's ass more times than any of us could ever know. So I made it an important part of my administrative business to make sure that crew chiefs' quarters were well maintained, that chow was good, and that they were kept off the strictly bullshit details.

Those first several months of 1969, the enemy in III Corps avoided, when they could, any large-scale military actions. The Tet Offensive of 1968 had cost the NVA so much in human casualties and matériel losses that they had pulled remaining manpower back behind the Cambodian border to lick their wounds. Charlie employed mostly sapper actions, small force ambushes, and standoff attacks with rockets and mortars to disrupt allied operations.

Using these kinds of methods to conserve manpower and equipment, the enemy was hard to find banded together in any numbers. Therefore, most of our aeroscout VR missions went out to search the 1st Division's TAOR, trying to find, fix, and hold these small enemy elements for their intelligence value.

Since I was used to finding the enemy only in either singles or very small groups, I was shocked at what I saw while flying over fire support base Gela early on the morning of 13 May 1969.

I had been asleep when the CQ came into the hootch and awakened the Firefly team (a Huey equipped with searchlights and night flares, and two Cobra gunship crews). I roused myself and looked at my watch. It was 0230. I heard the CQ tell the groggy pilots, "Gela is under attack . . . need to scramble a team north."

I was marked up as scout Scramble 1 for first light that morning, but, lacking a full complement of navigational instruments, OH-6s did not fly at night. When a scramble call came in during the dark hours, a red team (two Cobras) responded along with a Huey flare ship.

I couldn't get back to sleep after the Cobra crews took

off, so I finally just got up, dressed, and went over to troop operations. I wanted to see what was going on. Besides, it wouldn't be long before daybreak. After a few minutes of listening to the radios and checking out the operational maps and condition boards, I began to get an idea of what had happened.

The 1st Battalion of the 28th Infantry was positioned at Gela, a fire support base located south of the Michelin and just east of an area we called the Onion. At 0143, an enemy force of unknown size had hit Gela with heavy 82mm mortar fire, followed by a strong ground attack that had made its way into the perimeter wire.

The scrambled Firefly and gun team had arrived at the scene, and the ops room radios blared the high-pitched talk between the infantry commander on the ground and the gun pilots circling overhead.

With first light at Phu Loi, my Cobra cover (Dean Sinor, Three One) and I got off as Scramble 1 and headed to Gela. It was about 0600.

Arriving on station, we fell into trail with Mike Woods, Three Five, and Bruce Foster, Three Two, the red team of guns that had been scrambled at 0230.

Woods and Foster gave us a situation report (sitrep) as we circled and looked down on the still-smoldering fire base. "OK. The attack occurred at 0143 and continued through the night. They took some initial fire down on the southeastern side of the compound from the tree line at seventy-five yards. Fire was returned. But the heavy enemy attack came from the northwest with a supporting attack out of the tree line on the northeast. The enemy got as far as the wire. There are bodies in the wire, multiple dead on the outside of the wire. They did not reach the perimeter. They had sniper fire . . . most of fire was returned. Base artillery is now cold.

"We have engaged one heavy machine gun and two recoilless rifles due north of the compound at seventy-five yards and another heavy machine gun southeast of the

compound at one hundred fifty yards. All known gun locations have been hit by our air strikes or Spooky [AC-47
aircraft armed with miniguns and illumination flares] and
some tac air. Ground wants to get a scout down over the
base and fan out in concentric circles for a BDA and body
count. Try to find the enemy guns, and make sure there
aren't a lot more people out there still kicking around
between the jungle and fire base."

I rogered all that and then got my rules of engagement.

"OK, One Six, you got friendlies on the inside of the
wire. You have no friendlies on the outside of the wire. I
say again, no friendlies outside the wire. You have a complete free-fire outside the wire."

Before I headed down, Sinor came up on FM to the
infantry commander on the ground. "Four Six, this is
Darkhorse Three One. I'd like to get you to hold your
external fires, hold your indirect fires. I'm going to put the
scout down now directly over the base and let him work
outward to give us a bomb damage assessment and also try
to locate survivors, wounded, and the direction of enemy
retreat."

I monitored Four Six's response. "Darkhorse, roger. We
see the scout on station. We're going to hold our external
and indirect fires. Last fire received on the perimeter was
from the direction of three two zero degrees at two hundred yards—light automatic weapons fire. Haven't had any
fifty or recoilless rifle fire since you guys took out that
position about three minutes ago. We've got a Dustoff
inbound, and while fire is shut down for the scout we'll go
ahead and bring in Dustoff if you'll be good enough to
cover him."

"Roger, Four Six, I'm putting the scout down. I'll cover
the Dustoff insertion. Your contact this frequency for the
scout is Darkhorse One Six."

Then Sinor came back to me. "OK, One Six, are you
ready to go down? You've got free-fire but use caution
toward the friendlies. Any questions?"

"No, I've got what I need."

From fifteen hundred feet, Gela looked like a five-pointed deputy's badge lying on the ground, with a wreath of three strands of concertina wire around it. Dropping down on top of the base, I could see that each star point was protected with gun positions that swept—with a wide field of cross fire—anything that came across the clearing and into the wire.

The adrenaline always flowed as I dropped down onto a target. You never knew who or what was down there. I made my first couple of passes at about forty feet, smokin' between eighty and ninety knots. That gave me a quick look around out to the base perimeter without much worry of getting rounds into my bird.

"My God!" I murmured as I slowed and dropped down on Gela's perimeter wire. This had to have been one hell of a fight. There were bodies everywhere!

Grotesquely entangled on the barbs of the concertina were numerous enemy corpses—ripped, bloodied bodies dressed in black shorts and pajamas, blue tops, and Ho Chi Minh sandals, AK-47s still gripped tightly in their hands. The sight burned an image in my mind.

Taking in the devastation, my crew chief, Crockett, hit the intercom. "Shit, sir, look at all the bad guys. They're everywhere! There's more enemy below us right now than I've seen altogether in 'Nam since I got here!"

I was thinking the same thing. This was the first time I had ever seen this kind of enemy concentration. I wondered if the bad guys had decided to come out of Cambodia in larger force and start hitting us in strength.

Fixated on the battle scene below me, I suddenly realized that I needed to get away from the wire and start looking for any live enemy who might be around. Our infantry in Gela needed answers to some questions: Was the base still under siege? If not, where did Charlie go? How many dead did he drag away? What kind of weapons were out there? Could the base finally come down off full alert?

I moved my orbit out to the tree line. It looked as though Gela had been completely surrounded by the enemy, with the major attack coming out of the northwest. At three two zero degrees, I saw many body drag marks and blood trails leading off into the jungle. The enemy usually tried to recover his dead and wounded from the battlefield by dragging them back along their route of attack. By leaving as few casualties as possible on the field, he hoped to confuse U.S. and ARVN forces as to the extent of his losses.

Following this well-beaten trail off to the northwest, I soon spotted their hastily dug mass graves back in the jungle, and the location of the seventy-five recoilless and .50 caliber that covered their main attack. The guns weren't there now, though; they had been dragged away, too.

The fresh, heavy foot trails through the jungle definitely headed back toward the Michelin. Charlie was probably holed up there by now, licking his wounds.

As I made my orbits, I kept up a constant stream of talk to Sinor on what I was seeing. His front-seater logged it on the map and radioed the information to the infantry ground commander and back to troop operations.

This was the first time I had seen the results of a large unit action, of the enemy coming in after us. The U.S. forces were hunkered down behind the fortifications of their fire support base, which was totally out in the open with no jungle overhead cover whatsoever. The enemy— possibly a unit of the 7th NVA Division's 165th Infantry Regiment, known to be operating in the vicinity of the Michelin rubber plantation—was probably attempting to execute what we called a "hugging" tactic, that is, trying to overpower an installation by quickly charging their soldiers in so close under the artillery that our heavy firepower was nullified by the extremely short range.

But to no avail at Gela. Caught in the cleared, open

area between the fire base outer wire and the jungle tree line, the enemy was pounded by our mortar, artillery canister rounds, and aerial ordnance. The bare earth outside the wire had been pulverized by hundreds, if not thousands, of projectiles, then scorched by napalm from the tac air, and by Phougas drums of jellied gasoline half-buried in defensive positions around the perimeter and pointed to explode liquid fire onto incoming attackers. The enemy bodies beyond the wire looked like ripped and burned rag dolls. Many had made it as far as the wire before being caught in the deadly defensive small-arms fire generated from within the fire base.

God, what a battle! I thought over and over to myself.

Official after-action reports listed three U.S. soldiers killed in the attack, twenty wounded, and forty-one enemy killed. But forty-one bodies were all the enemy left to be counted; as my observation had confirmed, scores of their dead and wounded had been dragged from the field and left hastily buried just a few yards into the jungle.

I have often heard it said that an aviator fights an impersonal war, that he never sees, hears, or smells the close-up reality of the battlefield. But on 13 May 1969, looking down into that pit of death and devastation at Gela, Crockett and I knew the reality of war.

CHAPTER 7

WHERE IS ONE FIVE?

By May 1969, division G-2 estimated enemy strength in the 1st Division area at ten thousand personnel, with another four thousand people providing logistical support for the field troops.

Our picture of the enemy was getting clearer. With more experience, the scouts could now tell who and what we had found on the ground. We could, for instance, identify the NVA troops, generally natives of North Vietnam, members of the legally constituted, trained, and equipped people's army of the North Vietnamese government. Outfitted in his green and tan fatigue uniform, including thick-soled boots, Soviet web gear, and Russian-designed weapons, the NVA soldier was a professional—well-equipped, trained, and disciplined. His basic weapon was the Soviet Kalashnikov AK-47 assault rifle, though many were armed with either the RPG-7 or RPG-2 portable rocket launcher. He was a worthy foe on the battlefield.

The Viet Cong guerrillas, on the other hand, were generally natives of South Vietnam but not sympathetic to the government of the Republic of Vietnam. Their loyalty was to the national liberation movement of South Vietnam, and to the NVA who had come from the north to help them in their cause.

Though many times thought of as wandering guerrilla bands, the VC, in reality, were highly organized in their military resistance efforts. Main force VC units in the 1st Division area included combat outfits such as the Dong Nai Regiment, Song Be Battalion, and the SR-4 (strategic region) battalions of the Thu Duc Regiment. In addition, they had their own artillery units, such as the 74th and 96th artillery regiments, along with K33, K34, and K35 arty battalions.

Instead of the highly militarized uniforms of the NVA, the VC normally wore dark blue or jet black pajama tops and bottoms. Sometimes the pants would be to the ankle, but black shorts were common. Unless he had come across a pair of U.S. jungle boots, VC always wore Ho Chi Minh sandals, cut out of vehicle tires.

Many wore scarfs fashioned from strips of camouflage parachute cloth. Larger pieces of this same cloth were tied around the neck and used as capes. The scarf served to hide the head and face and keep away insects; the cape provided excellent camouflage as the guerrilla moved through the terrain. When a VC ran, the cape flapped out behind him like a banner.

The things needed to sustain a VC in the field were mostly carried on his back: generally a lightweight sleeping bag around his shoulders, web pouch or bandolier of ammo across his chest, and a roll of rice around his neck. He carried an AK-47 assault rifle, sometimes a Russian 7.62mm SKS (Simonov) carbine. On occasion, it was an American M-16 scavenged from the field, as well as a supply of U.S. hand grenades.

The main force VC were nearly on a par with NVA regulars in their fighting capability. They were well-organized, employed good tactics, had excellent weapons, and were tenacious as hell.

As an aviator, I noticed one difference between the NVA and VC that held true in most instances. That was in fire control. In scouting over an enemy contact area, if I began to catch ground fire from a considerable distance, it was a probable assumption that I had jumped VC troops. If the fire opened up right under me, you could take odds that the shooters were NVA soldiers. The more battlewise NVA regulars didn't expose their positions as readily, and realized that waiting to shoot meant a better chance at knocking the low, slow-flying scout ship out of the sky.

The lowest organized component of VC combat troops was the local force unit. The main forces were organized to regimental strength; the smaller VC local force units generally did not exceed platoon and company-sized elements. Though these small units were numbered (C-61 Company, D-368, K-10), many times they were identified by the name of the village or area from which the people manning the unit came, for example, the Ben Cat Company or the An Loc Platoon.

The men and women making up these local forces could be seen around their villages one day doing their jobs; the next day they would be gone, having disappeared to join their VC units for some guerrilla operation. When the mission was accomplished, they'd return as quietly and discreetly as they had left.

The local force VC most often carried older weapons. Being at the bottom of the supply distribution schedule, they had to use whatever weapons were available to them. This included old French MAT-49 submachine guns, U.S. BARs (Browning automatic rifles), Thompson submachine guns, and .30-caliber M-1 carbines.

It was very difficult to tell any of the Vietnamese soldiers apart, and nearly impossible to determine individual political persuasions. Only our Kit Carson scouts could positively tell the good guys from the bad.

The NVA and the VC lived the same way in the field. They ate their rice and fish and built bunkers in their areas of operations. Bunkers were important for storing supplies, providing overhead cover, and establishing field bases from which to operate.

As aerial scouts, we were always on the lookout for cooking fires, especially early in the morning when Charlie might be boiling his rice and fish for breakfast. We also looked for their fish traps in the many rivers and tributaries. There was generally someone around to tend the traps, and you could be pretty sure that the "someone" was Charlie.

Most fliers would not have known these details about the enemy. They had no reason to. But scouts were different—we had to know the enemy's habits and personality. We were down low and slow looking for them every day, and knowing these things helped us locate the enemy.

So I could know Charlie's ways even better, I arranged with Four Six (ARP leader Bob Harris) to go out into the field with the ARPs on my days off. This way I could actually see enemy bunkers and study how they were built, talk to captured enemy personnel through interpreters, and go into their tunnels and hootches to discover how they lived in the field.

Up to this time, the scout platoon worked in the south around the Iron T, Trapezoid, and Michelin. The terrain around those areas was flat and open, and occupied mostly by VC forces. But, in late May, our services were required up north to help keep elements of the 7th NVA Division under close surveillance.

We all disliked working up north on Thunder Road (Highway 13) around An Loc and Quan Loi because it meant trying to see through triple-canopy jungle. There was also the good prospect of running into the NVA regulars who operated out of nearby Cambodian sanctuaries. The whole area was hot as a firecracker.

From An Loc–Quan Loi it was only about twenty kilometers north and west to the Cambodian border and an area we called the Fishhook. When we worked up there we generally took a flight of six (three scouts and three Cobras) out of Phu Loi and up to Quan Loi early in the morning. Then we'd work out of that base and return to Phu Loi before dark.

Though the entire border area was crawling with NVA, the main problem was the terrain—the tall, layered, dense, and dark jungle. To see anything at all from the air, we had to fly right down on top of the trees, then slow down to nearly a hover—a point where we were easy pickings for the many heavy tripod-mounted .30- and .50-caliber anti-aircraft machine guns that the North Vietnamese had dug into the jungle.

On 22 May we were working west out of An Loc–Quan Loi on reconnaissance to provide information on enemy activity to the base camp commander. The VR-1 that day was Bob Davis (One Three). He was down in his search pattern lowin' and slowin' away when all hell broke loose. Enemy .50-caliber rounds suddenly came bursting up out of the jungle and tore into Davis's OH-6.

The sound of any kind of fire tearing through the bird is frightening, but the sound of .50s finding their mark is terrifying. Especially when you can't see the gun or its muzzle blast, and have no idea where the fire is coming from.

Fortunately, neither Davis nor his crew chief was hit by the sudden barrage. With some careful nursing, One Three was able to get his ship back to Quan Loi and safely set her down. There were numerous big, ripping slug tears through the cabin and tail boom of the aircraft. It was the first time since I had been in the troop that any of our Loaches had ever been engaged and hit by .50-caliber fire.

Davis told me the general area where he had run into trouble, and I headed out with my gun cover to see if I could find the emplacement. I had no luck at all. Peering down into the deep, dark jungle revealed not a trace of any enemy activity other than a few old foot trails. The score near the Cambodian border quickly became NVA one, Darkhorse scouts zero.

Not long after the incident, Jim Ameigh (One Five) was

scouting the same area and found the .50 pit that apparently had fired at Davis. We called those pits "donuts" because they were circular, with a platform of earth left in the center where the gun rested. This way, the firing team could track targets 360 degrees on the tripod without having to physically move the machine gun.

When Ameigh found the donut, the gun was gone. Once the enemy had exposed their position, they didn't wait around. They knew that U.S. air would be back soon on a hosing down mission.

The incident left us all with an ominous, foreboding feeling about the area. We knew that the entire region to the west of An Loc was infested with NVA, and that the difficult terrain wouldn't let us find them easily.

On 26 May, we were back up around An Loc–Quan Loi to work a routine VR mission out west toward the Fishhook. Crockett was getting ready to rotate back home, so I was flying again with Al Farrar as my crew chief.

As we pulled out behind Darkhorse Three Eight (Phil Carriss's Cobra), Farrar keyed the intercom. "Where we headed today, Lieutenant?"

As we passed over the Phu Loi perimeter fence, I heard him arm his M-60. "Just sit back and relax, Al," I responded. "We've got a few klicks to ride up to Quan Loi, then probably on out toward the Fishhook for a little looksee at what the bad guys are up to."

"I hear it can get pretty hot up there, sir. But, you know, I love flying scouts. I haven't been a crew chief very long now, but I'm learning real good and getting better every day."

"How about a little radio fifty-four as we ride, Al?" I said back into the intercom. Without waiting for his answer, I flipped on the automatic direction finder (ADF) so we could catch the armed forces AM radio on the long flight up to Quan Loi. As was becoming my habit also, I took my right foot off the pedal and propped it on the lower door frame outside the aircraft. Finding that I could easily handle level flight with just the left pedal, wiggling my right foot out the door was a comfortable diversion.

"I really have been looking forward to flying more with you, sir," Farrar said over the music. "Since I'm just learning, I sure would appreciate anything you can do to help me along."

"If you think you've drawn the master card to learn everything on this flight, you're in deep trouble, Al, because we're both learning. So, if we cooperate and graduate together, we might get this thing done right."

"I sure do roger that, Lieutenant."

As we flew into an area northwest of the An Loc rubber plantation, Carriss in the Cobra broke on VHF to me. "OK, One Six, we're coming up on the area that Quan Loi wants us to take a look at. How do you feel about it?"

"OK, Three Eight, let's go," I responded.

"All right, One Six. I want you to go down on the large open clearing on the crest of the hill at about your four o'clock. Have you got that in sight?"

With my head cocked out the door, I picked up the hill with a valley leading off to the west. "Roger that . . . in sight."

"OK," Carriss followed up, "then begin your runs to the west, working to the north. We'll call your breaks for you. You've got free-fire."

I keyed the intercom and asked Farrar if he was ready to go to work. With excitement clear in his voice, he came back, "Yes, sir, Lieutenant, let's do it!"

I kicked right pedal and whipped the cyclic over, forcing the little Loach into a tight right-hand descending turn. We swirled down to about a kilometer away from the hilltop where I was to start my pattern.

Pulling out at fifteen to twenty feet above the treetops, I headed for the hill from zero nine zero degrees so I could pass over that specific terrain feature and start my run in the cardinal direction of west. I headed up the valley at about forty knots, making 360-degree turns over things I wanted to look at again.

As I neared my westerly mark, the Cobra front-seater called, "Western limit, One Six."

With that message, I did a right turn north for fifty to sixty yards, then another right, heading me back east to work a return search.

As I circled over what looked to be an old deserted bunker, looking for foot traffic patterns, I was interrupted by Carriss. "Hey, One Six, we've lost you. Where are you?"

Knowing full well how difficult it was to see me against the dense jungle from fifteen hundred feet, I kidded back, "I'm right down here, Three Eight. I can see you. Why in the hell can't you see me?"

"Move out into a little clearing for a second, One Six, so I can see if I can pick you up."

Moving into an area that offered some terrain contrast to the back of my bird, I keyed back, "Have you got me yet, or do you want me to drop a yellow smoke?"

"We've got you, One Six. Don't need a smoke . . . move back into your pattern."

On about the third route west, I noticed that we were coming up on what looked like a small valley within the valley. There were fairly high wooded hills on each side that extended from about halfway up the main valley to what appeared to be about the western limit of my search leg. I headed between them, more than a little apprehensive about flying into such tight quarters. I started my three-sixties just as soon as I entered the eastern end of the valley.

Though you never knew where you'd find bad guys, this looked like a perfect place for trouble. Besides, my built-in warning alarm was going off in the nape of my neck, telling me I needed to be extra careful in here. I keyed the intercom. "I've got a funny feeling about this place, Al. Keep your eyes peeled and your 60 cocked."

I had no sooner gotten the words out of my mouth when I passed over a fairly heavy wire strung across the valley. A wire? I thought. If it is, it's sure as hell out of place in the middle of this jungle. I swung around to take another look. "What do you make of that wire that just went under our nose?" I asked Farrar.

"I see it, Lieutenant. Looks like it's tied to trees across the valley from each other. I don't know what the hell—"

"You know what I think we got, Al? Could that be a radio antenna?"

Punctuating my question was a tremendous burst of ground fire coming up on the front and left side of the aircraft. Not from just one weapon, but from AK-47s and .30- and .50-caliber machine guns.

As I jerked a hard right turn and tried to dive for the treetops, I screamed into the radio, "I'm taking fire . . . taking fire!" Farrar's 60 went off in response.

Just as I turned, I caught new fire from across the valley coming up at me from twelve o'clock dead ahead. I was getting hit . . . I could feel the hits in the airplane. All the time Farrar's M-60 kept firing.

"Son of a bitch!" I yelled. "We must have found a god-damned NVA radio station on the end of that wire, or they were just waiting to ambush us!"

Meeting the new fire head-on, I instinctively pulled another hard right. Fortunately I still had forty to fifty knots of speed to help get our asses out of there. However, my last right turn headed us right back into another blanket of enemy fire, coming up again from the opposite side of the valley. Also, I had caused Carriss to abort his rocket run on the targets because I had pulled right in front of him. He had to yank up his nose to avoid hitting me.

I had let go a blast of the minigun and Farrar was still giving them hell, his 60 blazing. He was leaning out of the airplane, down under the tail boom, and shooting 60 lead out behind us.

Going like a bat out of hell, I pulled away from the

ambush kill zone. "Hit 'em," I yelled at Carriss. "Hit the bastards! I'm clear . . . I'm clear!"

"Did you get a smoke out?" asked Carriss.

"Shit," I muttered, and looked back at Farrar. His eyes were as big as billiard balls. "Lieutenant, sir, I ain't going back in there for nothin'. If you're going back in there, you can just let me out."

I keyed Carriss back. "No, we didn't get a smoke out."

"Ah-h-h, One Six, I think I spotted the source of your fires. I'm going to roll in and put some rockets down. What have you got down there?"

"I've never seen an enemy radio station before, Three Eight, but I think I've got one. While you expend your load, I'm going to start a spiral climb to altitude."

"Roger, One Six. I'm in hot." I watched Carriss break for his run.

Coming into fifteen hundred feet of altitude, I began to have trouble with the aircraft. Scanning the instrument panel, I saw that my turbine outlet temperature (TOT) gauge was running in the yellow and pushing the red line at nearly 749 degrees centigrade. Torque pressure was low and dropping. It was obvious that some of the enemy rounds had gone through my engine combuster. I wouldn't be able to stay in the air much longer.

As Carriss came back up after his run on the ambush targets, I told him I was going to have to get back to Quan Loi and put the ship down. There wasn't any question that I had taken a bunch of hits.

He wanted to escort me back to base, but I suggested that he stay on the NVA radio station and bring in some artillery and tac air. Carriss argued, but I assured him that I could already see the "plantation strip" (our name for the Quan Loi base runway) and that I really thought I could nurse the Loach in. He pulled back toward the target to set up some big stuff.

When the airplane was down safely at plantation, Farrar and I counted nineteen bullet holes in the ship. The rotor blades were hit. The nose was hit. The belly was hit. The tail boom had been hit, and there were about four rounds through the crew compartment, any one of which could have gone through Farrar.

Damn, I thought as I crawled underneath the Loach's belly, we just about got our asses shot off! Once again, I was amazed at the little OH-6's ability to take that kind of punishment and still get us back to base in one piece. But it was obvious that there was no way this aircraft would fly again in the shape she was in.

Farrar was still contemplating the four holes near his seat position, and I could see that his hands were shaking. His head was also shaking, but when he saw me he started laughing.

I looked down at my own hands. My whole body was shaking like a leaf. We both stood there on the tarmac, shaking and laughing uncontrollably.

Farrar broke the moment. "Son of a bitch, sir. You know a man could get killed doing this." I threw my arm around his shoulder and we walked away to see if we could hitch a Huey ride home.

I had been platoon leader of the Outcasts less than a month, gaining more confidence every day in my aircraft, in my scouting ability, and in my scouts. But the stress had a way of building, also. Though I was getting shot at almost every day, I never got used to it. But getting shot at was usually the way a scout found the enemy, and finding the enemy was our basic job.

The army TO&E (Table of Organization and Equipment) called for ten scouts in the platoon. Six, or possibly eight, however, were all we ever had. A typical combat flying month would usually add up to between 130 and 160 hours in the air for each scout pilot. It meant that each scout was flying an average of five hours a day. Every day. Thirty days a month!

It was tough—flying constantly under pressure, constantly in fear—and it took its toll. It was a constant game of trying to second-guess the enemy. It was a constant worry—about your airplane, about your crew chief, about learning your scouting craft well enough to survive.

The aeroscout platoon worked wherever it was needed within the 1st Division's geographical area of tactical interest. For about ten days in the early part of June '69, the Outcasts were called upon to provide scout cover for the Rome plowing work that was being done for the opening of the Song Be Road, officially known as Highway 1A.

The initial roadbed was built by the French sometime during the nearly hundred years of their Vietnam occupation. Highway 1A started down around Phu Cuong (just west of our base at Phu Loi), and ran generally north up along the western extremity of War Zone D. It wound its way up through Dogleg Village and Claymore Corners (another American-named landmark so-called because it formed a giant intersection where highways 2A, 1A, and 16 all came together just east of Lai Khe), then over the Song Be River bridge just north of Claymore Corners, on up through Phuoc Vinh and Dong Xoai, and finally to Song Be somewhat south of the Cambodian border. From altitude, the narrow little red dirt road looked like a rust-colored snake, slithering up through the jungle, rubber plantations, and Vietnamese villages along the way.

For a distance of eighty to ninety kilometers, the jungle crowded right up to the road on both sides, which put any military or civilian traffic under constant enemy surveillance and potential ambush attack. To open the Song Be Road for our supply convoys and civilian traffic, it was necessary for the 1st Engineer Battalion to put out land-clearing companies to remove jungle growth for about two hundred yards on both sides of the road.

The Outcasts' job was to sweep ahead of the Rome plows, chaperon the tanks and armored personnel carriers (APCs), and scout for enemy mines, bunkers, and spider holes. The Rome plows could take a good deal of punishment, but the APCs were soft-bellied and didn't take too well to running over mines. The scout platoon was to work this mission under the operational control (opcon) of the 11th Armored Cavalry Regiment, whose headquarters at the time were located at fire support base Bunard, way out in the boondocks northeast of Dong Xoai.

I was called up there to get a briefing on the specifics of the scout assignment from elements of the regiment's command group. They were to direct me to where the regimental commander (none other than Col. George S. Patton III) wanted our air cav unit to work, since the aero-scouting mission was being split between us and the 11th's own Blackhorse troop.

On the appointed day, Dean Sinor (Three One) and I flew up as a team to FSB Bunard. It was 5 June. Since a fire support base was a crowded, busy place, Sinor got on the radio as soon as we had Bunard in sight to get our landing instructions. "Blackhorse Three, this is Darkhorse Three One. We're a flight of two coming up on station for a briefing. Where would you like us to put down?"

"Ah . . . OK, Darkhorse, this is Blackhorse Three. We've been taking a lot of fire this morning from the jungle. Recommend that you make a spiraling descent right into the base camp. No long approaches because we've got a bunch of sniper fire down here."

Sinor rogered that and then asked me how I felt about going in. Even from altitude I could tell there wasn't much room down there for a couple of birds to just drop in. So I keyed him back: "You know what, Three One? Why don't you go on in first and take all the room you need. I can put my bird down anywhere, but you'll have some trouble shoehorning that gunship inside the concertina wire. Then, after you're in and shut down, I'll just drop on into whatever space is left."

Sinor made a high overhead approach and circled down into an open area right in the middle of the fire base—the only space big enough to take his fifty-two feet, eleven inches of rotor-turning Cobra.

When he was in and shut down, I searched the camp for a spot where I could light. My Loach had a turning diameter of just over thirty-four feet, so I was looking for about a forty-foot niche inside the wire.

I spotted a small bare dirt area in between where Sinor had put down and what looked like a tent pitched out the backside of an armored personnel carrier. It would be tight, but that's all there was.

I went into a high overhead approach by spotting my ship directly over the point where I wanted to put down. Kicking the OH-6 over on her side, I entered a hard right-hand descending spiral. I continued falling out of trim until I was over the little bald spot next to the tent attached to the APC. Then I leveled off into a wider turn, flared, pulled pitch, and dropped the Loach to the ground right on the money.

Red dust swirled. Objects blew. I didn't see much with all the junk blowing, except to notice that my rotor wash had popped the tent loose from its moorings.

With ropes and stakes flying, the wind blast blew the tent and its belongings like a rumpled paper sack up over the top of the personnel carrier, then deposited the mess, inside out, at the other end of the APC. It looked like a huge pile of dirty clothes at a Chinese laundry.

When the dust settled, I looked over toward the APC. Two soldiers were sitting in lawn chairs, scowling at me. One had a huge mustache, which was twitching with anger. The other man had a great shock of gray hair, now totally askew from having his tent blown off the top of him.

I didn't immediately recognize the soldier with the mustache. But the gray-haired man . . . oh, shit! Though I had never met him, I knew exactly who he was: the regimental commander of the hard-fighting Blackhorse 11th ACR, George S. Patton III.

As I shut down, the enlisted man with the big mustache

got up out of his chair, put on his helmet, and walked toward my ship, looking as though he was going to eat me alive. I could hear him screaming as he got closer. "Goddamnit, Lieutenant, I guess you realize that you just blew away the regimental commander's tent!"

Just then I recognized the sergeant. His name was Wolf, and I remembered him from Fort Knox. He had been my first sergeant in the recon company at Knox after I graduated from OCS.

By this time, I had my helmet off and he recognized me. "How in the h-e-e-l-l are you, Lieutenant?" he said, the anger leaving his face. "How ya been?"

Realizing that I was probably in trouble anyway, I responded sarcastically: "I'm OK, but the regimental commander ought not park his goddamned tent in my landing zone."

"You want me to tell him that, Lieutenant?" said the sergeant major, smiling.

"You're damned right," I answered, thinking so far so good.

But the sergeant major was going to have the last laugh. He turned around and walked back to Colonel Patton. "Colonel, that young helicopter lieutenant out there wants to know why you got your goddamned tent in his landing zone."

Patton exploded with laughter. "Bring that obnoxious son of a bitch up here!"

That was my introduction to George Patton. Though the son of famed General Patton of World War II, George III was well known in his own right as an aggressive, fearless, and hard-hitting leader. He was also a man with a very much appreciated sense of humor.

The Outcasts were closely involved in the Song Be Road mission until it was completed ten days later, on 15 June. On that day, and in conjunction with the Big Red One's fifty-second service anniversary, a Song Be Road completion ceremony was held at Phuoc Vinh.

As our final assignment, I was asked to go up for the ribbon cutting, primarily to set up a couple of VR teams to cap and fly cover for the ceremony. It was a big occasion. Both Vietnamese civilians and allied military forces would now be able to traverse the full length of the road with much improved security.

I returned to Phu Loi that afternoon about 1500. After four straight hours of flying, I was ready for a shower and quiet dinner at the O club. I walked in my hootch door and parted the beaded curtains that separated Bob Davis's and my bunk areas from the rest of the hootch. I immediately noticed that my fan was running, my TV was playing, and perched right in the middle of my bunk was a black-haired lieutenant of infantry.

He had his boots off. He was scratching his bare foot with one hand, drinking a Coca-Cola out of my refrigerator with the other, watching my TV, and cooling his damned self with *my* fan! There were no possessions guarded more jealously than a man's fan, TV, stereo, and certain refinements of his bunk area. In fact, these items of luxury were so coveted by the pilots that they were actually willed to successors should the owner depart the country or be killed in action.

With as much composure as I could muster, I demanded, "Just what in the hell are you doing here?"

Completely unperturbed by my blast, the man responded, "I'm new to the troop. I'm assigned to this hootch, and I'm looking for a place to drop my gear."

"Well, this ain't the place, soldier," I shot back in a caustic tone of voice. But I realized that the guy had probably been waiting around in an empty hootch for two to three hours hoping someone would show up to help him find an empty bunk. Besides, I kind of liked his manner.

"Hey, there's an empty bunk right outside the beaded curtain. I'll help you move your gear, then after I shower up we can go down to the O club and catch dinner and a movie."

By this time he was on his feet and sticking out his hand. "My name is Rod Willis, Lieutenant Rod Willis. Are you a scout pilot?"

I shook his hand. "Well, yes . . . I'm Hugh Mills, One Six. Are you assigned to the scout platoon?"

"Yes, but it wasn't easy."

I liked Willis almost from the start. I got him introduced around the club and showed him the troop plaque lineup behind the bar. Each of the pilots in the troop had a plaque with his name and call sign on it. When a new guy came into the unit, his plaque was made up and put at the bottom of the group on the left side wall behind the bar. Plaques for the senior pilots were hung on the right side of the bar. As people DEROSed or otherwise left the troop, their plaques were taken down and everybody else moved up higher in the pecking order. Willis took a lot of kidding that night as he became the lowest man on the totem pole —a very visible position.

After supper, Bill Jones, Bob Davis, Willis (now to be the new One Seven), and I went back to the hootch and talked scouting for a couple of hours. Though Willis didn't do an awful lot of talking, we learned that he was an air force brat. His father, a thirty-year veteran (a senior master sergeant), and the family had lived all over the world. He had followed exactly the same army career path that I had: enlisted, basic training, OCS (infantry), flight school, and Vietnam.

When he processed into Vietnam, he was assigned to pilot Hueys in the 1st Division. He told us how he practically begged on bended knee to get the S-3 to change his orders from jockeying ash and trash to flying combat missions in the scouts.

The kinds of questions Willis asked that night showed me what kind of pilot he would be. "You guys fly real low, don't you?" "How often do you make enemy contact?" "How many kills are you getting?" "How much damage are the scouts doing to the enemy?" "How soon can I get transitioned into Loaches so I can get at the bastards?"

This guy's naturally aggressive style was perfect for the scouts. He acted and talked like an individualist, and individualists were what the scouts were all about. Plus, he didn't have a wife and family back home to worry about.

At about the same time that Willis came into the unit, we also got a new Darkhorse troop commander, a cavalry major by the name of Charles L. Moore. Not having met the man, I didn't know what to expect when the new CO called a meeting of all the platoon leaders in his private hootch after supper on the day of the change of command ceremony. Before the meeting, though, I did find out that Moore was a second tour veteran, had actually served as the Darkhorse XO during his first tour, and had good familiarity with troop organization and operations.

At precisely 1900, we all walked into Major Moore's hootch, snapped crisp salutes, and reported to the new commanding officer. The first thing that came across about him was that he was supercharged to the aggressive position, and somewhat spring-loaded to the pissed-off position. In other words, he was very aggressive, said exactly what he was thinking, and wanted it damned well understood that the mission of the troop was to seek out and destroy the enemy.

"It's our cavalry heritage," he said, "to find the enemy wherever the sons a bitches are. When we find 'em, we're going to kill 'em. Is that understood?"

"Yes, sir!" we responded simultaneously.

"And starting tomorrow, I'm going to be flying C and C on as many of your missions as possible, so I'll be there right on top of the contact to make whatever tactical decisions need to be made. Is *that* understood?"

Major Moore's attitude was like a breath of fresh air to me. I decided then and there to show him Joe Vad's new Outcast patch design.

Vad (Nine) was a rough, tough, street fighter from

Brooklyn, New York. He didn't care too much for the plain rectangular cloth patch that all the Outcasts wore over our right jacket pocket, so he had sketched a new design that he thought better typified the scout platoon's fighting spirit. It was a blood red disk with a big skull and crossed cavalry sabers in the middle. At the top was the word OUTCASTS; at the bottom written on a scroll were the words, LOW LEVEL HELL.

I had been waiting for the right opportunity to show the design to Major Cummings. As soon as Major Moore saw Vad's artwork, he approved it. He ordered patches be made and sewn on scout uniforms as soon as possible.

Though the motto on the new patch was Low Level Hell, the scout platoon was flying high. We knew our business. We all had miniguns strapped to our birds. We were scouring the countryside and finding the enemy every day. We were killing enemy every day. We hadn't lost a single man in the platoon as the result of combat action. And the Darkhorse reputation was spreading—we were a pretty damned hot bunch of fliers.

Our increasingly cavalier attitude didn't prepare us for what was about to happen.

A few days later, on 24 June, Jim Ameigh (One Five) and I were the scouts for two hunter-killer teams that had left Phu Loi early that morning to work an area around the Quan Loi airstrip. Captain Mike Woods (Three Five) was my gun pilot, and we worked for about ten hours with Ameigh and his gun, reconning from Quan Loi and An Loc in the south, on up Highway 13 to Loc Ninh in the north. We ended the operation about 1700, and the four of us met at Quan Loi for the flight back down Thunder Road to our base at Phu Loi.

On that day I was flying with an observer pilot in the left front seat instead of a crew chief in back. Artillery 1st Lt. Dwight Cheek had just recently come into the unit and was flying with me as a scout pilot in training. He already knew the OH-6 pretty well, having taken advanced training in the Loach and served some time as an OH-6 instructor pilot before coming to Vietnam.

Ameigh's door gunner for the day was an experienced young crew chief by the name of Jim Slater. On the ride home from Quan Loi, both Ameigh and Slater were especially elated because they had made contact with enemy patrols that day and had scored confirmed kills—Slater out the back door with his M-60, and Ameigh with his minigun.

As we climbed out of Quan Loi, Woods in the lead Cobra got on the artillery frequency and asked for a status report.

Quan Loi artillery came right back. "Roger, Darkhorse. Quan Loi is cold . . . negative outgoing fires. Contact Lai Khe artillery north Thunder Three for Lai Khe advisories. Lai Khe arty is currently shooting 105s to the south and southeast. Good day."

With Ameigh's bird tight on my left wing, we headed down Highway 13 at eighty to ninety knots. As we approached Thunder One, Woods called up again, asking arty status from Lai Khe artillery.

They responded: "OK, Darkhorse flight of four, we've got 105s shooting out of Lai Khe, max ord three thousand feet. You are cleared direct to Phu Loi as long as you stay along the highway, and under two thousand feet for a safety buffer."

Three Five rogered that with the comment that the guns were running at slightly under fifteen hundred feet and the scouts were down on the deck at a hundred feet or so off the ground. Ameigh and I were low because it was beginning to get dark, which gave us the opportunity to scout the road and maybe catch a bad guy planting a mine or digging a spider hole.

A couple of kilometers north of Lai Khe, Ameigh and I saw a group of our M-551 Sheridan tanks and M-113 ACAVs that were getting loggered in for the night. They were on the west side of the road and, in size, looked like about a troop or squadron-minus of armored cavalry.

As we flew over the tanks, Woods radioed from his fifteen-hundred-foot position. "Hey, One Six, Three Five. You guys are going to have to either turn on some lights or come up to altitude. I'm having trouble seeing you."

We knew he didn't expect us to turn on our navigation and anticollision lights. The large red-flashing anticollision light mounted on the belly of the OH-6 was so visible that we called it the "target." Woods really wanted us to come up and get into formation with the snakes.

I came up on UHF to Ameigh. "One Five, this is One Six. Let's take it up to altitude and get on the gun's wing." I waited for him to come back, or, at a minimum, respond by twice breaking squelch with his transmit switch. But nothing. I heard nothing back.

I was ready to key Ameigh again and repeat the message when Mike Woods broke back in. "One Six, where is One Five? I don't see your wingman. I say again, I do not see One Five. Is he with you?"

I twisted in my seat to look back where Ameigh's ship ought to have been, yelling, "One Five, this is One Six. Where are you? Come on, goddamnit, where in the hell are you?"

No response. I kicked right pedal, pulled full power, and slammed the cyclic right. Coming hard around in a tight descending, decelerating turn, I scoured the sky for Ameigh's bird. Nothing. He wasn't there.

I flew several large circles, looking around the immediate area. He had been right there on my wing; now he was gone. Not a sign of him anywhere.

Mike Woods on VHF and I on UHF both appealed to Ameigh to come up on either frequency. Nothing.

On about my fourth circle around the area, I caught sight of a wisp of white smoke trailing up out of the jungle. A cold chill went through me. I moved directly over the smoke and tried to see through the trees. Suddenly I was nearly overcome by the smell of CS gas. The stream of smoke coming up from the jungle floor was riot gas, apparently from a burning CS canister. All the scout OH-6s carried CS canisters.

Eyes heavily watering from the gas fumes, I looked down and saw a hole in the jungle with tops of trees chopped off all around it, as if a giant woodsman had taken a blunt ax and splintered them away.

It was getting so dark that seeing all the way to the ground was almost impossible. But something white caught my eye. Straining through the faint light I could tell that it was definitely the open engine cowl door of an OH-6. The inside engine compartment of all OH-6s is painted white. And the only OH-6 not accounted for at that moment was Jim Ameigh's.

"Three Five, One Six. I've got the bird—he's down in the jungle. No apparent fire, but a CS gas canister must be popped. I see no sign of life. The aircraft is on its side. I can't see very well, but I think the bird's engine is still running because I can also smell JP-4 exhaust."

By this time Woods was circling above me and had informed Darkhorse ops at Phu Loi that Ameigh was down. He keyed me and asked, "Do you want me to scramble the ARPs?"

"Negative, let's hold on that. There's no lima zulu to put 'em down. It's getting too dark and it's too far from Thunder Road to put them in there and expect they'd find the bird out here in the jungle. We gotta do something quicker than that."

"OK, I roger that, One Six. How about those tanks we just passed back on Thunder. Do you suppose they could get in here to the wreck?"

"I don't know, but it's worth a try," I answered. "Let's get over to them."

Woods gave me a steer. The tanks we had passed were about two kilometers to the north and west. I also needed a frequency to talk to them. Since Cobras worked with all the ground units routinely, Three Five came right back with the FM push and call sign.

I hit it immediately. "Tanker, Tanker, this is Darkhorse on fox mike. Any unit in vicinity Thunder Road south of tango one [FSB Thunder I], please come up this push and talk to me."

Almost immediately a voice answered. "This is Tanker Six. What do you need, Darkhorse?"

"Tanker Six, this is Darkhorse One Six. We've got a downed bird just south and east of your logger location. Aircraft with pilot and crew chief down. I cannot get to them. I need you to bust a trail through the jungle. Can you do it?"

Immediately and unhesitatingly, Tanker Six responded. "Roger, stand by. Is that you in the little bird?"

"Yes, I'm in the little bird with a heavy gun team over me."

"Roger, Darkhorse. Lead on. I'll get my guys up on our frequency, and I'll follow you on this push."

Tanker left the frequency momentarily as I circled low overhead. Then, suddenly, all hell broke loose amidst the armored vehicles below. Tank crewmen who had been lounging around on the backs of their vehicles and ACAVs in all states of dress and undress sprang up, donned flak jackets, grabbed M-16s and helmets, and disappeared into their armored vehicles.

In just seconds, engines were fired up and the column began moving out of its night defensive position. The lead Sheridan steered right up onto Highway 13 and toward me where I was now hovering just south of their logger area.

As his column formed up on the road, Tanker came back on the FM frequency. "Darkhorse One Six, Tanker Six. What are the circumstances of the crash? Do we have enemy ground fire?"

"Negative, Tanker Six. If we had enemy ground fire, I did not hear it. Circumstances are unknown why the bird is down. Two souls on board, a pilot and a gunner."

"Roger, Darkhorse. We'll follow you and try to bust a trail to the site."

I headed off south down the road with the armored column following, sending up a swirl of red dust. When I reached a point on the road that was approximately ninety degrees and adjacent to the crash site, I pulled up and hit the radio to Tanker. "I'm going to leave you here. I'll hang east and go directly to the downed bird and hover over it. You can aim on me as you come off the road, but I'll be back overhead to correct your steering as you bust toward the site.

"Be aware that CS is coming up from what may be a ruptured canister. There is also hot ordnance on board. The aircraft engine appears to still be running, and the bird's tanks are full of JP-4."

As if all that made his job any easier, Tanker Six rogered my transmission and sent his lead Sheridan off the road into the jungle.

I flew on over to the crash site, circled a few times trying to see down into the dark jungle hole, then returned to the armored column to see how they were doing. The Sheridan out front was knocking down everything in its path. Trees fell and the low vegetation was being ground to pulp under the heavy tank treads. The ACAVs followed the big M-551 toward Ameigh's downed ship.

Every once in a while I keyed Tanker to alter his course a few degrees one way or the other, until the column finally gained a position about forty meters out from the crash site. "OK, Tanker," I said, "let's stop the lead track here and put some of your people on foot so your column doesn't overrun the aircraft. The downed bird is now about forty meters directly to your front."

The lead tank rolled to a halt. Several soldiers jumped off the 113s and took up positions out front and to the sides of the big Sheridan. Then the column started moving slowly ahead.

It was now very, very dark. I could hardly see the armored column when it stopped again, this time about fifteen meters from Ameigh's battered OH-6. As the rest of the soldiers poured out of the ACAVs, I moved my bird into a wider orbit around the crash site so the sound of my aircraft would not disrupt what they were trying to do on the ground.

Suddenly my FM radio crackled. "Darkhorse, Darkhorse, this is Tanker. We're at the bird. The aircraft is still running . . . say again . . . still running. It sounds like a full-bore runaway jet engine that could explode any second. What should we do?"

"What's the condition of the aircraft?" I asked.

"The chopper appears to be on its side, possibly upside down. The rotors have been torn off, and the engine is going max RPMs. Can't see pilot or door gunner. We're afraid the whole thing could go up any minute. Can you tell us how to shut down the engine? Need instructions."

I thought for a second. There was no way I could explain to those soldiers how to get into the cockpit and turn off that aircraft. I had to get down there and do it myself.

I went back to Tanker. "You'll never find the engine controls. I need to get down there myself. Can you bust me a landing zone so I can put this Loach down?"

"Sure can," he answered. "How much of an LZ do you need?"

Without any light to help guide me down into a hole in the jungle, I needed a spot at least fifty feet diameter, as close to the wreck as possible. I also told him that my other crewman was a pilot, and one way or another we'd get in and out of there.

Seconds later, the lead Sheridan cranked up and began to neutral-steer where it was. The tank growled, twisted, and turned in the little area, tearing down trees and bamboo. In three to four minutes, there was a landing zone just a few feet from Ameigh's aircraft. The LZ wasn't flat, not with all those knocked-down trees and other vegetation forming the floor. But when Tanker asked if his freshly carved lima zulu was OK, I told him to back off his Sheridan and let me give it a try.

I turned to Dwight Cheek. "I'm going to set this thing down in that spot the Sheridan just busted, then I'm going to get out of the ship. When I do, I'd like you to hold it at a hover. We'll be right on top of a bunch of torn-down trees—no solid ground, no firm footing—you'll have to be *very easy* until I can get over and check out the wreck and see if I can shut down that engine. Do you have any problem with that?" Dwight didn't bat an eye.

I went around to the west and started a run into the LZ at almost a dead hover. Once over the jungle hole, I began to let down vertically, with Cheek and me hanging out the aircraft doors to make sure the tail was clear.

I set her down as lightly as I could on a precarious perch of broken tree limbs and stumps. The little OH-6 began to totter. I lifted her up, turned about three feet to the right, and set her down again.

"OK, Dwight, you've got it. Pull in a little pitch and just hold her right here. I'll be back as quick as I can. Now be ready for a change in weight when I get out of the aircraft."

I disconnected my helmet and seat belt and slid my right leg out the door. Then I lifted my left leg up and over my cyclic stick, which Cheek was controlling now from his side, and jumped out of the ship.

I landed on a tree limb sticking up about two feet off the ground. Doing a quick balancing act, I worked my way through the branches and into the arms of a couple of troopers who had run over to help me.

They grabbed me and led the way to Ameigh's smashed aircraft. I could hear the high-pitched whine of the jet engine that was still running wild amidst a white cloud of choking CS gas.

Reaching the wreck, I had to momentarily turn away because my eyes were watering so badly. Tears ran down my face, and my nose and mucous membranes poured. I arm-swiped my face with the sleeves of my fatigue jacket.

All the troopers around me were in the same condition. One of them was trying to get relief by standing with his face up in the OH-6's rotor wash, trying to flush out some of the CS gas.

I approached the aircraft and could see that the engine cowl on the right-hand side was open and the ship was lying almost on its back. The noise was almost unbearable. With the downed bird's engine running full blast, the ACAV motors going, and Cheek's Loach hovering, the nearby armored crewman could hardly hear me yell into his ear, "Get me some help in here. We're going to try to lift the ship up enough so I can crawl into the left side of the cabin and get at the engine controls."

The fuel valve control knob and the battery off-on switch were both located on the console circuit breaker panel between the seats. By going into the left side of the cabin, I could probably get at those switches easier because the left seat was vacant. All I would have to do is find the fuel switch and pull it out; that would immediately cut off the fuel supply to the engine and shut it down.

With the help of about five troopers braving the CS gas, we lifted the left side of the aircraft about eighteen inches off the ground. The armor guys held it there momentarily, and I slithered into the cabin. I immediately started feeling around to get a fix on where things were.

It was black as pitch. My initial reaction was that absolutely nothing was where it ought to be in a normal Loach cockpit. Things were torn loose. Everything seemed crushed over on top of itself, accordion style. Finding that fuel cutoff was going to be some kind of trick. Damn! If I could only see something. This mother could go sky high any second!

With the fingers of my right hand, I felt my way up over what should have been the back of the left front seat. Then on to where the console and the circuit breaker panel were between the seats, where, with a little luck, I'd find the push-pull fuel shutoff valve control.

God, it was eerie in there! Everything bashed to hell, Jim Ameigh and Slater in there someplace, in what condition I couldn't imagine, and the aircraft's engine running red-line and tearing itself apart.

Groping wildly now, my fingers suddenly touched the fuel valve. I yanked it hard, and to my utter horror the whole switch assembly—valve, cable, and all—tore loose out of the panel and into my hand.

The engine whined on. My eyes burned from CS gas and from the sheer frustration of the ripped-out valve. My thoughts raced, trying to figure out what I could do now.

A last resort occurred to me—try to shut her down at the engine itself. I backed out of the aircraft. The soldiers helped me relift the OH-6 so I could crawl into the engine cowl door.

I really couldn't tell what I was dealing with in there, but I felt a push-pull tube on the fuel control that seemed to be the throttle linkage. When I pulled and turned it, the fuel shut off. The engine wound down and stopped.

Now I had to get back into the wreck and see about Ameigh and Slater. As I crawled into the rear cargo compartment, one of the soldiers wiggled in behind me. He didn't have a shirt on, but a medical bag was tied around his neck.

"I'm the medic," he said. "How many casualties have you got, sir?"

"I don't know, I can't tell yet, but the crew chief should be right here."

Groping in the dark, I suddenly brushed against a leg. I assumed it was Jim Slater's. He was still strapped into the gunner's seat, his upper body bent forward where the caved-in engine and transmission had pushed him. With the wrecked aircraft inverted, he was hanging upside down from the roof.

I reached up and held Slater around the waist as I

punched the automatic seat belt release. I kept jabbing at
the release but nothing came loose. The damned thing
must have jammed. I was frantic. What I didn't realize was
that Slater was also attached to his monkey strap, which
was still holding him securely in place.

I moved around to the right and Doc came up into the
cargo hold with me. There was about three feet of
headroom, with our knees on the ground.

I pulled out my survival knife, and with both Doc and
me cradling him, I cut through Slater's belts. His body fell
into our arms like a heavy sack of wheat. We yelled to the
soldiers outside to lift the aircraft again so we could pull
Slater out.

Dragging him into the open, Doc tried to rip away the
top of Slater's flight suit to start working on him, but the
chicken plate was in the way. Doc had never seen a
chicken plate before, so I reached down with my knife and
cut it loose.

Doc quickly checked all the vital signs, then looked up
at me. "I'm sorry, sir, he's dead."

It took a moment for the realization to sink in. "OK,
then, let's go back. We've still got a pilot in there."

I knew Ameigh had to be on the right side of the aircraft, which was still against the ground. "Everybody!" I
yelled. "I need everybody over here to turn this bird over."
In seconds a dozen or more soldiers were lifting and pushing.

As the aircraft moved, a hand fell out of the pilot's
cabin door. I let go of the aircraft and grabbed the hand to
search for a pulse. My heart nearly jumped into my throat.
I felt a pulse—a strong but irregular beating against my
trembling fingertips. "This man's alive," I screamed. "Push
this thing up . . . get the airplane up . . . and be careful
as hell!"

Ameigh was still strapped in, but sideways in his seat.
The aircraft had rolled over on him. Doc was at my side
again as I reached for Ameigh's seat belt and shoulder

harness release. When I popped it, he fell loose into our arms and free of the aircraft.

As Doc and the others started working over Ameigh, I ran back over to Cheek, who was still hovering precariously over the fallen tree limbs of the LZ. I leaned in the cabin door, plugged in my helmet, and hit the intercom button. "Three Five, this is One Six. We've got the charlie echo kilo [crew chief-engineer dead]. Charlie echo is kilo. One Five is still alive. Let's get a Dustoff. Scramble a Dustoff. We've got Ameigh still alive down here. Get Dustoff over here as fast as you can." I rushed back over to Ameigh. "How's he doing?"

The medic looked up at me. "I don't know . . . it's touch and go."

I told him I had called Dustoff, but that maybe both Doc and Ameigh could get into the back of my Loach for the short lift over to Doctor Delta (Lai Khe hospital).

Doc quickly turned down my offer. "Negative. I want him in a litter. I don't want to curl him up—he's had massive internal injuries."

"Can you keep him alive?" I pleaded.

"I think I can if we can get a Dustoff in here and not waste any time getting him over to the hospital."

Doc and another one of the soldiers strapped what looked like a tourniquet around Ameigh's lower body, then hooked up an IV. Ameigh was a really handsome guy with black wavy hair. Standing there looking into his ashen face, I just couldn't believe that he had been on my wing one second, then gone without a trace. Now this!

I went back to the hovering Loach and got on the radio just in time to hear Mike Woods say, "One Six, Dustoff is coming off Doctor Delta right now. I need to get your Loach out of there and get Dustoff down in your lima zulu. Will the Huey fit?"

Looking around me, I said, "Yeah, it's big enough for a Huey, if he's good. Dustoff can make it in here, but it'll be tight as hell."

Then I turned to Cheek. "Dwight, I'm going to go with Ameigh in Dustoff. Can you get this bird out of here, then get up on Three Five's wing and take this ship home?"

"Sure. Roger. Do you need any help?"

"No, I just need room down here for Dustoff. Get up on Mike's tail and stay with him. Do what he tells you and you'll have no problem."

I backed away and watched the OH-6 climb up into the night. Seconds later, Dustoff arrived and started descending into the jungle hole just vacated by Cheek. Then its light came on, illuminating the whole area in a blinding white glare.

As the ship floated down, the jungle began to rumble and roar. The rotor wash of that Huey blew things all over the place. Soldiers grabbed for their hats and other gear. I saw Doc lean down over Ameigh to protect him from the fury.

The air ambulance couldn't set down on that pile of torn-up forest any better than we could. So the ship hovered, and a medic jumped out and helped Doc work over Ameigh for three or four minutes. Then Ameigh was lifted onto a Stokes litter and we carried him over to Dustoff.

The crew chief turned to me. "What about your dead?" he asked.

"No time . . . let's take care of the living. We'll come back for Slater."

He signaled the pilot to get going, and we lifted up into the night. Lai Khe was only a couple of minutes away. We were no more than up when Dustoff's light came on again and we settled down onto the Doctor Delta pad, with a huge red cross painted in the middle of it.

Waiting at the medical pad were five or six hospital people with a gurney. A wooden ramp went directly from the pad over to a Quonset hut with double doors.

The instant Dustoff touched down, Ameigh was transferred to the gurney and a doctor bent down over him with a stethoscope. I followed behind the gurney as it moved toward the double doors. The medical people were all in their gleaming hospital whites; I was still in flight gear with helmet, chicken plate, survival vest, and gun belt.

When they kicked open the double doors, we were suddenly in an operating room with emergency medical equipment all over the place. Still nobody told me what to do, so I stepped aside and watched the flurry of activity. As they lifted Ameigh off the gurney and onto an operating table, I whispered, "God, please save him."

The team worked feverishly. Then, suddenly, CPR was ordered. I began to feel very nervous, light-headed, and almost nauseous. I steadied myself against the wall. My God, I thought, Ameigh's not going to make it.

For eight to ten minutes more, the medical team worked over Ameigh. Then, as suddenly as they had begun their lifesaving efforts, they stopped. I heard the lead doctor say quietly to his associates, "OK, that's it."

The doctor had apparently noticed me standing nearby. He pulled off his face mask and rubber gloves, and stood motionless over Ameigh for a moment. Then he walked over to me. "I'm sorry, we've lost him. There's nothing more we can do."

I nodded and looked past the doctor at Ameigh lying there on the table. I felt totally lost. With my flight helmet still in my hands, I turned and walked out the door of the emergency room. There was a bench there, and I sank down on it.

For what seemed like an eternity, I sat there listening to the muffled blasts of artillery shooting into the night out of Lai Khe. I could see flares bursting over the Iron Triangle. I could hear the cracks of small-arms fire in the direction of Ben Cat. Then my world went silent.

For the first time since the ordeal had begun, I realized that my body was drained. All my energy was gone. My senses were dull. I was dead tired.

* * *

I don't know how long I sat there on that bench outside the emergency room before one of the Dustoff pilots walked up and snapped me back to reality. He told me that the hospital had received an FM radio message that Darkhorse was sending its C and C Huey to take me back to the troop.

I thanked him and continued to sit there staring. I smoked a cigarette and thought about what had happened. I still couldn't believe that one second Ameigh and I were flying and talking together, and the next second he was gone. Irretrievably gone. I just couldn't believe it!

About fifteen minutes later, the troop C and C landed, and just behind that ship came Dustoff returning from its second trip to the crash scene with Jim Slater's body. Realizing that there was nothing more for me to do at the hospital, I climbed aboard the C and C ship for the trip back to Phu Loi.

Wayne McAdoo (Two Six) and Bob Holmes (Two Nine) were the pilots, and they wasted no time asking me, "How's Ameigh? Is he OK?"

"No," I mumbled. "Ameigh's dead . . . Slater's dead . . . they're both dead."

There was a long pause while my announcement sank in. Then McAdoo turned to me. "What should we do?"

All I could say was, "Let's go home . . . that's all we *can* do."

Without another word said, the Huey lifted off from Lai Khe, leveled off at fifteen hundred feet, and headed southeast to Phu Loi.

I sat on the floor with my legs drawn up, my arms folded over my knees, and my head cradled in my arms. The wind rushed through the open rear compartment doors and the Huey's rotors beat a steady rhythm in my ears.

My body demanded sleep, but the pictures in my mind of Ameigh and Slater kept playing over and over again.

Even in the misty fog of my exhaustion, I kept thinking just how fragile life really is. This was my first close-up exposure to death, and it was a deep, hurting shock to my twenty-one-year-old mind.

CHAPTER 8

MAD CHARLIE

Rod Willis (One Seven) completed his scout training flights and moved onto the active flying roster, taking the place of Jim Ameigh. Jim Morrison had left the scout platoon for troop maintenance, so there was another vacancy in the Outcasts. Filling that slot was a new pilot, Bob Calloway, who took the scout platoon call sign One Zero. I made it a point to fly with new pilots coming into the troop as often as I could.

Calloway had been flying as door gunner for about a week, getting the feel of things. On 7 July, I decided to take him out on a pilot training mission, with him doing the flying out of the right seat and me riding along as observer in the left seat. I chose an area where I felt we could work without a great deal of danger—out along the Saigon River north and west of the Mushroom.

At that time of year, the Vietnamese were harvesting their rice crop and planting a new crop right behind it. In the area where Calloway and I were to fly that day, there were lots of U.S. Army and ARVN troops, protecting the farmers while they harvested and planted their rice. I felt, therefore, that the area would be relatively free of bad guys and potential combat situations. Besides, there were old forts, winding trails, Highway 14, various types of bun-

kers, tiny villages, and rice paddies on which Calloway
could practice scouting techniques.

When we reached the area, I asked our Cobra pilot,
Paul Fishman (Three Four), to put us down over a small
open field. I wanted Calloway to practice how to drop out
of altitude into a low search pattern, orbit a given area,
and report everything he saw to the gun pilot.

I counseled One Zero, remembering that not so long
ago, *I* was the trainee. "The good scout pilot never stops
talking to his gun from the moment he goes down out of
altitude until he comes back up again. It not only keeps
the Cobra happy and informed, but it tends to keep your
own guts stabilized when you're down low working and, at
any instant, could catch a bellyful of AK-47 fire."

Then, while Calloway practiced, I relaxed. I hung my
left foot out of the aircraft and let it flap in the breeze. I lit
a cigarette and began watching the ground out the left side
of the ship.

I noticed a group of people working a rice paddy out to
the west, just off the east bank of the Big Blue (Saigon
River). It looked like about thirty Vietnamese men and
women all wearing the usual conical hats and traditional
pajama tops and bottoms, pants rolled up above their
knees.

Calloway didn't see them at first because he was looking
straight down in his right-hand orbits over the field. But
each time we came around, I watched their progress as the
group waded through the paddy, all heading in the same
direction and working in almost perfect unison.

It was fascinating to see how smoothly and quickly they
worked. They had bags of rice shoots strapped to their
backs. With each step, they'd withdraw a shoot from their
pack, plunge the shoot into water up to their elbows, leaving it standing erect in the mud, then move on to insert the
next shoot. I was momentarily captivated by their almost
military cadence as they moved down the watery furrows.

Then, the little alarm twitch in the back of my neck went

off. Something about the group was just not right. I couldn't figure it out.

My attention began to center on one of the workers near the middle of the group. He didn't seem to be doing things the way the others did. As he moved forward with the group, he seemed also to be inching his way ninety degrees out of the knot of workers and toward the river-bank.

He didn't have a hat on, and all the other workers were wearing hats. I studied his face. He appeared to be about military age, not very young or very old, like the rest of the workers. While they marched steadily on, planting their rice and paying absolutely no attention to our orbiting air-craft, this person kept nervously glancing up at us, keeping close watch on where we were and what we were doing.

To distract him from the fact that we were keeping an eye on him, from our orbits over the adjacent field, I dropped a couple of smokes. I hoped that would make him think we were interested in something right beneath the airplane.

But he was too nervous to take the bait. Every moment or two he glanced over his shoulder at us—all the time trying to give the appearance of feverishly planting rice—while hurrying his movement across the main body of the group to make his exit.

That did it for me. I got on the radio to the gun. "Three Four, this is One Six. We got a guy over there in the middle of those farmers who's planting rice the wrong way and looking suspicious as hell."

"What do you think you've got, One Six?" Fishman came back.

"I don't know, Paul," I answered. "But I don't think he's a farmer. I think we've got a dink over there who's trying to look like he's planting rice, while trying to pull a *didi-mau* out the other side and make a run for the river."

"What do you want to do, One Six?"

"I'm going to tell Calloway to go over there and make a

few passes near them to see what this person does. Then I'll let you know. In the meantime, why don't you get up on the ARVN push and find out who the controlling agency is for this area, so we can bring an interpreter in here and run a few questions by this guy."

Three Four rogered that and I pushed the intercom button to Calloway. "OK, Bobby, roll out of here easy and move on over to that group of farmers. Then take up an orbit at a respectable distance away, not directly over their heads. There's a guy acting weird. We're going to see what the hell he's doing in there and nail his ass if he keeps looking phony."

Just as we were getting to the group of farmers, Fishman came back up on VHF. "Sorry, One Six. None of our friendlies in the area have anybody right now they can plug into this area to pick up your guy and interrogate him. What do you want to do now?"

I thought for a minute while we watched below. Calloway now had the bird in right-hand turns about twenty feet off the ground, just to the west and on the river side of the group.

Our bareheaded rice planter was looking more suspicious than ever, glancing over his shoulder to make sure that he knew our every move. The other farmers were ignoring us, planting their rice without ever breaking stride.

I was convinced by this time that the fellow didn't belong in that group of farmers, so I suggested that Fishman call up the troop and scramble the ARPs. We could put them down somewhere around here and they could take the guy into custody and find out what he was up to.

In less than a minute, Fishman was back to let me know that the ARPs were on strip alert for an infantry operation someplace else in the 1st Division area. So they weren't available to us for anything other than a major priority situation.

Well, damn! I thought. I keyed the gun back. "OK,

Three Four, cover me, please. We're going in there and land, and I'm going to get that sucker myself."

"You really want to do that?" Fishman responded.

"Well, he's right out there in the middle of that rice paddy, and it doesn't look like too big a deal to me to take my M-16 and round him up. Then we can fly him to the ARVN unit just down the river and they can talk to him."

With that, I pointed Calloway to a thin dike in the flooded paddy near the group of farmers. "Make a circle and drop the bird on the dike just as close to that guy as you can. Then just hold her right there while I get out and get him."

Flying beautifully, Calloway settled the Loach on the little bare piece of ground. I jumped out of the aircraft, carrying my M-16 with a thirty-round magazine in it. As usual, I was dressed in my Nomex flight suit and was wearing my chicken plate, which alone weighed about thirty pounds. Then my survival vest on top of that. My APH-5 flying helmet, flight gloves, a pistol belt with my .45 Colt and survival knife hooked onto it, plus a shoulder holster where I carried my own personal Python 357.

I walked in front of the aircraft, where I could look over the heads of a couple of rows of farmers and right into the face of my fidgety suspect. Since I didn't know how to say, "Get your ass over here" in Vietnamese, I simply pointed my finger directly at him and motioned for him to come to me. He looked back at me with an "In your face!" grin.

So I waved to him again, this time using the M-16 instead of my finger. I looked him straight in the eyes and snarled, "Come over here to me!"

By this time you would have thought that all the people in the rice paddy would have stopped what they were doing to watch the confrontation. But, not so. They paid no attention to me or to him; they just went on planting their rice more furiously than before.

This was their obvious signal to me that this guy was no part of their operation, that the rest of the group wanted nothing to do with him, with me, or with whatever we were arguing about.

I motioned to him a third time and said again, as sternly as I could make it sound, "Come over here to me right now!" He looked at me with that stupid, toothy grin and slowly shook his head. Then he started backing away from me, as though he was looking for a fast way out of this deal.

"OK, you little son of a bitch," I yelled. I dropped to one knee, leveled the M-16, and let three quick rounds fly, aimed at a spot right in front of him. Mud and water kicked up in his face.

Immediately his hands went up over his head and he started walking toward me, nodding and grinning like a Cheshire cat. When he got to me at the dike, I patted him down for weapons, forced his hands behind his head, and made him lock his fingers together. Putting my hands over his, I pushed and prodded him around the front of the aircraft. My intention was to put him in the crew chief's jump seat and strap him in so he couldn't go anyplace.

As I laid my M-16 in the left front seat, he suddenly twisted out of my grasp and bolted away from the airplane. He darted underneath the tail boom, just missing the still-turning tail rotor, and made a running jump back into the rice paddy.

"You little son of a bitch!" I screamed, as I grabbed the M-16 back out of the front seat and ran around to the rear of the aircraft. I intended to fire one round over his head to make him stop and come back to me.

In my haste, I jerked the selector of the M-16 to full automatic, inadvertently firing all twenty-seven rounds that I had left in the magazine. "Damn!" I muttered in disgust.

I watched for an instant as my adversary bounded through the paddy toward a tree line that separated the paddy from the river. He was getting away, and all I had

was an empty M-16 and a mind-set—I was either going to
get that little bastard or bust my ass trying!

With all my gear on, I probably weighed two hundred
pounds or more. But I jumped in the paddy to go after
him . . . and immediately sank to my waist in that water
buffalo shit-stinking muck!

I could hardly move. Waving my empty M-16 above my
head, I yelled, "Stop! Come back here or I'll let you have
it!" He wouldn't know that I had a dry weapon.

But I was losing him. In desperation I turned back to
Calloway, who was still holding the idling Loach on the
dike. I pointed to the guy and shouted, "Go get him . . .
run him down!"

Calloway, I learned fast, was the kind of pilot you didn't
have to tell twice. He picked up the aircraft and took off at
a dead gallop, holding the Loach about two feet off the
ground.

He cut an arc right over the heads of the rice planters,
who started diving into the water in every direction. It
made a tremendous splash as all thirty of them screamed
(probably a choice Vietnamese obscenity) and simultaneously hit the deck.

My guy was running through the water for all he was
worth, with Calloway hot on his trail. I could only watch—
my boots were so deeply mired in the slimy gunk at the
bottom of the rice paddy that I could hardly move.

I managed to struggle forward a couple of steps while
Calloway tried to corner the running Vietnamese. Bob had
caught up with the suspect and circled above his head a
couple of times, to let him know that he wasn't going anyplace. Then Calloway dropped the helicopter down right
in front of him to cut off his route of escape. Rotor wash
made the paddy look like a full-blown geyser in Yellow-
stone Park.

Every time the Loach let down in front of the Vietnamese, he would change direction, like a halfback doing a
fancy piece of broken field running. Calloway's OH-6

looked like a yo-yo on a string as he jerked the little Loach up and down, always managing to get down again right in front of the fleeing man and block his progress. Bob, through some damned skillful flying, had the man cornered like a rat in a trap.

As I made my way toward the sparring Loach and the frustrated escapee, I heard a sound in the water very near me. Then I noticed little splashes of rice paddy water kicking up on both sides of me, not more than a few inches away.

What in the hell is that? I thought. Then it quickly occurred to me: Those were bullets hitting the water, obviously aimed at me!

Looking toward the riverbank, about 150 yards away, my eye caught a pair of muzzle flashes coming from the tree line, no doubt a couple of AK-47s winking right at me.

So there I was, standing ass-deep in the rice paddy with an empty M-16 and no spare ammo, and no way I could tell either the Cobra or scout ship that I was being fired on.

Determined to do *something*, I reached down into the water and fumbled with the holster flap of my .45. Withdrawing the dripping weapon, I let fly with a couple of rounds toward the river, before realizing how futile it was. Using my .45 at that distance was like fighting a fire a hundred and fifty yards away with a twenty-five-yard hose.

Calloway in the scout ship was about twenty yards away from me by then. He was making diving passes at the prey, forcing him to fall flat down into the water each time he brought the ship around. Every time the man got up to run, Bob would turn his ship sideways in front of him, then rock his skids back and forth, slamming them into the man. Using the side of the skid like a boxing glove, Bob kept knocking the guy ass-over-appetite back into the water.

Having dropped the worn-out man several times, Calloway then expertly maneuvered the Loach over the flailing suspect until one skid rested across the Vietnamese's shoulders, pinning him to the bottom of the rice paddy.

As Bob held the man down in the water, I finally made it to the hovering ship and crawled up to the rear crew compartment. Plugging in my helmet mike, I keyed Fishman: "Three Four, I've got bad guys on the bank of the river at six o'clock right off our tail. They're shooting at me out here. Can you hose down that riverbank before they close in on us?"

With my last word, Fishman rolled in, making a rocket pass down the tree line. When I saw that Paul's rocks were right where I needed them, I backed out of the airplane and told Calloway to raise the ship off the guy while I jumped down to get him.

As the Loach lifted, I was back in the water reaching for the SOB. His eyes bugged as I grabbed him by his shirt collar with one hand and punched him in the face with the other. His eyes rolled back in his head and he went out like a light, his limp body falling into the water.

Calloway moved the Loach in closer so I could pick the guy up and dump him in the back of the aircraft. I didn't even tie him in, just grabbed a cargo strap and bound his arms and legs behind him. He was still unconscious, so he didn't give me any more trouble.

Jumping back in the left front seat of the bird, I grabbed the controls and told Calloway, "I've got it. Let's get out of here!"

As we lifted off the paddy, Calloway looked over at me, his nose crinkled up. "Jesus! You smell like shit!"

"Thanks a lot! By the way, for a student pilot, you did one hell of a job flying back there. A hell of a job . . . and I appreciate it very much."

We flew our suspect down the river to an ARVN compound, where he was quickly identified as a major from a VC division located near Dau Tieng. More than that, his interrogation revealed that he was a VC tax collector. It was his job to go out among the local civilian population in that area along the Saigon River and force them to pay taxes to support the VC. He'd hit up the farmers for food and money, and even pressed them into service to carry supplies to the Viet Cong forces. This guy was a pretty big fish to capture—a damned lucky stroke for us, since we were on a routine training mission.

This incident actually provided excellent training. I could have thought forever and never come up with a better example of one of aerial scouting's most basic principles—contrast, or, what's wrong with what you see below you? What's in the picture that *shouldn't* be there? What's not there that *should* be there?

In the case of our VC major–tax collector, all the clues were there. The farmers were all planting rice in one direction; this single person was going off in a different direction, moving away from them. Everyone in the group of farmers wore a conical hat; this guy was bareheaded. The farmers paid no attention to our aircraft as we orbited nearby; this person kept sneaking glimpses at us over his shoulder and was moving away from the aircraft. Everybody else in the group was either very old or very young; this man was of military age.

When we got back on the ground at Phu Loi, Fishman came running over from his Cobra. He couldn't believe that the enemy soldier in the rice paddy had turned out to be a VC major. Paul slapped us both on the back. "A *VC* major? Jesus Christ, I can't believe you guys . . . I just can't believe you guys!"

The crew chief of our airplane had a different reaction, however. He came over to me with a thoroughly disgusted look on his face. "Shit, sir, have you looked at the back of my aircraft? There's blood, swamp water, water buffalo shit, and all kinds of other crud back there. Ah, shit, sir . . ."

But that was a mild reprimand compared to what I got when I arrived at my hootch to shower and change clothes.

As I walked in the door, Mai, our hootch maid, immediately stopped what she was doing and looked at me. There I was, still soaking wet from my jousting match in the rice paddy. My boots were fouled. Nastiness dripped from my flight suit and made a smelly, dark-colored puddle on the floor.

Mai's nose curled up and she came at me with an upraised broom. "Ding-wee! You stink bad. You smell like water buffalo. Get out and take shower, and no come back anymore until you no smell so nasty!"

Over the next week or so, the troop got a lot of feedback on the VC major–tax collector incident. Division G-2 and ARVN G-2 were ecstatic about having a VC field grade officer to interrogate. It turned out that he was the *chief* tax collector for that area, so he was able to tell interrogators where all the local and main force VC units in the area were located. He also knew all the shadow government and chain of command in the villages along his stretch of the river.

For his absolutely masterful piece of flying that day, Bob Calloway was awarded the Air Medal. But the thing that made the episode really unique was the fact that Calloway received this meritorious award for flying the OH-6 . . . before he was even signed off in the Loach as a scout pilot.

We had a little saying around the troop, which was probably common among American forces all over Vietnam: "We own the day; he [Victor Charlie] owns the night."

During the day the American soldiers and our allies generally controlled the war. We were the aggressors; in daylight we usually had tactical advantage over the enemy. At night, however, when our forces went back into defensive positions, Charlie stayed out in the jungle. He used the night as a cover for his resupplying and offensive actions. He couldn't stand against us during the day, but he sure could cause us a lot of difficulty once darkness set in.

We received a lot of night mortar and rocket attacks on

our base at Phu Loi. Scouts didn't fly operationally after dark, and we valued a good night's sleep to be ready for those first light VRs, which had us in the air by 5 or 5:30 in the morning. The VC seemed to have some insight into this fact. When they hit us after dark, the scout pilots would have to spend the night in bunkers instead of in our hootch bunks. It was cold and damp in those damned bunkers, and the only place to sleep was on hard, rough board benches. Not conducive, you can be sure, to a decent night's rest.

Since it was not unusual for us to catch a few rounds of enemy mortar fire during the night, we'd sometimes just stay in our hootch bunks and try to sleep through it. Rockets were another story, however. Russia supplied Charlie with an individual heavy 122mm rocket that weighed 112 pounds, had a 42-pound warhead, and had a range of ten miles. This weapon could be fired from an easily made and highly portable launching stand. The enemy could set it up in short order by resting the body of the weapon on top of two crossed tree branch supports, preaiming it, and then arming the rocket to fire when two wires made contact after the pan of water they were in evaporated.

One night, after softening us up with a few rounds of 81mm mortar fire, Charlie let us have a few rockets. I was just about asleep in my bunk when a rocket hit out near the runway. The resulting explosion actually lifted the roof right off my hootch. I could see starlight through the gap between the roof and the sidewall! Needless to say all of us spent the rest of that night in the bunker, hard board benches and all.

Trying desperately to sleep that night, I couldn't help but think about those enemy rockets and what it must have taken to get them from their initial supply point to a spot where they could be fired into our airfield at Phu Loi.

Charlie's supply system was rudimentary, but with his dogged tenacity, somehow he was able to transport 122mm rockets—about the size of a telephone pole and

weighing every bit as much—from an arsenal somewhere
near Hanoi all the way down to Phu Loi. Through mon-
soons, B-52 strikes, snake-infested streams . . . along
dust-choking trails. Amazingly, these rockets reached a
Viet Cong encampment in American III Corps area. All to
keep American aerial scout pilots in Phu Loi from sleeping at night.

It didn't take us long to understand what our new troop
commander, Major Moore, meant when he told us on that
first day that he was going to be involved in everyday combat operations. The previous commander had essentially
run the troop from his office desk. Major Charles Moore
liked to be in the air in his command and control bird,
right above the action.

I found this out in spades on 8 July, the day immediately
following the "swimming" experience with the VC major
in the rice paddy.

On that day, Chuck Koranda (Three Nine) and I received a frag order for a hunter-killer team to assist the 2d
Squadron, 11th Armored Cavalry on a sweep mission near
the Dead Man, a terrain feature located just south of
Boundary Road and west of Highway 13. Our first step
was to fly into the 2d Squadron's night defensive position
to get briefed on what they wanted us to do for them. They
were located up Highway 13 north of Lai Khe in the general vicinity of our Thunder I base camp.

Koranda and I landed outside the wire, shut down, and
walked together into the NDP. Chuck met with the squadron's S-2 and got all the map coordinates, details of the
operation that 2/11 was about to launch, and the latest
information on enemy activity in the area. There was to be
a 2d Squadron sweep-and-destroy mission into an enemy
base camp thought to be located immediately south of
Boundary Road. The intent was to push an armored column up from the southeast to hit the south end of Charlie's base camp. Additional tanks and infantry were posi-

tioned to patrol Boundary Road on the north of the camp. This would put the enemy in a vice if he tried to escape through the back door.

Our job was to get out ahead of the main column, guide it through the jungle, and screen to its front and flanks. As the aerial scout, I was to stay on the FM radio and keep Strider Eight (the armored column's CO) continuously informed as to what I was seeing around him.

As the crow flies, it was about ten kilometers from Thunder I northwest up to the enemy base camp area. As the column got under way, Koranda and I took off to circle it a few times and make sure the area was clear.

From my position twenty to thirty feet above the armor, I was fascinated watching the column work its way through the jungle. Out in the lead were five or six M-48A3 diesel-powered tanks with their 90mm main gun turrets pointed forward. The flanking tanks had their turrets turned to the side. The ACAVs (M-113A-1s), with their infantry troops, were in the middle.

Mixed in with the ACAVs were several Zippo tracks, which were M113s with a turret on top that carried a flame dispenser. The flamethrowers were used on bunkers and a variety of other targets when their special kind of devastation was needed. The Zippo tracks were particularly vulnerable to enemy ground fire, however. All loaded up with jellied fuel and tanks of compressed air, they were a choice target for an enemy RPG round.

My door gunner that day was Al Farrar, and as we neared the base camp I told him to be especially alert because we weren't sure whether the bunkers were occupied. The jungle was very thick, double canopy reaching up eighty to a hundred feet. Because of the dense jungle, Koranda told me that he couldn't see where the base camp actually was. I asked Farrar to get a yellow smoke ready to mark the area.

Al reached up to the wire strung across the back of the bulkhead and pulled off one of the smoke canisters. He

popped the pin and held it outside the airplane, tipping
the top of it toward me so I could verify the yellow color.
The color of the smoke we dropped and the color I told
Koranda to look for had to match, for obvious reasons.

As we passed over the center of the base camp area, I
told Farrar, "R-e-a-d-y . . . NOW!" He threw the grenade straight down from the aircraft. Yellow smoke boiled
up out of the jungle, telling Koranda exactly where to
mark the bunker positions on his map.

As we passed over, it was apparent to both Farrar and
me that there were people down there. We didn't see any
bad guys out in the open, but there were plenty of fresh
traffic signs. The trails and the general area were well
beaten down; the camouflage strewn around looked all
freshly cut; a few pots and pans were lying around; even
some clothing was hanging out to dry on lines underneath
the trees.

After dropping the smoke, I headed back to the column,
which was still several klicks away to the southeast. I
needed to keep them on a straight-line course to the base
camp, as well as scout the area around them again. With
the main guns of the tanks pointed either to the dead front
or flanks, the vulnerable point for ambush appeared to me
to be the immediate left and right front of the column.

I also had to keep a close watch on the north side of the
base camp. If Charlie decided to bolt out the back door to
the north, I needed to immediately alert the tanks patrolling along Boundary Road.

Running back and forth to check the base camp and
check the progress of the column kept on through two
Loach fuel loads. Each time I got low on JP-4, Bob Davis
and Bruce Foster would come up from our staging area at
Lai Khe and take over until I could get back on station.

I had just come back from Lai Khe with my third fuel
load when I learned that the troop C and C Huey with
Major Moore aboard had pulled in above us. The new
troop CO especially liked to watch his hunter-killer teams

work during enemy contact and action. With the armor nearing the southern outskirts of the enemy base camp, Moore probably thought that sparks were about to fly.

Moore was a dynamic man who liked to talk on the UHF radio to his aerial teams, especially the scouts. He acted almost like a cheerleader from the sidelines, spurring on his people.

I liked Moore. I didn't mind him suddenly appearing overhead in the C and C ship, to be on hand "to make troop command decisions" when he felt they were necessary. But what *did* bother me—and most of the other scouts—was his almost continuous use of the UHF radio. The aerial scout talked to his gunship on UHF, and the gun spoke back to his scout on VHF. By using different radios, there was never a voice overlap and no words were ever garbled. Charlie Moore's UHF cheerleading screwed up the equation, because the gun pilot couldn't always hear what his scout was saying.

Just back on station with my third load of fuel, I made a pass through the enemy base camp to see what was happening. Our armor was drawing near from the south.

Just as I rounded the northwest corner of the base camp, Farrar's M-60 opened up in several quick bursts. Shooting with one hand and keying his intercom with the other, Farrar yelled, "I got dinks under me, lots of them, sir. And they're running north out of the camp."

I had to immediately alert Koranda, as well as the tanks patrolling the back door along Boundary Road, so I keyed Three Nine on UHF. As soon as Major Moore heard us say we had seen enemy and taken them under fire, he opened up on UHF from his command and control ship. Right in the middle of my transmission to the gun pilot, and completely overriding what I was saying to Koranda, Major Moore began hollering, "Where are they, One Six? Go get 'em! Knock 'em down . . . kill the little bastards. Get in there, One Six . . . shoot their asses off, Mills. Get the fuckers!"

Seeing the impossibility of trying to outscream the Old Man over UHF, I flipped off the toggle switch for UHF, put the selector on VHF, and came up to Koranda. "Three Niner, this is One Six. I'm on Victor. Can you hear me now?"

Koranda came back, "OK, One Six, good copy. Glad you switched. I couldn't hear a damned thing you were saying."

Now, without "Mad Charlie" screaming in my ear, I pulled the Loach around hard in a decelerating right turn and looked straight down at where Farrar had fired.

There they were! Probably fifteen to twenty VC, dressed in brown, green, and blue uniforms, some with camouflage cloaks, all wearing Ho Chi Minh sandals, carrying weapons, and running like hell to the northwest out the back door of the base camp.

Farrar's M-60 began to chatter. Two VC dropped instantly, one right out in an open area, the other crumpled up under a tree. Continuing bursts from Farrar's gun nearly drowned out my FM transmission to the armor, telling Strider Eight that we had people running from the base.

The column commander, about 150 yards out by then, responded, "OK, One Six, let's back off. We're going to recon by fire."

One of the things that low-flying scout birds had to be very careful of while working around our armor was their 90mm main gun canister rounds. The shells were essentially filled with lead pellets, perhaps an inch in length, about three-quarters of an inch in diameter, and shaped like a miniature soup can. There were hundreds of them in a single 90mm canister round. When our tanks let go with canister fire, everything in front of the main guns went to hell in a hurry. It cut down trees, mowed the grass, and neutralized everything in the area. An aerial scout had to be sure he didn't catch a bellyful of pellets. So I immediately pulled back to the rear of the column and did figure eights, watching the enemy base camp area literally explode.

After a few rounds forward by the lead tank, Strider Eight in the second M-48 came up on FM. "Darkhorse, we're taking a little AK fire now that we're starting to enter the bunker complex. Can you . . ."

There was a long pause in Strider's transmission. Then he went on, "OK, Darkhorse, I'm back. We've got a slight problem down here. One of our tankers has hit an obstruction and thrown a track. We're going to circle the wagons around him and get some people reshoeing. Keep us covered and we'll get it fixed as fast as we can."

Reconnecting a tank track is difficult even on a good day. In jungle terrain and oppressive heat, I knew that they had their work cut out for them. While that job was going on, I worked back into a 360-degree orbit over the armor, letting my circles out just enough so that I could sweep a corridor all around the halted column.

I was on my third pass around when Farrar hit the intercom. "My God, sir, there's gooks down there!"

"Where?" I shot back.

"Right in front of the lead tank."

"No," I answered, "that's our guys working on the tracks." Just a second before, I had looked down and seen one of our people with a tanker bar in his hand wave to me as we went over. I was sure that was what Farrar had seen, also.

"No, sir," Al shouted back at me, "they're dinks . . . they're dinks! Go back, go back!"

I swung around hard and looked straight down. What I saw was a VC antitank team . . . two people! One man had an RPG-7 rocket launcher in his hands, camouflage cape on his back, and a back-mounted carrier for extra RPG rockets. The other Victor Charlie was carrying an AK-47 assault rifle and was wearing the same paraphernalia on his chest and back as the first guy. He was the loader.

During the lull after the tank firing, while our guys were working on the busted track, these sons of bitches had sneaked in to within fifteen to twenty meters of the lead tank. And there they were, getting ready to blow M-48s!

Farrar opened up again with his M-60. As I swung around, I let go a blast with the minigun. Everybody in the tank column dove for cover.

Strider Eight shouted at me over the radio, "We're friendlies down here, for Christ's sake! Knock off the shooting. Do you read, Darkhorse? Check fire! Check fire!"

I swung the ship abruptly away from the point of contact and keyed Strider. "Negative! Negative! RPG team to your direct front. Danger close. Depress and shoot everything you've got—twelve o'clock!"

I could hear Strider Eight's order to the column. "Full depression . . . main guns . . . fire canister . . . twelve o'clock!"

I wasn't able to get the Loach any farther away than the middle of the armor column when the whole jungle to the front exploded. All three forward vehicles in the column fired canister. At the exact same time, the enemy team let go with an RPG round.

The best place for me was right where I was—over the middle of the armor column doing tight three-sixties to stay out of the way of those canister rounds.

After the lead vehicles had fired, all the other tanks let go with canister that literally sliced down the entire circumference of jungle around the column. Flame erupted, trees flew, debris rained down, dust and smoke billowed up in almost a perfect circle. And I continued my tight little orbits, right above the center of it all.

Suddenly my FM radio came back alive with Strider Eight. "OK, Darkhorse," he said, "we're going to check fire. We'd like One Six to jump out there in front and see what you've got now."

I pulled the OH-6 out of the protective circles and

headed back over the lead tanks toward the spot where Farrar had spotted the RPG team. Looking down, I came back up to Strider. "You've got five or six bad guys down here; all appear KIA. One of them has on a red scarf—damned if that's not the first guy with a red scarf I've ever seen in 'Nam. They are all not more than fifteen meters dead front of your lead vehicle. You'll need to send your infantry up to check 'em out. I'm going to continue on over to the base camp to see what the live Charlies are doing."

I arrived at Boundary Road just as the enemy fleeing out of the base camp was making contact with the blocking armor patrolling the road. This put Charlie in a hell of a fix. He was now caught between the advancing armor-infantry column on the south and the tanks waiting for him on the north.

With the ground forces now fully committed, there was not much more Koranda and I could contribute. But we could give Charlie one more kick in the ass before departing station. I re-marked the area with smoke and asked the Cobra to expend his ordnance in a good hosedown of the entire base camp.

I also contacted the Sidewinder FAC, who brought up a flight of F-100s with napalm, as well as an ARVN flight of Douglas A-1 Skyraiders. After watching them put down their ordnance, Koranda and I broke station and headed back to Phu Loi, knowing that we'd be back in a day or two to make a BDA of the entire area.

It took about three days for our ground friendlies to finish mopping up the enemy contingent that had occupied the base camp. Most of the VC had to be flushed out of their bunkers. Those who wouldn't flush were dealt with by 2/11's M-48s. They would simply poke the muzzle of the main gun into the bunker entrance and let go with a single 90mm canister round.

The ground guys found—not more than ten meters in front of the lead tank—the five dead bad guys that we had spotted and engaged from the air. There were actually three RPG gunners and two loaders armed with AK-47s. If there was a third loader, he either got away or was vaporized in the hullabaloo.

The three RPG weapons and gunners meant that Charlie was setting up to knock down the three lead tanks in the column. If that had happened, the rest of the column would have stalled behind the halted lead elements, then, one by one, been disposed of with RPG rounds.

Another interesting thing the ground guys discovered was that our tank 90s and the first RPG round from the enemy had indeed fired almost at the same instant. The lead tank had a huge gouge cut into the armor plate on the left side of the vehicle's turret. The hastily aimed RPG round had actually hit the tank, but with only a glancing blow. The projectile did not penetrate or detonate when it hit. The nasty scar it left, however, was witness to the massive destructive punch that the Russian RPG-7 carried, even in a near miss.

I learned something from the experience, as I did every single time I flew in the aircraft in combat. I discovered that an up and running armored column can take a lot of the heat off a noisy helicopter. When tanks are nearby, they not only terrify the enemy, they also make so damned much noise that the helicopter overhead can't be heard—thereby shifting Charlie's attention from me to them. I was fairly certain that that was the case with the enemy RPG team.

A short time after the base camp incident, I learned that I had been recommended to receive the Air Medal with "V" device for discovering the enemy RPG team. I decided that it was time to grind an old troop-policy ax that had bothered me (and Bob Davis) for as long as we had been in aerial scouts. Policy was that when an aircraft commander was put in for an award, the copilot was automatically put in for an award one step down from the pilot. Then the crew chief generally was recommended for an award one level down from the copilot. In the case of the scout platoon, where we did not normally carry a co-pilot-observer, the crew chief was recognized right under the pilot. In other words, if the pilot was put in for a DFC, the crew chief might be awarded an Air Medal with "V" device for the same action.

Bob Davis and I both thought that it was a stupid way to handle the awards situation, particularly since that crew chief was up there in the same aircraft, yet had no control over his destiny. He was totally at the mercy of the pilot. If a pilot made a mistake that cost him his life, the crew chief generally died too. On the other hand, in order for the pilot to do his job effectively, he had to have a good crew chief who would keep the enemy's head down, knock out enemy gun positions before they could come to bear, and provide a second pair of sharp eyes to help spot trouble.

As scout platoon leader, I told Davis that I would write up a new policy and present it to the Old Man. That new policy simply stated that I would no longer endorse any awards for combat flight unless the crew chief got the same award as the pilot. If the pilot got a Silver Star, the crew chief got a Silver Star.

Major Moore agreed.

CHAPTER 9

THE CRATER

Stuff really began to hit the fan in late July and August of 1969, as far as enemy activity was concerned. We believed that the war in Vietnam was close to being over just a month before. But things had changed.

Instead of looking all day and seldom finding the enemy, the scout platoon was making two, three, or more solid enemy contacts a day. We were beginning to find bigger groups of enemy soldiers in the field—more NVA soldiers than Viet Cong. We were beginning to get more people in the troop hurt and killed as a result of the increased enemy contact. And more scout helicopters were being wrecked and lost due to heavier ground fire from a determined enemy.

We were finding that our OH-6As never got to three hundred hours for regular maintenance. We were darned lucky to get to one hundred hours before handing it over to the maintenance people—generally in pieces. There were, in fact, many times that we didn't even have a chance to get a new factory-fresh bird painted with troop markings before it was pressed into scout service to replace one shot up beyond flyable use.

The enemy was getting busy as hell in the 1st Infantry Division area, and none of us really knew the reasons why.

We speculated, of course. President Johnson had stopped the bombings of North Vietnam on 1 November 1968, and we figured that this had allowed Charlie time to rebuild forces decimated in their last big Tet offensive. With forces and supplies so strengthened, more and more enemy troops were probably heading into the field from their protected Cambodian sanctuaries.

There was also the fact that newly elected President Nixon had formally announced a schedule of planned withdrawals of American forces from Vietnam, beginning 8 July. With some of the Americans starting to leave, and ARVN forces replacing them in the ranks, the unfriendlies may have felt that the moment was right to rekindle their offensive.

It could have been one, none, or all of these factors. But we were just taking the days as they came. Flying every day, up to 130 hours or more a month, and doing what we could to find and bloody Charlie's nose every chance we got.

We took a little bloodying, too. Bob Harris's aerorifle platoon took 30 percent casualties in one day's fighting while holed up in an old B-52 bomb crater in the western Trapezoid.

It all started with a report from VR-1 that an abandoned base camp just south of the Michelin and west of the Onion was showing some evidence of rehabilitation and reoccupation by the enemy.

Scout pilot Bob Calloway was first up that morning on VR-1, and had reported seeing a platoon-sized group of VC move into a heavily wooded area near the old base camp. At this time in 1969 finding a platoon or larger element of enemy all together in a single group was unusual, and Calloway's report immediately caught the attention of G-2. The intelligence people wanted the troop to insert the ARPs ASAP to do ground reconnaissance and check out the enemy situation.

Even though Calloway wasn't a seasoned scout pilot, he

still recognized the potential danger of the situation. After making two passes over the site and seeing the enemy running from the open area into the woods, Calloway radioed his Cobra. "Don't put the ARPs in. I think there are a lot of bad people in here."

On this day I was scheduled to fly VR-2. While Calloway was up on VR-1, I was training another new scout pilot in the unit, a warrant by the name of Jim Bruton. While I was doing some chalkboarding and maneuvers with Bruton around the base area, I was also monitoring the radio conversations between VR-1 and Darkhorse operations.

It wasn't long before Major Moore was in the ops bunker and personally involved in the situation. He radioed Calloway's snake driver. "Look, if there are a lot of people down there, we need to put in the ARPs. Let's get Four Six on the ground and see what's going on."

At that point, Calloway made another pass over the area and again reported to his Cobra. "There are a lot of people down here. I don't think you ought to put in the ARPs."

The Cobra responded, "Do you see anybody down there, One Zero?"

"Negative," Calloway came back.

Since no additional movement of enemy troops was seen and the scout was not taking any fire, the decision was made to scramble the ARPs for a ground sweep and investigation of the area. Since it was a scramble alert for the ARPs, Bob Harris didn't get a mission briefing before lift-off; therefore, he had not heard about the size of the enemy force. Wayne McAdoo and his platoon of slicks whisked the ARPs out of Phu Loi in short order and headed up the Saigon River toward the western Trapezoid.

Harris, following his normal procedure, was in the lead slick listening for any radio information that would help him size up the ground tactical situation. If he had known that a platoon of enemy troops was involved, Harris probably would have called for a reinforcing company of infantry. This was routine in order to provide the normal three to one numerical advantage, which the attacker is traditionally deemed to need over a defending force.

Once out of the Hueys and about three hundred meters to the west of the objective area, ARP Sgt. Jim Gratton and Specialist Mitchell took the point and led the platoon toward the wooded area. Gratton had his usual shirt full of frag grenades and carried a shotgun. Mitchell had an M-16.

Harris waved his Kit Carsons forward to take up positions near Gratton and Mitchell. The situation called for cautious movement because the aeroscout had seen enemy in the area, and there was always the possibility of booby traps. The Kit Carson scouts, being former Viet Cong themselves, were generally better at spotting booby-trap situations than our people.

As the ARP formation reached the edge of the wooded area objective, Gratton sensed real danger. The Kit Carsons were beside themselves with fear. The point got on the radio to Harris, who was just in back of the lead element.

"There's a lot of people around here, in the woods. We think this thing is occupied."

Four Six radioed that information back to Phu Loi ops and was again told that he should move in and make contact with the enemy, to fix them in place. If necessary, additional forces would be brought in to support the twenty-eight ARPs already on the ground.

With that order understood, Harris pressed the platoon on into the woods, fully expecting to begin receiving fire at any moment. But, strangely enough, no enemy fire came.

Four Six radioed his point men again. "Why aren't we getting shot at? What's it look like up there?"

Of course, Harris knew that Gratton couldn't see much through the dense vegetation. No one in the formation could see more than a few inches in any direction. There was no way to detect enemy positions or firing lanes. Daylight itself was almost shut off by the thick growth of the stifling jungle foliage.

Without realizing it, Harris's ARPs had pressed about halfway into the enemy base camp. Charlie was sitting in his bunkers all the way around the ARP formation—waiting, watching, allowing the whole platoon to enter the lair before slamming shut the ambush door. Harris's men, though properly deployed and proceeding with all the skill and jungle savvy at their command, didn't have the slightest tip-off that they were already amidst the cunningly camouflaged enemy bunkers.

Suddenly, Harris's riflemen were deep enough into the trap. With a sharp staccato, AK-47 rounds abruptly tore into the column. Enemy fire came from their front and both flanks. Everybody hit the ground, but nobody knew where to shoot back because of the density of the jungle and total inability to see an enemy target.

It took only a moment to discover that any movement among the ARPs drew fire. Obviously the enemy could see.

Realizing that there was no way to attack an enemy he couldn't see, Harris concerned himself with finding cover and getting his men out of the killing zone. Most of the unit was right next to a bomb crater left by a 750- or 1,000-pound bomb from one of our B-52 raids. It looked like the only cover available. Rolling into the crater with his RTO, Harris contacted the other elements of his unit and told them to do the same.

It was then that he learned that both of his point men, Gratton and Mitchell, were down. They had been caught by the first eruption of enemy fire. It was impossible to tell if they were OK, wounded, or dead. Suddenly, in a lull in the withering fire, Harris could hear Mitchell cry out, then moan.

Harris immediately ordered his left flanking element to crawl forward and try to get to Gratton and Mitchell. But as soon as the effort began, enemy fire opened up on the men, pinning them to the jungle floor.

Lieutenant Harris then radioed his flanking element on the right side, "Left flank is pinned. We think Mitchell on the point is wounded. See if you can crawl up there slowly; try to either recover Mitchell or lay down a base of fire that will allow Gratton to recover him."

With Pfc. August Hamilton on the point, the right flanking element started to advance. They had crawled forward only a couple of feet when VC fire opened up on them. One of the enemy rounds went cleanly through the front of Hamilton's helmet and struck him squarely in the forehead.

Seeing Hamilton hit, the man crawling right behind him grabbed his legs and pulled him back out of the line of fire. Harris then learned that his right flank couldn't move forward either. They couldn't see who was shooting at them, so they couldn't effectively return the fire.

Now knowing that Hamilton was badly hit, Four Six ordered his right flank element to get the wounded man back to the cover of the bomb crater, where the medic could take a look at him.

Private First Class Hamilton was pulled, pushed, lifted, and finally lowered into the cover of the crater. Doc told Four Six that the man was losing blood fast. The supply of blood expander wouldn't last long, and more blood would be needed very soon or Hamilton would die.

During these initial tactical problems on the ground, Bob Calloway in the scout ship above was completely dumbfounded by the situation. There wasn't a thing he could do to help.

He couldn't call in his Cobra to shoot up the bunkers because the ARPs were caught right in the middle of the base camp complex. He couldn't call in an artillery strike to blast the place with heavy high-explosive rounds for the same reason.

All Calloway could do was fly circles over the contact

point and provide information to his Cobra, who, in turn, relayed it back to troop ops. It wasn't long before Calloway had to give up even that because of intense fire from the bunkers below. He either had to vacate the area or risk getting himself shot out of the sky.

By this time, I was in my hootch talking aeroscout tactics with Jim Bruton. I had stopped monitoring the radios when I left the ship on the ramp, and I had no idea how the ARP mission was going in the western Trap.

As Bruton and I talked, the hootch door burst open and a runner from operations came in. "Lieutenant Mills, sir, it's coming over the radio that Four Six is in heavy contact with the enemy south of the Michelin. You'd better get over to the operations bunker right away."

Rushing into the bunker, I was just in time to hear Bob Calloway's Cobra pilot come up on VHF to ops saying, "The ARPs are pinned down. They're separated into at least two or three groups and the vegetation on the ground is so dense that Four Six is unable to tell where all his people are. They're all trapped in a bomb crater and every time anybody sticks his head out, he gets shot at."

The ops officer questioned back, "What about casualties?"

Cobra answered, "Four Six doesn't know about his point men, since he can't see them and he can't get anybody up to them. They were caught in the first blast of gook fire. He does have one man, however, who has been hit in the head with an AK round. He's in the crater and bleeding badly."

Standing there listening to those radio reports, I thought immediately of the many times I had been on ground missions with Bob Harris and his ARPs. I had gone with them as often as I could to sharpen my scouting skills. Those experiences had helped tremendously my understanding of the ARP's world. I had found out right away that an aeroscout on the ground is totally out of his element.

In the air, the wind roared through the cockpit, making lots of noise and blowing the heat away. Also, you could see what was happening for several hundred yards in every direction.

On the ground, there was silence. The ARPs gave and received their instructions by hand and arm signals. Nobody talked unless the situation demanded it, and then only in quick, terse, all-business words. The heat was searing. Bodies were soaked with sweat and the beads ran down in their eyes—burning, blurring, and drawing swirling insects. Everybody carried at least two canteens of water on a mission, and guarded every drop.

But the most frustrating disadvantage of being on the ground was that you couldn't see anything and had no idea what was going on around you. The grass, the jungle closed in on you like opaque walls. The infantryman was lucky if he could see three feet in any direction. It was the *unseen* enemy that posed the greatest threat to the ground soldiers' good health and peace of mind.

So, standing there listening in the ops room, I had more than a minimal understanding of the mess Harris's platoon was in. I leaned in close to the radio speakers and hung on each word coming through.

The ops officer continued talking with the Cobra. "What help do you need up there? What help can we give you?"

The frustration in the Cobra pilot's voice showed. "I can't roll in with rocks because the ARPs are pinned right in the middle of the base camp. The scout door gunner has shot selectively but fears hitting friendlies. I got a Dustoff up here in the area to evac the head wound, but Four Six doesn't want to risk the Huey hovering in, knowing that it would make an irresistible target for the unfriendlies. You better get another hunter-killer team up here though. One Zero needs gas. Better roll Scramble 1."

The Scramble 1 scout that day was Bob Davis (One Three). He and his Cobra were launched immediately and were quickly at the contact scene to join up with VR-1 for briefing.

Davis was known in the troop for his happy-go-lucky, charismatic radio chatter, but when I heard him call his Cobra, I knew the situation was bad. When he dropped down in the contact area Davis lost his cool. "Holy shit . . . h-o-oly s-h-e-e-it! I'm taking lots of ground fire. But look at the dinks! I got dinks everywhere down here. I got bunkers everywhere. Everywhere I look there's bunkers and everywhere I look there's people! There must be a hundred unfriendly sons a bitches in here!"

While he was talking, I could hear the M-60 chatter in the background as Davis's crew chief, John Studer, fired out the rear cabin door. Then Davis came back up on the intercom to his crew chief. "Quit firing! Quit firing! We don't know where the ARPs are; we can't shoot!"

Then Davis's Cobra broke in. "One Three, you don't have to stay down there if it's too hot. It's your call." Davis responded that he would stay down, keep circling, and see if he could get a handle on how big the enemy base camp was.

Faced with the facts that his ARP platoon was pinned down, that Cobra gunships on the scene couldn't shoot, and that artillery could not be called in, the troop commander decided to go airborne in his C and C and size up the tactical situation at the crater for himself. Once over the contact area, Major Moore elected to call in the infantry reaction force. This was an infantry unit of about company size that the troop could activate when ARPs on the ground needed backup. They were on combat standby and available within a fifteen- to twenty-minute time frame. With Major Moore's decision, they were immediately loaded and transported directly to the contact area.

Jumping out of their slicks at the LZ and rushing across low scrub and underbrush to relieve Lieutenant Harris, the backup company was stopped cold in its tracks. The enemy opened up on them from the base camp and cut

Hugh Mills and LOH #927. Note the XM27E1 minigun and the early 1969 Darkhorse marking on the engine cowl door. The revetment protected the helicopter from mortar and rocket attacks.

Captains Hugh Mills (*left*) and Rod Willis at the end of Hugh's last tour in Vietnam. "Miss Clawd IV" was his final mount. OH-6A 17340 is now preserved in the U.S. Army Aviation Museum at Fort Rucker, Alabama.

The pilot occupied the right front seat of the OH-6A with the door gunner/observer in the right rear. While the pilot's seat had some built-in armor plate, the gunner had only an armor plate strapped beneath his seat.

The minigun occupied the left rear of the cabin, its weight counteracted by the pilot and gunner. When no gun was carried, a third crewman occupied the left front seat.

Mills's OH-6A en route to a mission, as viewed from the Cobra's cockpit. Scouts flew "wing" on the Cobras to and from the contact area. The scout pilot depended on the Cobra's frontseater for map guidance while at low level. *Photo by Larry Kauffman.*

Dean Sinor's AH-1G, "Satan Snake." The wing stores mounted M159 19-shot rocket pods inboard and 158 7-shot pods outboard. The turret contained a minigun and 40mm grenade launcher.

A Darkhorse OH-6A over the ARPs in the Iron Triangle. The area had been extensively Rome-plowed, but was honeycombed with twenty years' worth of tunnels and bunkers.

Hugh Mills and Jim Parker scramble from Lai Khe to relieve a crew in contact over the Michelin plantation. A CH-47 Chinook carrying fuel bladders is on approach.

Wayne McAdoo heads the "Four Horsemen" as they deliver the ARPs to the location of a VNAF A-1H Skyraider shot down south of Saigon in February 1969.

The Horsemen trail red smoke indicating kills by the ARPs. Rear area personnel enjoyed these impromptu air shows.

Outcasts OH-6A at a 1st Division fire base. These bases generally supported battalion-size units with fire and logistics.

Scout pilot Rod Willis checks the delinker-feeder of the General Electric M134 7.62mm minigun. Above the gun is the ammo box and colored smoke grenades for marking targets. *Photo by Rod Willis.*

Cobra pilot Dean Sinor, Darkhorse 31, and Hugh Mills. The rope around Sinor's neck is tied to his radio and frequency code-book, called SOI (signal operations instructions). Both pilots carry side-arms and Colt CAR-15 submachine-guns. The pouch mounted on Mills's shoulder holster contains a strobe light for emergency signaling.

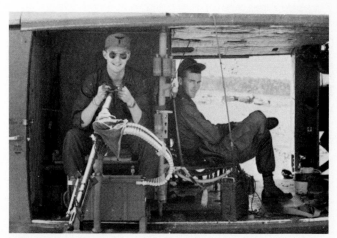

Mills and Horsemen platoon leader Wayne McAdoo on a slick. The weapon is an M60D 7.62mm door gun used by the UH-1H gunner and crew chief. McAdoo listens to the progress of the hunter-killer teams on the PRC-25 radio next to him.

Rod Willis and Mills "hunt tanks" in the troop area. The weapon is a Soviet RPG-7 rocket-propelled grenade launcher.

Darkhorse pilots and ARPs inspect weapons captured after Mills and Jim Parker interdicted and destroyed an NVA 28-man heavy weapons platoon. Scout pilot Fred Jennings (*far right*) carries a Thompson M1A submachine-gun.

Mills and Capt. John Gott, Darkhorse 3. Troop operations controlled the unit's aircraft throughout the division's area of operations. Note the posted mission statement.

After-action photo: Hugh Mills, Stu Harrell, and Rod Willis. Harrell's riflemen had held off the determined advance of an NVA battalion with help from the hunter-killer teams. The patch on Harrell's right shoulder indicates prior combat service with the 82d Airborne Division. *Photo by Stu Harrell.*

The ARPs move rapidly from the Horsemen's Hueys on a combat assault. The UH-1s are most vulnerable on the ground and limit this time to seconds. *Photo by Bob Harris.*

Darkhorse ARPs prior to an insertion. Each man carries extra ammo for the unit's four M60 machine-guns. The soldier in the foreground is Thuong, a Kit Carson scout. *Photo by Bob Harris.*

The M60 machine-guns were the ARPs' heavy firepower. The gunners carried nearly eighty pounds of gun, extra barrels, and ammo. *Photo by Bob Harris.*

ARPs practice rappelling from a UH-1H, then climbing back aboard on a troop ladder. In confined areas, rappelling might be the quickest way in and the troop ladder the only way out.

The Horsemen, in trail, descend into a landing zone for ground reconnaissance following a B-52 Arc Light strike. Note the craters, made by the 750-pound iron bombs from the B-52 Stratofortress.

ARP team leaders mark the landing location for the UH-1H with colored smoke and a colored panel. Other ARPs face outward from the LZ to guard against attack.

Mills and Jim Parker fly low level over the Iron Triangle. Scouting missions were flown low and slow; high-speed travel was at a higher elevation.

Armored cavalry assault vehicles (ACAVs) and M106 mortar carriers of the 11th Armored Cavalry Regiment beat down jungle, guided by a Darkhorse aeroscout. *Photo by Al Farrar.*

Rod Willis's OH-6A, one of several he crashed. The truss A-frame of the OH-6A made it the most survivable helicopter in a crash. Pilots and gunners were rarely injured unless the ship went in vertically.

Blood-spattered cockpit of Mills's LOH, shot down near FSB Tennessee.

The bubble of Mills's OH-6A, shattered by a tree strike. Dead trees were a constant threat at the altitudes at which the Outcasts flew; this photo is a testimonial to the structural strength of the OH-6A.

Cobra-eye view of an ambush on a convoy along Highway 13 by the NVA. The highway was the principal line from Dian to Quan Loi and An Loc.

Brig. Gen. Herbert Smith of the 1st Infantry Division presents Hugh Mills the Distinguished Flying Cross following "Impact Award" actions.

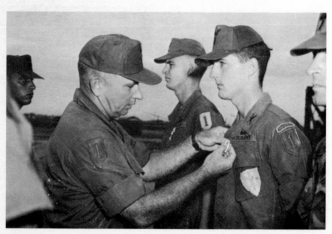

Maj. Gen. A. E. "Ernie" Milloy presents Mills with his third Silver Star for his actions over Stu Harrell's ARP platoon. *U.S. Army photo.*

Harris's relief to pieces! The infantry company, now stung by the hail of accurate enemy fire, began shooting back into the base camp area.

I could hear Bob Harris yelling into his radio. "Cease firing! Cease firing! Goddamnit, you're shooting into my people! You're shooting into our guys!"

Confusion reigned, and I couldn't stand it any longer. I turned to Darkhorse Three. "I'm going up there. I'm taking my remaining scouts to Dau Tieng so we can react to the fight." I burst out of the ops bunker and headed back to the hootch to get Jim Bruton and crew chief, Jim Downing. It seemed like just seconds before we were on the pad, in the bird, and off with Chuck Koranda (Three Nine) piloting my Cobra.

Just as soon as we got to the contact point, I dropped down low and got on One Three's tail so he could brief me. We had to maintain sixty to seventy knots because VC rounds were coming from all over the place. Ground fire out of that enemy base camp was as bad or worse than any I had ever seen. Davis was beside himself as he filled me in on the critical situation below. His voice was up about three octaves.

"Holy shit, One Six, there's nothing we can do down here except get our asses shot off! There's dinks everywhere! It's all screwed up. Four Six is pinned down in the crater with a badly wounded guy who's been shot in the head and needs more blood. They're going to lose him if he doesn't get more blood. And now we've got the reaction company of infantry pinned down with them, shooting back into our own people in the base camp. Man, we just plain got a shit pot full of trouble right here in Dodge!"

The words were no sooner out of One Three's mouth when over the net came the troop commander's voice. He had been flying around in his C and C Huey somewhere near the contact point. "I'm going on the ground to take command of the operation," said Major Moore very succinctly. "One Six, find me a lima zulu!"

My first reaction was that Major Moore was a cavalry officer. What in the hell was he going to do down on the ground in a strictly infantry situation? He ought to stay in his C and C and call his shots from there. But as that old saying goes, he's the boss.

I left Davis and scouted out a place big enough to get Six's Huey in and out, and that would provide some cover from the base camp's line of fire.

The C and C ship hovered into the LZ, landed, and out went Six and his artillery observer, Lieutenant Allen. Allen had his PRC-25 radio with him, and they hadn't moved fifteen feet from their helicopter when Major Moore's now more concerned voice came back up on the radio.

"This is Darkhorse Six. They're all around us! We're taking fire. We're pinned down!"

"Well, shit!" I muttered.

So now, besides the ARP platoon and the backup infantry company, we had the troop commander and his artillery observer down and ineffective. Here I was on station over all of this mess, and there didn't seem to be one damned thing I could do to help the situation.

Not knowing where else to start, I radioed Bob Harris. "Four Six, this is One Six. I'm just coming on station. Seems to me that you guys in the ARPs get all the no-sweat details. How's it looking down there?"

He came right back. "This is Four Six, One Six. Good to hear your voice. We're in a world of hurt! One man's hit—shot in the head. We've used all our blood expander. Doc says he's still alive but we need a blood expander kit fast or he's not going to make it."

"How's everybody else?" I asked.

"I've got point and his element out there somewhere in front of me," Harris continued. "I can't see them . . . I don't know where they are. I don't know if they're dead or alive, but we can hear a man moaning, and every time he moans, Charlie shoots."

"How can I help you?"

"You can start by seeing if you can find Gratton and his point backup. Also see if you can get Dustoff in here to pick up my head wound. That Huey will make a hell of a target, but he needs help fast. We've got to try to get Dustoff in here."

Before I could respond to Harris, Koranda in the Cobra broke in, "Four Six, this is Three Niner. That's a roger on Dustoff. I'll work on getting a medevac up here." Then Koranda went off frequency to get that process started again.

I began looking for Sergeant Gratton. I dropped down to about forty feet, making tight little circles over the area to the front of the crater. Maintaining my airspeed at about sixty knots, I jinked to the left and right, trying to make the little OH-6 a more elusive target.

There was plenty of ground fire coming up, but I was jinking and moving fast enough that rounds aimed right at the ship were actually passing in back of my tail. Thank God, I thought, Charlie hasn't quite got the hang of leading a target!

I was cussing to myself because I couldn't return any of that ground fire. The friendlies and enemy were too close together for us to shoot. We could see all kinds of Cong in their bunkers and the trenches that connected their firing positions, and it was frustrating not to be able to blow them away.

The enemy had really played it cool. They had allowed Harris's men to walk right into the middle of the base camp before springing the ambush, and they knew that we couldn't shoot at them without hitting our own people.

I couldn't fire in any case because the minigun had been removed from my bird before leaving Phu Loi. We had to reduce weight to make room to carry Jim Bruton, who was flying as an observer in the left front seat. Jim Downing's M-60 in the back cabin was all the firepower we had.

After two passes, I spotted Four Six's point men. They were lying about forty meters northeast of Harris's crater, one on his back looking up at me and the other face down on the ground. I knew Gratton from the times I had been on ground missions with the ARPs. He was the one on his back.

I slowed and nodded my head vigorously to let him know that I had seen him. He tried to wave back without giving away his position, and then rolled back over on his stomach to use his weapon again.

The other man with Gratton must have been Mitchell. He was face down and not moving, so I didn't know whether he was dead or alive.

Located right in back of Gratton and Mitchell was an enemy bunker. Fire from that position was what had the point men pinned down.

I immediately keyed the FM frequency to Harris. "Four Six, this is One Six. I found Gratton. He and his other point man are about forty meters out to your northeast. They're down near a little mound in the earth that's giving them some protection. Gratton looks OK and knows that we've found him. I think the other guy is hit. For right now they're OK where they are. They can't get back to you anyway because there's a hot gook bunker located right behind them. You copy?"

The same bunker that was blocking Gratton's retreat suddenly decided that my little bird was getting entirely too nosy. Every time I made a pass over the area, he'd open up, and his fire was beginning to get pretty accurate! I could hear and feel an occasional hit.

Realizing that I was taking fire, Koranda came up on VHF from the Cobra and told me to get out of there. But I decided to stay down to keep a cover on Harris's gang. I told Koranda I would try to go fast enough to avoid giving the bad guys a good shot.

Jim Bruton was getting a hell of an introduction to flying scouts. Having just gotten to the troop, he probably couldn't follow what was going on, but he could feel me jinking that little bird all over the sky and see the muzzle

flashes that were sending up enemy rounds, and feel them
tearing through the ship. Bruton was probably scared to
death. But so were the pilot and crew chief, perhaps more
so.

I was impressed with the way Bruton handled himself
while on the receiving end of the first shots ever fired at
him. He never said a word as he sat in the left seat, doing
the best he could to help the situation.

Even experience didn't keep Jim Downing from being
amazed at the enemy beehive below us. He kept keying
the intercom: "Jesus, sir, there's dinks everywhere! Bunkers everywhere. Three o'clock low . . . bunkers. Man
with an AK at twelve o'clock low . . . bunker with SGM.
Shit, Lieutenant!"

All I could say was, "OK, OK, Jim. I got it. I got it!" I
kept the airspeed up to about sixty knots and kept jinking
the ship to give Charlie a different look every time I came
around for another pass.

I rolled back in over Gratton's position to see how he
was doing. He was over on his back again and had an
M-16 magazine on his chest. Each time I came over, Gratton looked at us and jabbed his finger at the magazine.

Downing was quick to figure out the sign language. "He
needs ammo, sir, for the M-16. He's dry!"

"OK," I answered, "how many bandoliers do you have
with you back there, Jim?" Downing carried a backup
M-16, which he stowed under his seat, and I knew that he
would have some extra ammo.

"About six, Lieutenant."

"OK," I said. "Get three of them. We'll come in and
hover over Gratton and drop him the ammo.

"Now, Jim," I continued, "I'll have to come in slow and
hover down easy. You're going to have to bull's-eye the
first time. If we miss, I don't know what kind of chance
we'll have to try it again. OK?"

"I understand, Lieutenant," he answered. "I'll do my
best."

I went in right on the trees. Downing was hanging out of the cabin door with the bandoliers in his hand waiting for the right moment to throw them down. I kept the left side of the aircraft toward the VC bunker so that Downing would make less of a target. We slid in right over Gratton and hovered down as low as I could get. Then Downing let go of the ammo.

The bandoliers landed right between Gratton and Mitchell. Bull's-eye! Gratton rolled over, reloaded the M-16, and started squeezing off short bursts at Charlie again.

As I regained altitude, taking a couple more AK hits in the tail boom, Koranda called me.

"Nice shot, One Six. I've got Dustoff coming in, right about now. Let's try and get him to send a stretcher down and pick up the head wound."

Flipping to FM so that both the Cobra and Bob Harris on the ground could hear, I answered. "Four Six, this is One Six. Three Niner says that Dustoff will be here right away and wants us to try and get the Huey in. I don't think that the bad guys will let a medevac in without blowing them to pieces. How do you feel about it?"

Harris came right back. "Let's get him in here if we can, One Six. Earlier I waved away one Dustoff feeling that he'd never be able to hover in here and stay in one piece. Now Doc says he's bingo on blood expander for Hamilton and he's bleeding to death. Let's do it!"

By this time, Dustoff was coming in at altitude, and wanting to know where to make the pickup. I came up on Uniform to give him directions. "Dustoff, this is Darkhorse One Six. We need you to hover into the base camp over the bomb crater, drop a litter, and extract a bad head wound. Can you handle that?"

"Darkhorse One Six, this is Dustoff. I don't know but we'll try. We understand that the area is not controlled— that it is still hot."

"You copy right . . . the area is still hot. In fact, it's

very hot. But we've got a soldier down who needs blood fast and he won't make it unless we get you in there."

"I'll give it our best shot, Darkhorse," he came back. "Mark my area."

"Roger, Dustoff. Get on my tail and I'll lead you in the best way. When I say, 'mark, mark,' you'll be right over the bomb crater. Drop down and make the pickup."

Dustoff rogered and fell in behind me. I took him down low on the trees and circled around once to get the Huey in on an approach that avoided as many of the major VC gun emplacements as I could. As we came in over the bomb crater at about forty knots, I called to Dustoff, "Now . . . mark, mark!" Then I pulled a hard right and watched the Huey skid to a hover right over the crater and Harris's ARPs.

The moment Dustoff decelerated, the base camp below erupted with what seemed to be every weapon the VC had.

"Taking fire!" the Huey pilot screamed. "Goda-mighty! I'm taking fire . . . heavy fire!"

I instantly jerked the Loach into a tight right bank around the medevac ship and keyed the intercom. "Dustoff will never make it out of there, Jim, unless you get Charlie's head down. Get on the M-60 and start shooting. Be careful firing into our friendlies. Just spray to keep VC heads down, not to hit anybody."

Downing opened up. He poured several long bursts into the base camp below, doing his best to make Charlie duck while the medevac ship struggled for altitude.

With Downing still shooting to cover its retreat, Dustoff staggered off to the northwest toward Dau Tieng. The Huey had taken all the punishment it could handle and still stay airborne.

I then came up on FM to Harris. "Four Six, this just isn't gonna work. We've got another Dustoff flying into a nearby ARVN base camp to stand by, but to bring him in here would be murder. What do you think?"

"Roger, One Six," Harris came back, "but Doc says that Hamilton won't last another ten minutes unless he gets whole blood. We've got to do something!"

I thought as I circled another time or two. Then I made up my mind and got on the intercom to Bruton and Downing. "Look, this OH-6 is a hell of a lot more agile and a smaller target than that Huey. I think we can get in and out of there before Charlie can get us. So I'm going to go over to the Dustoff that's waiting at the ARVN base camp, get the blood, and we'll come back and drop it in."

I didn't ask them. I just told them that we had no choice and that we were going to give it a try. Nonetheless, it felt good when I got their instant replies almost in unison. "OK, Lieutenant, let's do it."

In the minute or two that it took us to get to the waiting Dustoff, I made plans with my crew chief. "OK, Downing, just as soon as we touch down, you jump out and get the blood from the Huey. Then when we get back over the crater, you're going to drop it to Doc. You got that?"

"Yes, sir, Lieutenant, I understand," Downing answered.

I gave Bruton his instructions. "Now Jim, I know that this whole experience may be a little new to you, but with you aboard, and no minigun, you're the only cover I'll have. Downing will have the blood kits and probably won't be able to use his M-60. You better poke that M-16 of yours out the door and be ready to shoot at anything that gives us a bad time."

When I told Koranda in the Cobra what I was going to do, he didn't mince words: "You're crazy, One Six!"

By that time, we were at the ARVN base camp. I landed right beside the idling Dustoff, waited while Downing ran over to pick up the blood, and then lifted off again.

I had never seen blood kits before, and had no idea that they came packed in a box the size of a milk crate. Downing sat in the back with that big box balanced on his lap.

I came in on the treetops and did tight, fast three-sixties

over the area while I checked out the situation in the
crater. There was some ground fire but it didn't seem directed at us this time. Charlie must have felt we couldn't
do anything to them anyway, so why waste ammo on such
a little bird.

Watching below me I could see that the ARPs were not
able to get their heads up over the rim of the crater without drawing instant fire. So they were lobbing grenades
when they could and sticking their weapons over the top
edge of the shell hole to snap off a few quick rounds.

As I slowed and came around for the third time, I felt
the ship's center of gravity shift dramatically. A quick
glimpse over my right shoulder told me that Downing had
eased himself completely out of the airplane and was cen-
tering the box of blood kits on the right skid. Bruton was
sitting right beside me with his M-16 pointed out his door.
He was sure getting a hell of an indoctrination.

Suddenly my intercom roared at me. It was Downing's
voice straining to be heard over the wild rush of wind that
was hitting his helmet mike. "Forward . . . forward . . .
a little more. Now right . . . right, sir . . . a hair more
to the right," he said, directing me into position over the
crater.

Looking between my feet through the OH-6's chin bubble, I could see Bob Harris lying face up in the shell hole.
He was also talking to me on FM: "OK, One Six, straight
ahead . . . straighter . . . now right. That's it . . . now
hold it . . . hold it right there."

At that exact moment, hovering twenty to thirty feet off
the ground, with Downing hanging outside the ship ready
to drop the box, I glanced out the door toward my right
front. About thirty feet away from me was a section of
trench line cut into the jungle floor, which apparently connected some of the enemy bunkers. As my eye fleetingly
traced the length of the trough, I was suddenly electrified
to see a VC in a dark blue uniform rise up out of the

middle of the trench. He was holding an AK-47 and was looking straight at me.

His eyes met mine for an instant. Then he raised his assault rifle and aimed it at my head. I was sure that my heart actually stopped beating as I waited for him to pull the trigger.

There was nothing I could do. I was hovering a 2,160-pound aircraft just inches above a shell hole full of our own people. Downing was hanging out of the airplane waiting to drop the blood. Bruton was looking out the other side of the ship completely oblivious to what was happening on my side. I felt my lips move as I repeated to myself, "God, don't let him shoot . . . don't let him shoot!"

We stared eye to eye for a moment that seemed an eternity long. He didn't appear to have a weapon malfunction. Nobody seemed to be shooting at him. He had me dead to rights, but he hesitated. He didn't pull the trigger. Only God knows why.

The moment of horror was suddenly interrupted by the intercom. Downing shouted, "That's it, Lieutenant, they've got the box. Let's didi this place!"

Feeling the hot beads of sweat on my forehead, I broke my fixation with the muzzle of the assault rifle. I yanked the collective stick all the way to stop and shoved the cyclic forward. The agile little bird responded instantly. It jumped for height and forward speed so positively that it pinned my backside solidly against the armored pilot's seat. Then the VC in the trench opened up with several quick bursts from his AK.

While I was in a hover, he had me cold in his sights long enough to blow my head off. But, for some reason, he waited until we began to clear the crater before cutting loose. When he finally shot, his aim wasn't bad either. I heard the thumps of three or four solid hits aft of the back cabin in the engine area.

I keyed the FM to Harris. "I'm out, Four Six. That's all I

can do for you right now. I'm hit. I'm going home for another bird, but I'll be back."

"Roger, One Six. I see smoke from your engine compartment. We've got the blood kits and Doc's working on Hamilton. Thank you, One Six. I'll see you later."

I then radioed Koranda in the Cobra and told him that he better get another scout team up there right away because I was heading back to Phu Loi with a sick bird.

The shot-up OH-6 made it back to base, but just barely. I had taken two rounds right through the compressor section, and the engine was trashed.

Next followed an almost unbelievable blur of events. As I was coming back into Phu Loi with my crippled ship, I passed Rod Willis (One Seven) and his Cobra (Dean Sinor, Three One), who were scrambling northwest to replace me over the contact area.

I wasn't able to wait around to brief Willis before I had to pull out, but as we passed in the air, I radioed him. "OK, One Seven, do you understand what you're getting into out there?"

"Roger, One Six," he responded. "I've been in the ops bunker listening to the radios. I'm up on the action."

"OK, Rod, you'll find the ARPs northwest of the tree line in the shell hole about thirty to forty meters into the jungle. They're mostly pinned in the crater and Charlie is shooting at anything that moves. For God's sake, don't slow down. Whatever you do, keep your speed up. Don't slow down over the contact area. You got it?"

Rod came back with a simple acknowledgment. "Right . . . don't slow down. I copy, One Six. On my way."

As soon as I got on the ground at Phu Loi, I grabbed my gear and headed for a replacement Loach. Jim Downing and I started to climb in when the executive officer, Joe Perkins (Darkhorse Five), ran up. "Hey, Mills, I'm going with you. I'm replacing your crew chief."

"What?"

"Downing can stay here. I'm going with you," he repeated.

Anxious to get off, I agreed. "OK, Five, you're the exec. Climb in back."

I nodded to Downing. "Jim, you stay here with Mr. Bruton. Get the platoon sergeant, and you three take over to get every aircraft that we have ready for combat. Get 'em all out, ready to go, all with plenty of ammo and topped off with fuel."

Perkins and I cleared with the tower and lifted off. As we passed over the base fence I switched the minigun to "fire normal" and told Perkins to arm his M-60. I poured the coal to the Loach. We were about six minutes from the contact area if I stayed low and didn't waste time going to altitude.

With armament systems activated, I next switched tower frequency to troop Uniform to catch up on what was happening with the ARPs in the crater. I no more than came up on the push when I was shocked to hear Willis's voice.

"I'm taking fire . . . I'm taking hits . . . I'm going down!"

"Son of a bitch," I hissed.

Then Dean Sinor, Willis's Cobra, came up. "One Six, One Six, this is Three One. Where in the hell are you?"

"Three One, One Six. I'm just coming off the pad now. What's happening?"

"OK, One Six, get your ass up here. We just lost One Seven. He's going down in flames."

I pushed the Loach to the red line. As I approached the base camp area from the southeast, my radio crackled again. "One Six, where are you now?"

"I'm on the deck heading three one five degrees. Whatcha got?"

"One Seven's down in the LZ," Sinor said. "Can you see his smoke?"

I rolled into a low-level right turn and circled the landing zone where we had originally put in the ARP Hueys.

At the far northwestern edge of the little patch of open ground, I saw wisps of smoke curling up where Willis had ditched his bird. I didn't see any flames, but the nose of the bird had been plowed into the ground and the tail boom was sticking almost straight up out of the elephant grass, looking to all the world like a giant lawn dart.

As I passed over the wreck I could see that Rod and Ken Stormer, his crew chief, were both out of the aircraft, busily removing their gear. I motioned that I saw them and would come in and pick them up.

I keyed the intercom and told Perkins my plan. He realized, I'm sure, that we'd be overloaded, with four people in the little Loach plus the weight of the minigun. But he nodded, knowing, as I did, that the OH-6 was a miracle machine. The aircraft could tolerate a gross bending of the rules, when necessary, and still give back nine cents change out of your dime.

So, with Perkins and Willis in the back and Ken Stormer in the front left seat, I made directly for the nearby ARVN base. Jim Bruton could bring Rod a replacement ship from Phu Loi.

Leaving Rod and Ken, I hurried back to the crater area to see how Harris was doing. Four Six told me that if someone wasn't successful in breaking through to him soon, he'd have to make plans for a night pullout.

We both knew that this would be a last resort. The VC were in their own base camp totally familiar with every inch of the ground. Their knowledge of the area gave them a tremendous advantage during the day, and that same advantage increased dramatically after dark. A night withdrawal would be extremely risky.

Within twenty minutes, Willis and Stormer were back. We circled for about thirty minutes before making another run over the base camp area. With Willis following close behind, I turned in for a fast run, staying on the trees and hitting about seventy knots. As we ripped over the crater, Rod gave me a call.

"Hey, man, maybe they're asleep or dry down there. Nobody shot at me."

"Me neither," I answered. "So let's slow 'er down a little, make another pass, and see if anybody's still kicking."

This time we came in from a different direction and dropped airspeed to about forty knots. We were almost over Harris's shell hole when the base camp came alive with ground fire, apparently saved up from our previous high-speed run-by.

I didn't hear or feel any hits to my ship, but just at that moment, my radio crackled again. "I'm taking fire . . . I'm taking hits. I'm going down!"

I looked around just in time to see One Seven veer off my tail, start to smoke, and head for the LZ again.

I couldn't believe it. Willis was going down again. Shot right off my tail and heading back into the landing zone, almost at the same spot as before!

"You OK, Rod?" I yelled at him. "Can you make it in? Get her down and I'll run your flanks with the minigun to keep Charlie off your back. Take it easy."

All I heard back was, "Hurry up, man, those guys mean business. Going down!"

I followed Willis until he was on the ground. He and Stormer jumped out of the ship and began removing their gear while I made runs down both flanks, squirting minigun fire.

As I hosed down the area, I got back on the radio to the C and C ship, telling them I needed their help again. I asked them to make a run into the LZ, pick up Willis and Stormer, and, while they were at it, also pick up Major Moore and Lieutenant Allen.

The C and C ship announced that they'd be right in. "OK, Two Niner," I said. "Take everybody back to Phu Loi. And tell Willis, if he and Stormer aren't banged up too bad, to get into another Loach and get the hell back up here as soon as they can."

With Willis gone we still had One Three, One Zero, me, and four Cobras left on the scene. But none of us could figure out how to get the ARPs out of the mess they were in. It was about four o'clock in the afternoon and Four Six's spot was getting tighter all the time.

After circling for a while, I got back in touch with the C and C ship and Major Moore. By that time, they were nearing Phu Loi. "Darkhorse Six, this is One Six. The day's going to run out on us, Major, if we don't get some help to these guys while there's still some light left. Is there any armor nearby that you can get to bust into them?"

Six came back, "OK, One Six, hang onto the help you've got up there now. Keep Four Six covered the best you can. I'll get some armor coming."

A few minutes later Six came back up on the radio. "All right, One Six, we've got armor coming. They're on their way now and will be there right away. They're coming down the road from Dau Tieng and you need to send someone over to pick them up and guide them into the base camp."

As I rogered Six's transmission, I looked over and saw Willis, now in Loach number *three,* burning back in on the trees hell-bent for election. After today, Willis would *really* be known as an "enemy ace." I radioed him. "One Seven, I need you to get over to the Dau Tieng Road and pick up the armor column. They're close by now and need you to lead them into the base camp area. Be sure they know who they're shooting at when they come in down there. Our friendlies have already had their share of shit for today."

In just a few minutes, Rod returned with the mechanized infantry company and an attached platoon of M-48A3 tanks, leading them into the southern end of the base area. In the meantime, we had marked the enemy positions the best we could with red smoke so that the tankers would know where to shoot.

The very second the armored column entered the base

camp, all hell broke loose. The relief column began to take horrendous fire from the bunkers. Willis and I were over the ARP crater trying to mark the friendlies when enemy fire seemed to explode from the base camp into one huge flaming ball. Rounds were flying everywhere. I could hear them hitting my ship as I goosed the Loach to get out of there. But not before I heard the now-familiar radio call.

"Ah, sheeit! I'm taking hits . . . I'm going down!"

"*Goddamn!*" I screamed. "Rod again!" Down he went. With smoke trailing.

Bob Davis came up on the radio as he watched Willis's third OH-6 pile into the LZ. "Why don't you just leave the son of a bitch down there? We haven't got any more aircraft for him to crash!"

I tried to take over guiding the tankers into the camp, but I couldn't get my FM radio to work. So, with Willis down and my FM not transmitting or receiving, I fed instructions to the C and C ship over UHF, who, in turn, relayed them to the tankers below.

In seconds, the armor began blowing the hell out of everything. They literally blasted their way into the base camp to link up with the beleaguered ARPs in the shell hole. As they moved forward, the M-48s depressed their main guns and stuck their muzzles point blank into the bunkers' firing ports, then pulled the triggers. The resulting canister round explosions blew the tops off the bunkers, sent debris showering everywhere, and completely vaporized everything within.

As the holocaust continued, I could see Four Six's flank and point elements finally get out of their pinned-down positions and low-crawl their way back into the crater with the rest of the ARPs.

After about forty minutes of furious battle, the base camp suddenly fell silent. Charlie was apparently at the end of his rope. The tanks stopped firing while the mechanized infantrymen ran forward to secure the area and see about the trapped ARPs.

Still circling overhead, I watched Harris's men begin to stand up, move around, and shake the battle debris from their bodies. Though looking totally drained by the day's experience, they could still smile and clap each other on the back, thankful that their siege was finally over. After some quick looks around at the rubble of the VC bunkers that had held them hostage most of the day, the aerorifle-men began to filter back out of the base camp and toward the LZ.

The plan was to extract the ARPs back to Phu Loi and leave the armor and mech infantry guys at the base camp to mop up. We called the slicks back in to pick up Harris's men, in addition to asking the C and C ship—again—to retrieve Willis and Stormer from their last crash into the landing zone. This time the engine had been completely shot out of his aircraft. Miraculously, neither man had been seriously hurt in any of their shootdowns that day. But Stormer was heard to say later, "Now, no shit, you guys, I ain't doing this no more today."

I stayed over the base camp until everybody was loaded and well on the way back to Phu Loi. After one last look at the devastation below, I headed back to base myself.

By the time I set down the OH-6 on the pad back at Phu Loi, the sun was slipping over the western end of the field. Perkins quickly bailed out of the backseat but I just slumped in my seat and sat in the aircraft for a minute, letting my body try to relax. I had been flying since about eleven o'clock that morning. It was then 7:30 in the evening, and, after almost nine hours in the air, I had never been so bushed in my life.

The moment of calm ended abruptly, however, when Willis came running up to the ship and threw his arm around my shoulders, "Come on, ol' aeroscout buddie, haul your weary ass out of that seat and let's go find Four Six!"

By that time, all the scout and gun pilots were on the pad and we started walking together toward Harris's hootch. The ARPs joined us and everybody was hugging each other, laughing and joking around. We were like a long-lost family coming together for a fifty-year reunion.

The ARPs had suffered minor casualties considering the circumstances. Three of their people had been badly hit. The severely wounded Sp4c. August F. Hamilton did not make it, and we all mourned his loss.

The troop's scout platoon had lost four Loaches that were damaged beyond repair. Two crew chiefs were hurt: Stormer was banged up after being shot down three times, and Jim Downing had broken his hand at Phu Loi while he and Jim Bruton worked to get scout aircraft armed, fueled, and ready to fly.

A close look at the OH-6 I had flown back to base at the end of the day showed twenty-six bullet holes all over the ship. One of those rounds had gone through my FM radio apparatus. It was no wonder it wouldn't work when I needed it to guide the armor into the VC base camp.

Some decorations were subsequently awarded to the scouts for that day's activity. Jim Downing received the Silver Star medal for the heroic act of exposing himself to heavy enemy ground fire, while dropping the box of blood kits into the crater where the ARPs needed it. I also received a Silver Star for my participation in the aerial operation.

Rod Willis and Ken Stormer each received the Distinguished Flying Cross for being shot down three times in one day, and returning to the fight every time. Of course, I was of the strong opinion that it was Willis's misfortune of being shot down repeatedly in the landing zone that helped save the day. The VC in the bunkers must have been so astounded, watching him get shot down three times in the same place, that it diverted their attention from the other things we were doing to relieve the beleaguered ARPs!

* * *

After that action, it took several days for the troop to get back to normal. We had wounds to lick. The ARPs needed replacements. I needed four new ships in the scout platoon. Everybody was a little skinned up and nervous.

By the end of July, however, our preoccupation with the crater incident was broken, at least for Willis, me, and gun pilots Sinor and Koranda. The Old Man called me in and said that he wanted two hunter-killer teams to go to Di An and be briefed for a "special combat mission."

We couldn't figure out what they wanted with two combat-ready scout-gunship teams in this rear base area. But over we went on the morning of 30 July to get our briefing from a representative of the division G-3. He told us that he wanted our two teams to work for a couple of hours right around the immediate Di An base area.

We said, almost in unison, "But, sir, there isn't anything around here for us to work."

The G-3 nodded his head as if he understood. "Well, I want you to work it anyway . . . carefully, very closely. Look for mines, foot traffic, anything that might be out of line." He pointed to the map. "We want you to set up a screen in this immediate area just outside the base perimeter. Don't get closer than about five hundred meters to the perimeter, and don't get more than about a thousand out from it. Understood?"

As we rogered, he drew a tight little circle on the map around the Di An base area and dismissed us with a comment. "We've got VIPs coming to town, so keep a sharp eye out."

When it was time to start patrolling, Sinor and I took the first shift. It wasn't long before we saw a Huey off in the distance on an approach pattern into the Di An base. I listened on the radio as the Huey pilot contacted the Di An tower for landing. He was obviously expected at the base, and I wondered if these were the VIPs we were covering.

Since the ground below me was practically sterile as far as any indication of enemy activity, I watched the ship as it settled down into the middle of the base. It landed near a formation of soldiers, and a group of people got out. One soldier in the group had on army "greens." I hadn't seen anybody wearing a green dress uniform in the entire seven months I had been in Vietnam. I wondered who he was and where he had come from.

A brief ceremony was held, involving the formation of soldiers, then the group got back on board the Huey and it took off.

About the time the VIP bird departed, the G-3 came up on our frequency. "OK, Darkhorse, you are cleared to depart station. Your mission is completed and we appreciate your support."

Sinor acknowledged and asked, "Say, Ops, who was that VIP anyway? What was that all about?"

There was a slight pause. "That, gentlemen, was your commander in chief, President Nixon. Thanks again, Darkhorse, you can tell your grandkids that you flew cover for the president!"

When we got back to Phu Loi, Willis and I walked into the hootch. Bob Davis was lying on his bunk reading a magazine. Knowing that One Seven and I had been out on a special mission for Major Moore, Davis perked up and asked, "Where you guys been?"

Willis said, "Nowhere . . . no big deal."

"Ah, come on," Davis pleaded, "where you been? Did you get into anything hot?"

"Naw," Rod answered. "Very, very quiet . . . no big deal at all."

David could tell by then that we were yanking him around a little. "OK, cut the shit, you guys. What did you do and who were you flying for?"

"The president of the United States," I answered as nonchalantly.

Davis, by then, had had enough. "All right, you horses'
asses, quit bullshitting me and give it to me straight!"

"We're not shitting you, One Three," I said. "Oh, by the
way, Dick said to tell you hello when I got back to Phu
Loi."

"You didn't meet him. You really didn't get to meet the
president . . . come on, that's ridiculous!"

"Sure we met him," I answered. "We met him personally . . . got to shake his hand . . . even got our picture
taken with him!"

That did him in. Davis spent the rest of that day kicking
his butt for not getting to go on that mission . . . until he
found out that Willis and I never got closer than a half
kilometer from that VIP Huey, and couldn't have recognized anybody on the ground if we had tried. Not even the
president of the United States.

CHAPTER 10

COBRA DOWN

One Three (Bob Davis) was one of the most reliable scouts in the platoon. If he said he saw something on the ground, it was down there. He had good, quick eyes and could read sign like a book. But one day when we were working out of Lai Khe over the western Trapezoid, Davis ran across a bunker in an old enemy base camp that defied his best efforts to identify it.

When flying VRs out of the Trap, we generally took two scout teams to Lai Khe and used that as a base. On this day, Davis was out working an area northwest of FSB Lorraine when he radioed me at Lai Khe.

"Hey, One Six," he said, "I'm on my way back in, but don't you get off 'til I get there. I need to talk to you. I've got something out here and I can't figure it out. I'll talk to you when I set down."

A few minutes later Davis got in, and while his crew chief was refueling his ship, Davis trotted over to my bird. He told me he had found a bunker at X-Ray Tango 670420. "This thing is really big, probably twenty-five feet across and maybe forty feet long, a hell of a lot bigger than any VC bunkers we ever see.

"Besides," he went on, "this thing's got a corrugated tin

roof on it—no camouflage, no logs and dirt on top like every other bunker we see."

"Has it got gunports?" I cut in.

"Not exactly. There're open spaces under the roof that look like observation slits, but no gunports. When I back the bird off to a side and try to look in under the tin, I can see something down in there, but I'll go to hell if I know what it is!"

"OK," I told him, "I'll take a look. I'll be out there in six to seven minutes and give you a call."

When I got to the bunker, I saw what One Three meant. This thing was a hell of a lot bigger than anything we'd ever seen before, except for maybe a company or battalion bunker-type classroom. The enemy was known to have built some large bunkers where they were conducting training classes for their troops. They outfitted them with all sorts of American equipment and weapons that they had either stolen or picked up in the field, so their soldiers would have firsthand knowledge of our gear.

The enemy didn't fight from bunkers like that, however; they used them just for training. And these classroom bunkers were never located in small base camps, only in the larger, major base camps that were more secure.

After a little discussion over the radio, Davis and I agreed that a classroom bunker was what we had. We were excited about finding it because it meant that we had probably located a big and important enemy base camp. But before calling for an air strike, the decision was made to bring in the ARPs to do some reconning. We needed to determine if the base camp was occupied or if there were any fresh traffic signs around, and what was going on with the big bunker.

By that time, One Three had come back up to join me for another look, and to mark the big bunker with smokes to guide the ARPs.

As Bob Harris's aeroriflemen got on the ground and began to approach the strange-looking bunker, their Kit

Carson scouts got very excited. They found that every approach to the bunker was heavily booby-trapped and mined. There was no question now that the bunker was very important; otherwise Charlie wouldn't have gone to all this trouble to protect it.

Davis and I listened in on FM while the Kit Carsons slowly moved in and began dismantling the booby traps. It took some time before the area was cleared and Harris's men could get close to the tin-roofed pit.

Finally, Bob Harris's voice boomed into our phones. "One Six, this is Four Six. You're not going to believe what we've got down here in this friggin' bunker!"

"Four Six, One Six. Whatcha got?"

"We got a tank, buddy!" he shouted.

"Say again, Four Six, what do you have?"

"We've got a tank—a tango alpha november kilo—down here, One Six!"

"You gotta be kidding me," I ventured one more time.

"Believe it or not, you guys, there's a complete tank underneath this tin roof. Looks like Charlie dug the pit, drove the tank into it, and then built the roof over it. I'm not fooling you!"

I had never seen an enemy tank in Vietnam. "What kind of a tank is it?" I asked Harris.

"I can't tell," he came back. "This thing is too heavily booby-trapped. I'm not going any farther until we can get some engineers in here."

So our best guess had been completely out in left field. The bunker wasn't an enemy classroom; it was a shed for a tank!

Later, some Civilian Irregular Defense Group (CIDG) troops and elements of our 16th Infantry were pulled into the area. They occupied the base camp and provided security while a couple of officers from the 11th Armored Cav were flown in to make an ID on the tank. It turned out to be an old American M-41 Walker Bulldog light tank. It was complete with its 76mm main gun, but its .30 coaxial

and .50-caliber antiaircraft guns had been removed, probably to be used elsewhere. There were also some fifty-one
rounds of main gun ammunition, two hundred rounds of
.50 caliber, and seven hundred fifty rounds of .30-caliber
ammunition still in the tank. This baby was really loaded
for bear.

The tank had apparently been well maintained and appeared to be in excellent condition. The only questions left
were where it had come from, and how it had ever ended
up parked in an enemy jungle base camp.

These questions were ultimately answered when it was
learned that the tank had originally been given to the
ARVN forces by the United States early in the war. The
enemy captured it from an ARVN cavalry outfit when
their outpost at Ben Cat was overrun by the VC in May of
1966. The VC drove the tank away at that time and it
hadn't been seen since. Not until three years later, when
Bob Davis spotted its unusual parking garage.

On 11 August a long-range reconnaissance patrol
(LRRP) team went out of brigade HQ in Dau Tieng and
was inserted up on the eastern edge of the Michelin rubber plantation. LRRP teams usually consisted of six to
eight specially trained personnel. Their mission normally
was to be inserted into the jungle, set up an observation
post, and report enemy activities. They maintained con-
cealed positions and absolute silence while in the field,
except when executing an occasional ambush along an enemy trail. If they did execute an ambush, the LRRP unit
had to be extracted immediately. As a general rule, the
LRRPs tried to avoid heavy enemy contact because six to
eight lightly equipped soldiers had no chance to prevail in
a decisive encounter.

In this case, however, the LRRP team was hit and took
casualties the moment they stepped off their Huey. That,
in itself, was quite unusual because of the intensive planning that went into the missions and the precautions taken

by the Huey in putting the LRRPs down into an LZ. The transporting Huey would always make several false insertions, landing and then taking off from several spots all around the area, so that enemy observers would not be able to pinpoint the real insertion location.

As soon as the LRRPs ran into trouble, they hit the radio for immediate backup and extraction. Their mission had been compromised, they had people hit, and they had to get out of Dodge before getting wiped out entirely. Their call for help immediately scrambled the ARPs out of Phu Loi, along with the Scramble 1 scout team, Joe Vad (Nine), and his crew chief, Al Farrar.

When Harris and his riflemen were inserted about a kilometer away from the LRRPs, they also were hit by the enemy, pinned down in the LZ with two men killed. Scout Joe Vad moved in over the contact area, trying to locate enemy positions. His low, slow flying, however, immediately alerted Charlie to his presence, and Vad's bird began to take heavy ground fire.

There were NVA soldiers in dark green uniforms moving in all directions around the aeroriflemen and the LRRP unit. Farrar's M-60 blasted away at the host of targets while Vad twisted and turned the Loach to avoid taking vulnerable hits.

But to no avail. Ground fire ripped into the ship, causing an engine failure. There was nothing Vad could do. The bird plowed down into the far edge of the LZ where the ARPs had been put down just minutes before.

Amazingly, Joe Vad was not badly hurt when his Loach went in. Farrar was not so lucky. His knee and leg were twisted in the wreckage and he was in pain. Joe managed to help Al out of the aircraft, however, and they began to make their way toward the ARPs.

Back at Phu Loi, I was on alert as Scramble 2, with Jim Parker as my crew chief and Dean Sinor as my gun pilot. Receiving the call that Scramble 1 was down, we lifted off and started a fast run to the contact area to assume air control of the situation.

Behind us, the entire troop—including every other available scout bird, gunship, and slick—was scrambled to move up to the strip at Dau Tieng to provide immediate support from that nearby base.

While Sinor and I were inbound to the contact area, I got VHF traffic and learned that the supporting scouts from Phu Loi were closing on Dau Tieng and wanted further instructions. I radioed back, saying, "Wait ten minutes and then send me One Seven [Willis]; ten minutes after that, give me One Three [Davis]."

Since I was just approaching the scene, I didn't know the extent of the situation. I only knew that there was heavy enemy contact, that the LRRPs were isolated and pinned down with casualties, that the ARPs had been hit and had taken casualties in the LZ, and now we had the aeroscout down with at least one crewman hurt.

Arriving at the scene, I made one fast pass to try to get everybody's position on the ground. I saw Four Six (Bob Harris) and his medic working desperately over a couple of their downed soldiers. Here we go again, I thought.

As we made eye contact, Bob began making hand signals. He pointed to the northeast, touched his index and middle fingers to his eyes, then pointed again off to the northeast. That told me he saw the enemy in that direction.

When I moved off on the heading Harris had indicated, I saw the wreckage of Niner's OH-6. The aircraft was on its side, with a crumpled tail boom and all four blades gone. It was smoking but hadn't burned on impact.

As I made one circle over the crash, I saw Vad with his pistol drawn, half dragging and half carrying Farrar. Al was still hanging onto his M-60 and had a very long belt of ammunition dragging along behind him. It took more than a crash and twisted leg to separate a crew chief from his machine gun!

Wanting to make sure that they made it to cover, I stayed over Vad and Farrar until I saw a couple of ARP point men move out to escort them back into the middle of the ARP formation. Satisfied that the scout crew would be taken care of, I headed off in the direction that Four Six had indicated.

Hitting about sixty knots and flying about ten feet off the trees, I crossed over a tree line not far from the LZ. Immediately I began to draw heavy automatic weapons fire from all directions. The rounds coming up at me were from both .30- and .50-caliber enemy weapons, probably positioned in bunkers. My airspeed, and the fact that the gunners weren't leading me enough, kept me from taking any hits, however.

Parker opened up with his M-60, spraying the general area. I didn't ask him to check his fire, but I did remind him to be very careful, since we had a lot of friendlies down there.

After about three orbits, we spotted the LRRP unit huddled together at the base of a large tree. It looked as if three of the men had been hit. There was a small open area nearby, but it wasn't big enough for a rescue aircraft.

One of the soldiers had a radio in his hand but was apparently talking on a frequency I didn't have. I got off a quick call to Sinor, asking him to find out the FM push that the LRRP team was using. He was back to me right away, and I immediately called them.

"Ranger, Ranger, this is Darkhorse One Six. How do you hear?"

Normally those LRRP guys were pretty cool and collected over the radio, but this soldier was fairly screaming. "Roger, roger, Darkhorse! I've got you. I see you. Can you see the enemy? They're everywhere! They're all around us. You gotta get us out of here fast!"

"OK, Ranger, sit tight. I've got an infantry platoon on the ground about eight hundred yards to your southwest and they're moving toward you."

"Negative! Negative!" he shouted. "There are more enemy troops in here than that. They're company force . . . company *plus*. It's gonna take more than a platoon. Do you copy?"

"I roger that, Ranger, but you've got more than just any platoon to help you out. You've got the Darkhorse ARPs. Do you copy?"

Everybody in the 1st Division knew and respected the aerorifle platoon. It was made up of select infantrymen from all over the division who had distinguished themselves in combat and had volunteered for the ARPs. This multiskilled, multifaceted group of twenty-eight young men really knew their business.

The LRRP leader immediately understood that I wasn't just bullshitting him. "I copy, Darkhorse ARP platoon. So get us the hell out of here. We've got wounded. We need a doc for our wounded."

I rogered, "There's a medic on the ground. Sit tight where you are. The ARPs are moving toward you from your sierra whiskey, so control your fire to the southwest. Now give me a target for the gunships to hit."

"That's a roger, Darkhorse," he answered, "controlling fire to sierra whiskey. Can you see my cardinal direction for the ground fire . . . in this direction fifty to seventy-five meters? We're taking heavy .30- and .50-caliber machine-gun fire from bunkers. Can you get on them?"

"OK, Ranger. Can you give me a smoke?"

"Roger, Darkhorse . . . stand by."

A second later I saw the flash of the grenade fuse going off, then a puff of purple smoke. "OK, Darkhorse, smoke's out. Do you identify?"

I answered, "That's affirmative . . . I've got grape."

"Roger, Darkhorse, grape smoke is out. Enemy target from the smoke is fifty meters my direction . . . enemy bunkers. Give 'em hell!"

By this time, we had three Cobras over the contact area:

Sinor (Three One), Koranda (Three Nine), and Carriss (Three Eight).

"OK, guys," I came up to the guns. "LRRPs are pinned down by bunker fire. Grape smoke is out just north of the LRRP position. In trail, make your runs east to west with a south break . . . a left break. LRRPs are going to be danger close . . . watch your rocks and keep impact twenty to thirty meters north of smoke."

Sinor acknowledged for the Cobras, "Roger, One Six. East to west run with south break. You cover the ARPs while we get busy. Inbound hot . . . now!"

The Cobras made three firing passes, expending about twenty rockets. They put their rocks right on the money, and probably not more than forty to fifty feet to the LRRPs' front.

Seeing that the gunships had temporarily taken the heat off the LRRPs' position, I went back for a pass over the ARPs to see how they were doing. "Four Six, this is One Six. Snakes have got Charlie off Ranger's back for a minute. Have instructed Ranger to control fires to sierra whiskey your direction. Now, how are *you* doing?"

"Not good," Harris came back, "not good at all, One Six. I've got two men hit bad and down, and another not so bad. We need to medevac these people so we can move on up to our friendlies. Can you get a Dustoff in here?"

I immediately radioed Sinor, who was just back to altitude after hosing down the enemy bunkers. "OK, Three One, good rocks, good rocks. But right now Four Six has got three badly wounded. He needs a medevac before he can move up to the LRRP team. Get me a Dustoff in here as quick as you can.

"Also, Three One," I continued, "get hold of One Seven, who's on his way out here right now, and have him link up with Dustoff and escort the Huey into the LZ where the ARPs are down."

In just a few minutes my radio told me that Dustoff was inbound with Willis leading the way. I turned and saw the medevac Huey on short final with One Seven breaking over the LZ ahead. They had made good time.

While Dustoff was loading the ARP wounded, I briefed Willis on the LRRP position and enemy bunker locations. "All right, One Seven," I told Rod, "come on around and get on my tail. And for God's sake try for a change to *not* get your Texas ass shot out of the sky, OK?"

"That's one big roger, One Six," Willis drawled. "I am *on* your tail, pardner!"

We orbited the LRRP team position and found them all OK after the Cobra runs. In fact, they were looking up and smiling at us, indicating that they were not taking any more bunker fire.

I told Ranger that Dustoff was picking up the ARP wounded and would be right back to get his. All he had to do was sit tight until the aerorifle platoon got up to him with their medic. Then we'd pull them all back to the LZ for extraction. This all went like clockwork.

Just to be sure the enemy bunkers were out of business, the Sidewinder FAC was then called in. It wasn't long before he had fast movers on the target to massage the bunker complex with their hot stuff. Our work was done.

Not many missions involved the entire troop, but this was certainly one of them. Every available Darkhorse scout, gunship, and slick had been brought into action. Fine-tuned coordination and esprit de corps was typical of D Troop people—it was always there, in all our operations day in and day out. But it was especially keen when ground guys were in a tight spot and committed to a firefight. Or when an aircrew was down. These were high-priority situations.

Only a week later another Darkhorse aircrew was shot down by Charlie's heavy automatic weapons fire and ended up down and stranded. Only this time it was a Cobra gunship and not a Loach.

The OH-6 was the usual victim of enemy ground fire

because we flew right down on the deck, and slow enough
to make a juicy target. The Cobras were usually high, fast,
and heavily armed, so getting shot down by enemy ground
fire was not their greatest worry.

On 18 August, Dean Sinor (Three One) and I took off
on a routine VR mission up over the Saigon River near
the northwestern corner of the Iron Triangle. Larry Kauffman, a hootch mate of mine, was Sinor's front-seater in
the Cobra. Jim Parker was my crew chief.

As a flight of two we rolled out of Phu Loi at first light,
bound for the areas known as the Coliseum, the Onion,
and the Onion Stem, located between the Michelin rubber
plantation in the north and the Iron Triangle in the south.
Reaching station, we started in the north near the edge of
the Michelin and scouted in east–west legs on south down
to the Mushroom and the Saigon River. Other than an
occasional bunker and a few trails showing relatively fresh
traffic, we didn't see anything unusual or make any enemy
contact.

We intentionally did not fly any farther south than the
river because the Saigon was the boundary line between
the operational areas of the 1st and 25th divisions. Everything west of the Saigon belonged to the 25th; everything
east to the 1st. About the only thing that operated back
and forth over the river between the two divisions was
artillery. Many times 1st Division artillery fire was coordi-
nated at unfriendlies on the 25th side of the river, and vice
versa.

As we finished our VR and got ready to head back to
Phu Loi, Sinor ran his procedural radio check to see if any
friendly artillery was firing near our route of flight back
home. He found out that artillery was being fired south
out of Lai Khe in 1st Division OA, as well as rounds coming north out of the 25th Division base at Cu Chi, right
through our route of return.

Sinor came up to me on the radio. "One Six, we've got
an arty problem going home. We'll either have to take the

long way back to papa lima or go lima lima to Dogleg."
That is, we could either fly all the way around the artillery
that was crossing our return flight path, or we could drop
down to low level (lima lima) and fly all the way back on
the deck to Dogleg Village, which was the IP (initial point)
for the northern approach into Phu Loi.

We decided to take the short route. Though it was unusual for a Cobra to spend much time traveling down low,
it wasn't any big deal for a scout. We did it every day for a
living.

Kauffman checked his maps and plotted a heading of
one two zero degrees. The course would take us straight
south and east across the heart of the Iron Triangle, over
the Saigon River at Phu Cuong, north to Dogleg Village,
and then the short descent south into Phu Loi.

We dropped down out of altitude, took up one two zero,
and began zipping along at about a hundred knots.
Though fairly fast for the Loach, that speed was kind of
lumbering along for the Cobra.

We were in trail with me leading and running about
twenty to thirty feet off the ground. Since we hadn't
worked this particular area, we flew with guns hot and
everybody watching. With big bird in tow, we were being
especially cautious.

It couldn't have been more than three to four minutes
later when I looked down at the ground and was shocked
to see troops below in contact! U.S. ground pounders were
running through the marshy terrain and firing their weapons in the same direction.

As I passed over the American soldiers, I saw what they
were shooting at. Coming up under my nose were twenty
to thirty VC slogging through the mud and firing their
AK-47s like crazy back at the Americans.

I hit the mike button for Sinor and yelled, "Three One,
break right, break right now! I got gooks under me. Get
the hell out of here!"

As I spoke, I slammed hard right pedal and jerked the

cyclic to whip the Loach up and away from the danger zone, hoping that Sinor's Cobra would be right behind me.

At the same moment, Sinor shouted, "Three One's taking hits. I'm taking hits. We're hit!"

Still in my hard right turn, I looked around and saw Sinor veer off slightly to the left, then back to the right. I hoped nothing serious was wrong. Sinor was out of his element—actually hearing ground fire and seeing the people who were shooting. Maybe he was just overreacting.

No such luck. "One Six, they got my hydraulics. I've lost my hydraulics and I've got to put it down!"

I swung around behind him and got on his right wing. We would have to find a place fast to put her down before Sinor lost his accumulator auxiliary. When something caused hydraulic fluid to escape the aircraft's system, an emergency accumulator provided a small reservoir of fluid, which permitted some movement of the aircraft's hydraulic controls. But that emergency fluid was soon pumped right out the same hole in the lines that caused the initial loss. Sinor had to get his aircraft down before he lost complete control of his ship.

From my position on his right wing, I could see Sinor and Kauffman in the snake's cockpit wrestling with the now-hardening controls. In his struggle to help fly the aircraft, Kauffman had dropped his map and wasn't able to pinpoint a grid of our location. Well, I thought, I'll figure that out later.

Suddenly I saw a clearing ahead that looked big enough for the Cobra. The ground looked wet and soggy, and there was a tree or two, but otherwise it was OK, considering our state of affairs.

I circled around off Sinor's wing and keyed the mike. "All right, Dino, there's the clearing. I've got you covered. Go ahead and put her down. Watch the tree . . . watch your tail to the right, you've got a tree."

Three One powered the big bird down into a controlled landing. He must have used the last drop of fluid in his system before the accumulator locked up. I started breathing again.

I circled close above as Sinor cut emergency power and fuel switches and the rotors began to wind down. The aircraft, other than the skids being stuck down halfway in the mud, looked in pretty good shape. And the crew was OK; I saw both men unbuckle and throw open their individual canopies.

Kauffman exited on the left side with his CAR-15 in hand. He ran around the nose of the ship to Sinor, who was just jumping out on the right. The two men crawled underneath the ship's right rocket pod. Kauffman was down on all fours, getting his CAR-15 into firing position.

I couldn't believe where they had taken up their defensive position. The Cobra's fuel cell, containing probably three hundred to four hundred gallons of JP-4, was right over their heads. In addition, there were the two rocket pods, one on each wing, still full of thirty-eight 2.75-inch explosive rocket rounds. What a place to be with the possibility of somebody shooting at you!

As I looked down again, I noticed that Sinor was doing something funny with his right arm, kind of shaking it with short, choppy jerks. It looked as though something had happened to his arm or hand, probably when he put down the ship.

My speculation was interrupted by Kauffman, who had gotten his PRC-10 radio out of his emergency vest and was talking into it. "One Six, One Six." His voice was a bit shaky. "Are you there? Can you hear me, One Six? I'm on Guard freq. Come in, One Six!"

"I'm here," I answered. "I'm circling just to your sierra echo. Is Three One all right? Looks to me like he's hurt. Did he injure his hand or arm?"

"Nope, he's not hurt, One Six. He's just got his pistol caught in his sock and can't get it out."

Cobra pilots seldom had reason to use their personal weapons when they flew, so they carried their sidearm in their shoulder holster, wrapped in a sock. They'd clean, oil, and load the weapon (usually a Model 10, 4-inch-barrel Smith & Wesson revolver) and stick it into a sock to keep out dust and dirt. It worked well except when the knot in the top of the sock pulled tight and the weapon wouldn't come out.

With Sinor jerking away, Kauffman continued to set up a defensive firing position under the right wing of the Cobra—with thousands of pounds of fuel and ordnance over his head. I radioed again.

"OK, Larry, you and Dino get the hell away from that wing and move down to the tail of the aircraft where you won't have all that JP-4 and ammo on top of you. I'm going to sweep around the area and find out where Charlie is, then see what I can do about getting somebody to get you guys out of here. Sit tight for now."

I keyed Parker on the intercom. "Jimbo, get ready back there. We've gotta keep the bad guys from coming down this way and messin' up the rest of Sinor and Kauffman's day. I don't have a push on the friendlies up here, but I imagine they're 25th Division on this west side of the river. Watch out for them if you have to shoot."

I pointed the bird straight north from the downed Cobra and almost immediately began taking heavy AK-47 fire. I heard hits in the fuselage and the tail boom area.

"Sir," Parker yelled, "we're catching it but I can't see them! And I can't shoot because of the friendlies!"

My God, I thought, those gooks can't be more than seventy-five to a hundred meters away from Sinor. I whipped the Loach around in a sharp 180-degree turn to get back on top of the Cobra. I could see Sinor and Kauffman huddled underneath the tail boom, looking north, where they must have heard the AKs open up on me.

Their faces showed their predicament. They looked alone and scared. The airborne power, speed, and heavy armament of their AH-1G gunship were gone. Sinor and Kauffman were on the ground, with nothing more than a

rifle and a revolver (maybe still stuck in its sock) to try to
ward off an enemy that had obviously seen the Cobra go
down.

Having been in similar circumstances, I knew what they
were feeling. Every nerve ending in your body flashed red
hot, then ice cold, feeling like thousands of little pins repeatedly stabbing you. Your eyes strained, trying to penetrate the dense foliage and see the soldiers whom you
knew were closing in with their AKs. Tightening the
clammy grip on your weapon, you breathed in short little
gasps, wondering how you were going to get out of this
mess.

I knew I had to get somebody in there fast to snatch
these guys. It wasn't going to be long before the VC were
down on that Cobra. Sinor and Kauffman wouldn't have a
chance.

I got on the radio again to Sinor. "Three One, One Six.
They're close, Dino. Charlie's about a hundred meters to
your north front and headed your way. They may just want
to hug for security, knowing we can't shoot when they get
that close in on you, but I want you to stand by while I go
up on Guard to see what I can get in here to take the heat
off. Stay cool."

Before he could roger, I went back up on Guard freq.
"Break, break, any aircraft . . . any aircraft on Guard.
This is Darkhorse One Six. I have an aircraft down at the
northwest corner of the Iron T; crew is down. Any aircraft
vicinity of the Iron Triangle, come up on Guard. Over."

A voice came right back at me. I recognized it immediately as one of our Darkhorse snake drivers, Paul Fishman
(Three Four). He had been working farther up north that
day with scout Bob Davis.

"I got you, One Six," he said. "This is Three Four up on
Guard. Where are you?"

"Good to hear your voice, Three Four," I answered.
"I've got trouble. Three One is down. Crew is OK for now
but they're in close vicinity to a contact between U.S. and

Victor Charlie located about a hundred to a hundred and fifty meters north of their position."

"I don't have a grid," I continued, "but I'm at the northwest corner of the Iron Triangle, about two, check that . . . about six klicks south of fire base Tennessee, near fire support base Aachen. Do you copy my location, Three Four?"

"Good copy, One Six," Fishman came back. "We have your approximate location. We're up in the vicinity of Thunder III right now. We're going to start your way. Where are you in relation to Highway 14, One Six?" I tried to relay our position via landmarks.

"Roger, One Six," Fishman came back, "I got you covered. We're on the way, balls to the wall!"

"One more thing, Three Four, I'm lima lima and too low to make radio contact with the troop. Can you get hold of troop ops and scramble the ARPs? We need help up here fast before Charlie overruns Sinor and Kauffman."

"Roger that, One Six. We're en route and I'm scrambling the ARPs. Hang in there!"

Then my Guard freq crackled again, only this time in a deep Australian accent. "Hello there, Darkhorse One Six, this is Sidewinder One Five, your friendly neighborhood FAC. I hear you've got trouble, matie. I'm just coming off Dau Tieng with a full load of Willie Pete and guns on board. Can I be of any assistance?"

"Yep, you sure as hell can, Sidewinder," I answered the forward air controller in his OV-10. "We've got a helicopter and aircrew down danger close to a VC contact. We may have to do a RESCAP. You got any fast movers you can haul in here to put a cap on this thing?"

"Well, I don't know, mate. I'm just getting off and haven't checked in with my control yet. Stand by while I query. Meantime, I'm en route."

Then I heard Fishman go up on UHF to troop ops. "Darkhorse Three, this is Three Four . . . in the vicinity

of Quan Loi with a message from One Six. Darkhorse
Three One has been shot down in the area of grid X-Ray
Tango 660290. Crew is down near heavy contact between
VC and 25th Division troops. Need to extract immediately
before Cobra crew is overrun. Scramble the ARPs. Scramble gun teams 1 and 2. I'm en route and moving out ahead
of my scout to make contact."

While I waited, I mentally reviewed the situation. Sidewinder was on the way from Dau Tieng and was working
on RESCAP. Three Four was on his way from Quan Loi,
and scramble teams would soon be under way from Phu
Loi. If only any one or all could make it to the crash scene
before Charlie got on top of Sinor and Kauffman. This
would be close!

The Australian came back up on the Guard emergency
frequency and I heard him call in the blind: "This is Sidewinder One Five off of Dau Tieng at one zero past the
hour. A U.S. helicopter and crew are down. Who can help
me on a RESCAP operation?"

I overheard a series of transmissions back to Sidewinder
offering help. A flight of four VNAF (Vietnamese Air
Force) A-37 Dragonflies in the area northwest of Saigon
was diverting, a flight of four A-7 U.S. Navy aircraft operating somewhere to the northeast was en route, a flight of
F-4 U.S. Air Force fighter-bombers operating up on the
Cambodian border near the Fishhook was called in, and a
flight of Spads, or Vietnamese Air Force A-1s, was diverted from down south around VC Island.

Sidewinder logged in the transmissions from the reporting flights and assigned them to various altitudes over the
contact area. Knowing the basic characteristics and capabilities of each type of aircraft, Sidewinder stacked the
flights according to which planes could stay longer and
which had to do their thing fast and get out of the pattern.
As cool as a cucumber, the Australian sequenced and
layered all the air support over the contact point so that he
could use each type of aircraft to its fullest capability. I

had to hand it to him . . . he bloody well knew his business.

As all this was going on, I maintained a tight circle pattern over Sinor and Kauffman. For their own peace of mind, I wanted them to know that I was overhead and keeping an eye peeled for any sign that the bad guys were getting closer to their downed Cobra.

I really couldn't see what the VC were doing, however, so I decided to make a run up to the last contact point and check out the situation. I radioed Sinor. "Get your heads down and keep 'em down, you guys. I'm going to spread out my circles, see where the contact is, and try to find the U.S. troops. Be back in a minute."

In less than two orbits I saw the ground fight. The VC were withdrawing and moving south rapidly in the direction of Sinor and Kauffman. I also caught a glimpse of another VC force of about fifteen men south of the leading VC element. They looked as though they were trying to swing around and come up in back of the downed Cobra.

I keyed the intercom. "Get on 'em, Jimbo. Fire at will. If you can identify the target, fire at will."

It was difficult to distinguish between VC and U.S. troops because they were so intermingled on the ground. But I immediately began to hear Parker's M-60 open up in long bursts, and black shirts began falling. He would knock one VC down and without even releasing the trigger go on to another target and put him down.

"Keep stickin' 'em, Jimbo!" I yelled into the intercom. But I knew that nothing we could do from our bird would stem the tide of those VC. They were dodging, firing back at their pursuers, and running directly toward Sinor and Kauffman.

I flipped my radio over to Uniform and called Fishman. "Hey, Three Four, this is One Six. How you doin', man? We're in deep shit down here. How you doin'?"

"OK, One Six," Fishman answered. "I've left my scout

behind to catch up when he can. I'm hauling ass, coming up on Chon Thanh now."

"Hurry!" I shot back. "I'm scared we aren't gonna make it. I've got VC closing in on Thirty-one from their front and possibly their flank. We can't hold 'em off, and if somebody doesn't get here damned soon I'm not sure we can get the crew out."

"How about the friendlies on the ground? Can they get to the crew before the bad guys do?"

"Negative . . . negative," I answered. "No way can our guys leapfrog the VC and make it to Sinor first. Besides, I'm not even sure that the 25th people know we've got a ship down, although they should have seen Three One going down, and sure as hell should have seen our little bird flying around up here. What's your ETA here, Three Four?"

"Estimate eight to ten mikes, One Six," Fishman answered. No way, I thought.

Just then Wayne McAdoo, lift platoon leader, reported in. "One Six, this is Two Six. I have the ARPs on board and am just clear of papa lima. Estimate fifteen to sixteen mikes your location."

"Two Six, One Six copies. But you better put a burr under your saddle. I'm afraid we may just lose ourselves a gun crew if we don't shake it out. Sinor and Kauffman have got all kinds of bad guys knocking on the front door!

"Break, break," I kept on. "Three Four, I'm going to come up on Guard to the crew. Can you monitor? I need to tell them what's happening and how I want them to set up for your rocket runs."

Then I went immediately to Kauffman. "OK, Thirty-one, here's the good news. ARPs are en route and are about fourteen to fifteen mikes out. Fast movers are en route and Sidewinder will be stacking them over you as they arrive, ETA working. Three Four is en route and will be here in eight to ten mikes, but I gotta tell you that the dinks are falling back your way and are closing on you fast from the northwest."

"Damnit! Talk to me, One Six!" Kauffman obviously was not happy with the report. "How close are the bad guys?"

"Well, the bad news is that I'm beginning to take some random ground fire from Charlie now on the November edge of my orbits over you. They're close, maybe forty to fifty meters to your front. They're getting chased toward you by the 25th."

"OK, OK, One Six," Kauffman replied. "If it looks that bad, why don't you come in and get us? Land and pick us up in the Loach."

"Look," I came back, "if I have to do that, I will. But I'd rather stay up here and try to keep Charlie off your backs until we can get some help in here."

Worry showed in Kauffman's voice when he answered. "We roger that, One Six, but we aren't having any fun down here. Sinor's finally got his piece out of his sock . . . if that doesn't hold 'em off, maybe it'll scare 'em to death."

"Listen, here's what I want you to do. I need you to move away from the aircraft a little to your rear and get yourselves flat on the ground. Get your butts in defilade because when Three Four comes in here, I'm not even going to bring him around for a look-see pass. I'm gonna have him lay some rocks square between you and the bad guys, right from his inbound run."

Kauffman really sounded worried now. "How's Three Four gonna see where we are? We could end up with his rocks right in our laps!"

"Relax, Larry, don't worry so much," I consoled. Kauffman had just recently lost a wad of money in a hootch poker game bluff, so I needled him. "I wouldn't dare let the dinks or a few little 2.75 rockets take down a poker player as good as you."

"Fuck you, too," Kauffman said, but at least he chuck-led.

I keyed the UHF to Fishman. "Three Four, we aren't gonna make it. The way it looks, you're going to get in here about the same time as the bad guys. I'm going to swing around to the north and try to work on the dinks with the M-60 and my minigun. Maybe I can persuade some of the little folks that they don't want to come down on our crew."

"OK, One Six," Fishman acknowledged. "I'm pulling max power."

"I won't be able to hold 'em long with my firepower, so just as soon as you can see our general area, holler and I'll throw out some smoke. I'll put out two smokes and I'll want you to lay rocks in between the two markers for pro-tective fire to the crew." I knew that he'd be on the scene as fast as he could. He was probably pulling 130 to 140 knots in a fully loaded heavy hog.

I continued to fly right-hand orbits over the downed Cobra. Every second or third circle, I swept out north where I could hear the sound of ground fire over the whine and chop of my Loach engine. Each time I came around over the enemy, Parker opened up with his M-60, and a couple of bad guys would drop. I couldn't line up a minigun shot because I couldn't be quite as selective with that weapon and there were too many friendlies down there.

Those 25th Division guys must have wondered just who that little scout ship was and why it kept swooping in, killing a few enemy troops and then swooping out again. They probably still didn't realize that a downed Cobra with a grounded crew was out there just to their immedi-ate front.

As I looked down, though, it was evident that the VC were falling back fast. They may not have known either that a Cobra was down. Other than throwing a few pot-shots up at me, they were obviously most concerned with covering their own asses from behind. The U.S. troops were hot on their heels.

This is it, I thought as I watched the firefight below. No way will the ARPs get here in time to cover Sinor and Kauffman before the dinks are down on them.

I keyed the intercom. "We're out of time, Jimbo. I'm going to swing around to land and pick up the crew."

Without a sign of reluctance, Parker came right back. "OK, Lieutenant, I'm set, but it's going to overload the hell out of us. We haven't used up much ammo or fuel."

Parker was right. Every time we took a scout bird off the ground, we were at or over max gross weight because of all the fuel and ammo we crammed aboard. We never knew what we would be flying into, so we wanted to be able to scout and fight as long as possible.

"I know," I answered Parker. "We'll be putting another four hundred pounds in here with those two guys plus their weapons and body armor. We'll just have to dump everything out the door that we can get along without, and then hope to hell that the Loach will get us up out of there!"

Just as I was pulling around to go back and land, my radio snapped to life. "All right, One Six, this is Three Four. I'm just coming up on being able to observe your general area. Get your smoke out so I can shoot."

I touched my radio transmit button twice to let Paul know that I acknowledged. Then I pulled the Loach around in a sweeping right-hand turn. I keyed Parker again. "Get me a red . . . correction, get me two red smokes ready. We're going to mark the limits for Three Four's rocks."

Parker pulled two red smoke grenades off the bulkhead in front of him, pulled the pin on both, and held them straight out the cabin door. He threw one straight down on my command. "Now!" I shouted again, and he threw the second grenade straight down, marking each edge of a north–south corridor where I wanted Three Four to aim his rockets.

With the second smoke out, I broke right, then another hard right in order to cross back over the enemy-occupied corridor. Fishman's Cobra was still nowhere in sight, so I went back up on UHF. "Three Four, One Six. Smoke's out. It's right on top of the enemy. Give me rocks *between* the two red smokes. South edge of the corridor is the little clearing where the crew is down. You'll be danger close to them. Shoot between the smokes on your approach out of the north as soon as you can."

Three Four rogered and I circled back south to take up an orbit just beyond Sinor and Kauffman. Just on the horizon was Fishman's Cobra, a single snake with puffs of smoke beginning to erupt from the rocket pods beneath its wings. Pairs of Three Four's rocks slammed down right between the two red smokes and into the men withdrawing down the corridor.

Fishman broke out of his run, and I quickly circled back over the corridor to see if his 2.75s had slowed Charlie down. As the smoke and debris cleared, I saw that Three Four's rockets had killed about half of the enemy force. A few of the survivors looked dazed, but the rest were running in a frenzy toward the crew.

Just then my Guard frequency came back alive with Kauffman's shouts: "Here they come, One Six! We can see 'em . . . we can see the little bastards coming! We're going to get the hell out of here while we can!"

"Negative . . . negative . . . stand by, Three One," I shot back. "I'm coming in to get you. Be ready to jump on board . . . I'm coming in."

Then I let Fishman know my plan. "Your rocks were good, Three Four, but we're in deep shit down here. The Indians are closing in. I'm going to get the crew. I've got no choice . . . I'm going in to pick 'em up."

"OK, One Six," Paul came back. "I got you covered. How are you going in?"

"From east to west," I answered as I pulled the OH-6 around, "and I'll make a south break after I take the crew aboard. Keep Charlie occupied by putting a few more rocks in his way. Put 'em same place as last time, only come on down south about forty meters. Don't give us a haircut. We'll be danger close, danger close!"

Fishman swept around to set up another run on the corridor as I decelerated and started to put down. "Are you ready, Jimbo?"

"Ready, sir," he came back in his steady, impassive voice.

I picked my spot and began to settle down right beside Sinor and Kauffman's Cobra. As I was nearing touchdown, I heard Fishman's second round of rockets impacting about thirty to forty meters away. Then came the sound of shrapnel zinging through the air all around my ship. Fortunately, none of it caught us or the crew, who by then were crouched down, waiting to jump aboard.

My skids reached the ground and I waved to the two pilots. Big smiles slashed across their faces as they sprang toward the Loach and piled in—Sinor in the back with Parker, Kauffman squeezing over the minigun and into the front left seat.

As the two jumped aboard, I felt the ship sag. They were both two-hundred-pound guys with their chicken plate on, and the little OH-6 groaned under the new weight. I really didn't appreciate just how much we were over max gross weight until I felt the bird begin to settle.

I looked out my door at the landing gear and my gut tightened into a square knot as I watched the Loach's skids spread and slowly sink about a foot down into the soft, marshy ground.

"Son of a bitch!" I cursed. Everybody aboard looked at me as if to say, Well, what the hell do we do now? Good thing Fishman's second rocket pass had slowed the VC or they would have been all over us by that time.

I pulled up hard on the collective, knowing that I'd need

a surge of power to get off the ground. To my horror, nothing happened. The Loach seemed stuck solid in a foot of mud.

"Come on, baby," I coaxed. "Get us out of here. *Please* get us out of here!"

I pulled on more power. The rotors thundered. The ship vibrated. The engine tachometer climbed rapidly to 103 . . . 104 . . . then through 105 to near 107 percent. She was at max power, but the bird still didn't move . . . not a damned inch.

I punched the intercom and yelled at Parker. "Dump everything! Throw everything out you can, because we aren't gonna make it otherwise!"

He reached over and broke off his M-60 ammo belt, then kicked his nearly full ammunition box out the cabin door. Sinor and Kauffman ripped off their chicken plates and threw them out on the ground beside the ship. But it didn't help. We were still stuck.

I tore my eyes off the instruments long enough to see that Three Four had finished his second firing run and was headed out. By then the enemy troops had recovered from Paul's last rocket rounds and were rushing toward us. We could see them coming at us. But we couldn't shoot. My minigun was pointed in the wrong direction, and we'd just thrown Parker's M-60 ammo overboard.

I looked back at the instruments. Everything was passing through the yellow arcs and climbing toward the red lines. Screw it! If I don't get this bird out of here now, I ain't gonna get it out of here . . . ever! I applied all the collective that was left, beyond the governor and as high as it would go, then started pushing the cyclic stick forward and back. Maybe rocking the skids back and forth lengthwise would dislodge them.

Pilots are very sensitive about not exceeding the operating limits of an aircraft. So I felt the pricks of hot sweat stab my face when I looked back at the instruments and saw that my gauges were no longer in the yellow arc. They were in the red. Not just in the red—the needles were hard up against the red pegs. I didn't know what was keeping the OH-6 engine from blowing itself up.

As I pulled up harder on the collective, I sensed that the aircraft might have moved up a slight bit. I continued rocking the cyclic, pleading, "For God's sake, hold together, engine. Don't quit on me now. Please . . . *please* get us out of here!"

Suddenly I heard a loud, slurping, suction sound. Then all at once the ship broke loose and popped out of the mud. Under all that power, it literally catapulted fifty to sixty feet in the air, as though we had been shot out of a cannon.

"We're out!" I yelled. I kicked hard left pedal and yanked the cyclic over. Responding instantly, the bird went into a tight climbing left-hand turn to put my tail to the enemy.

Grins broke out all around. Kauffman reached over and gave me a grateful swat on the helmet. "Hey, man . . . all right! We did it . . . we're out!"

We all looked back at the little clearing where we had been just seconds before. Charlie had overrun the spot and his AK rounds trailed us as we squirted away.

Thinking that he had successfully cheated the hangman, Kauffman added his personal gesture of triumph to the moment. He leaned out the door, presented a stiff middle finger to the enemy, and yelled, "And fuck you, too!"

The brief celebration ended for me as I lowered the power on the engine and saw that my torque and TOT needles were still tight against the red pegs. That told me for sure. I had flat-out lunched the engine. God only knew how much power I was pulling when the OH-6A finally popped loose and lifted out of the mud. The army allowed you to operate—if necessary—up to thirty minutes in the yellow arc. But even in an emergency, the pilot was never to exceed five to ten seconds with indicators in the red. I wondered what the army would do to a pilot who had destroyed a $20,000 engine.

To hell with that, I thought. The amazing thing was that we were out of there, and the engine was still running, still carrying four heavy people back home to Phu Loi. And with the needles *still* in the red.

When everybody was home safe and sound, we learned that Two Six had put the ARPs down in the contact area and secured Sinor's airplane. Sidewinder had put in the fast movers, planting a lot of heavy ordnance on Charlie, chasing him out of the area. Pipe Smoke then went in and lifted out Sinor's crippled bird.

The Hughes tech rep examined my OH-6 with a fine-toothed comb, and he couldn't believe what he found under the engine cowling doors. Every piece of machinery in the hot end of the engine was burned to a crisp! He couldn't figure out how that engine continued to run without blowing up. Neither could I.

But it took Kauffman to provide the last word for the day. He came over to talk to me after we had set down at home plate. "Well, goddamnit, One Six, one thing you can be sure about. It'll be a long, cold day in hell before I ever fly around lima lima again behind a friggin' scout ship!"

CHAPTER 11

ENGINE OUT

Once in a while the Outcasts would catch a mission up on the Saigon River. On 22 August, Dean Sinor and I were assigned the VR-1 flight to recon a section of the Big Blue. The area started down around the Mushroom and FSB Tennessee, then went on up northwest to the outskirts of the village of Dau Tieng. Troop ops had briefed us that division was experiencing an increase in the enemy sampans infiltrating down the Saigon in that area. The sampans were known to be carrying soldiers and supplies downriver to support enemy operations against us in the northwest Trapezoid.

Our job was to put early morning aerial scout cover over the navy riverine and 1st Division engineer boats, to help them search out unauthorized river traffic and, more specifically, to track the ground movements of any bad guys who might have come ashore from enemy sampans. Along that stretch of the Big Blue, there were no settlements or villages, so no Vietnamese civilians should be out on the river. Also, no friendly military troops were authorized to travel the river between the Mushroom and Dau Tieng. Therefore, any craft or people discovered on or in the water, except our riverine boats on patrol, were immediately considered to be unfriendly.

None of the infiltrating enemy sampans risked traveling on the river during daylight hours. This would have exposed them to observation either by our aerial scouts or friendly ground troops. So the enemy moved on the river at night. By day they tied up, carefully camouflaged their sampans, then moved into the heavy foliage near the river.

Sinor and I left Phu Loi at about 5 A.M. It was still dark as we passed over the Iron Triangle en route to our search starting point near FSB Tennessee. From the air, Vietnam at night looked black and desolate, since the countryside was mostly without electricity. Therefore, the terrain below was totally unrecognizable.

The early morning, however, was always the best time for our aerial reconnaissance missions. The smoke and haze had cleared from the air and we could see much better.

As Sinor and I flew along at altitude, I lit another cigarette and decided that it was going to be a fine morning for checking Charlie on the river and seeing what mischief he might be up to. I didn't realize, watching that fine dawn, that I would still be along the Saigon River some sixteen hours later, watching the darkness envelop us again—from the ground.

Several U.S. fire support bases were strung along the eastern side of the Saigon in the area we were going to work: Junction City and Aachen were just downriver from the Mushroom, Tennessee was located right in the stem of the Mushroom, and Mahone (known after 14 September 1969 as FSB Kien, honoring ARVN Lt. Col. Thein Ta Kien, KIA) was situated upriver and located at the edge of a large rubber plantation just southeast of Dau Tieng. Troop ops had instructed me to drop out of altitude and pick up the river at the Mushroom, then move my search pattern to the northwest along the Saigon, checking out both banks and tributaries as I went, as well as creating a search corridor about four to five kilometers wide on the east side of the river.

As Sinor and I neared the Mushroom, I radioed him. "Hey, Thirty-one, will you be able to see me down there? It's still pretty dark."

"I think it will be OK, One Six," Sinor answered. "But if I can't track you when you get down, you can always turn on your anticollision lights."

Before heading down, I needed to set the shoot-not shoot guidelines for the day with Parker. I came up on the intercom. "We're ready to go lima lima . . . standard rules, Jimbo—if you see anything that looks like it's hostile, and it checks hostile, go ahead and open up, then we'll deal with it from there. Any questions?"

"Nope," Parker answered. "Let 'er rip, Lieutenant."

I kicked the ship over into a descending right-hand spiral. The drop-down put me at treetop level right in the middle of the Mushroom. I could see some small cooking fires and a few lights within fire support base Tennessee. Our guys were just beginning to crank up for the day. They waved as Parker and I zipped over the base at about thirty feet and seventy knots. Then I pulled an easy right turn that headed me back to the northwest, to a point on the Big Blue where the river began to form the western outline of the Mushroom. That's where I would begin my scouting orbits. At this point, also, Highway 14 snugged up close on the east side of the river. That gave me the opportunity to set up my scout pattern to sweep as far as the west riverbank on one end, then east past Highway 14 and two to three kilometers into the countryside beyond.

As the day brightened and we started our sweeps, the river was quiet. Moving our orbits farther north toward a fairly sharp bend in the river, we saw a pair of American boats pulled up tight against the west bank, just downstream from the bend. One boat was a navy patrol boat, riverine (PBR), working upriver from its base at Phu Cuong. The other was what we called a Swift boat. Larger than the PBR, it was reminiscent of an old Louisiana oil field construction boat. Both types of craft were jet propelled, had a shallow draft, and carried plenty of weapons. In addition, they were outfitted with Starlight Scopes and searchlights for operating along the river at night.

The two boats were situated so they could intercept any craft coming downriver around the bend. They had probably been stationed there most of the night, watching and waiting for anything on the river that tried to run the curfew.

We waved and the boat crewmen waved back. I moved our orbits to the north and lamented that so far we hadn't spotted a thing on or near the river.

As the Saigon snaked along under us toward the northwest, I noticed a small tributary (Rach Suoi) that emptied into the Big Blue. The stream was on the west bank of the river and headed off to the northwest into the 25th Division area of operations. Though technically the junction of the Rach Suoi and the Song Saigon was not in the 1st Division territory, boundary responsibility was, out of necessity, a little loose. The two divisions frequently worked back and forth with artillery and whatever other means were necessary to cover each other, and to keep Charlie from operating more freely at a point where U.S. tactical unit operations were split. So I lengthened the western swing of my orbit to take a look around this area. It paid off immediately.

As we dropped in low over the north bank of the tributary, both Parker and I spotted a group of sampans tied up not more than fifty meters back from where the two rivers joined. The vegetation was extremely heavy and grew right down to the riverbank. But we could still see the shapes of several sampans huddled in a niche of the shoreline and carefully covered with fresh nipa palm branches.

No people were around, though. I headed off over the tree line and searched in vain for several minutes. There were no signs of trails, camp fires, or bunkers—nothing that told us where the people from the sampans had gone.

But at least we had found six enemy boats, and it was time to go back and deal with them.

I keyed Parker on the intercom. "I don't want to waste the time or ammo trying to bust those boats with the M-60. Grab your M-79 and I'll hover over near the sampans while you thump 'em off with grenade rounds."

Parker reached under his jump seat where he stowed the 40mm M-79, and loaded up. I came in slowly, keeping the moored sampans about forty feet from my right door. As I came to a dead hover, I heard the first high-pitched c-r-u-m-p erupt from the back cabin. Then another . . . another . . . and then three more times. Six shots from Parker's grenade launcher, and six enemy sampans quickly settled to the muddy bottom of the Rach Suoi River. I looked over my right shoulder and gave Parker a sharp thumbs-up.

Circling back to the Saigon, we resumed our regular east–west search pattern. We saw no river traffic or signs of enemy activity ashore. It began to look as though six sampans would be our score for the day.

Finally, another seven kilometers up the river, we came to another tributary. This one took off north from the east bank of the Big Blue. Tom Chambers, my Cobra front-seater who read the maps, told me that this little stream was called Rach Can Nom. Since we had had some luck in the other tributary, I pulled in over Rach Can Nom at treetop level, looking for another jackpot.

But there was nothing doing. After a few orbits, I thought about canning the operation and heading back to the Saigon. Before doing that, however, I decided to move a little farther upstream and make a couple of patterns beyond the point where the tributary passed under the Highway 14 bridge. The stream turned back east right about there and passed by the little village of Ben Chui on the south and a large rubber plantation on the north. Just beyond the rubber trees to the north was our fire support base Mahone (Kien).

As I passed over the Highway 14 bridge, I was startled to see six more sampans and a motorized junk pulled up against the north bank. I keyed Parker. "Damn! Did you see that?"

"What do you suppose we got, Lieutenant?"

"That motorized junk must be thirty-five feet long, Jimbo—a hell of a good-sized riverboat to just be out on a little pleasure cruise. You can bet it's not friendly, and neither are the people who brought it in here."

Convinced that we had uncovered something pretty heavy, I radioed Sinor in the Cobra. "Bingo, Three One. We just found a small navy down here. We've got at least a thirty-five-foot inboard-outboard motorized junk, supported by six more sampans. They're pulled up on the north bank just beyond the bridge. I'm damned sure there's a whole lot of stuff down here, and it doesn't look friendly."

"See any people, One Six?"

"No people right around the boats, Three One. . . . Haven't had a chance to look around yet, but there's got to be a whole lot of bad guys on the ground near these boats. I recommend that you go ahead and roll the ARPs. Let's get 'em started out here because the hair on the back of my neck is telling me that there's trouble brewin'."

It was about 0610 by then. An ARP scramble that early in the morning might catch the troop before the lift Hueys had even been hovered out of their revetments. Once that loudspeaker blared "scramble," I knew that the ARPs would be on their way out in short order.

Since we had a few minutes to wait for the ARPs, I told Sinor that I was going to head up toward FSB Mahone and look around. Mahone was just a few hundred meters over the rubber trees to the north.

I left the river and took up tree-level orbits right over the plantation. Parker and I peered down into the trees, looking for any signs of the people from the boats.

Suddenly Parker came on the intercom. "I didn't shoot, sir, but we got bad guys under us."

I broke hard right to pull the Loach away from the spot. "What have you got?"

"There are bad guys under us in the rubber. They've got camouflage capes on their backs, and as we went over they ran east. I'm positive I saw 'em."

"OK, we're going back and take another look."

As I whipped a hard one-eighty, I remembered something that other aeroscouts had taught me earlier, something that had held true through my own scouting experience. When discovered in the field, the bad guys had a tendency to run for cover at the base of the largest, tallest tree in the area. Then they'd stay put until the danger was past.

With that little piece of G-2 in my mind, I returned to the spot where Parker had reported seeing the people. Then I decelerated and hovered over the biggest tree I could find. I looked down the trunk to the ground and there were four VC faces staring directly up at me. I jerked an armful of collective. The tail jumped up and the nose dipped as I hauled out.

Parker yelled, "You see 'em? You see 'em?"

"I see 'em. Did you see any weapons? They didn't shoot."

"I couldn't tell, it was too quick. I don't think I saw any guns," Parker answered.

My VHF blared as Sinor came up. "What's going on, One Six? I saw your tail kick . . . you OK?"

"Bad guys, Three One. We've got four enemy troops at the base of that tall tree. They didn't shoot. I'm going back in to check it again."

It didn't occur to me that I may have found just the tip of the iceberg. That motorized junk and the half dozen or so sampans on the riverbank should have instantly told me that a lot of people could have landed from those boats. More than the four VC at the base of that tree.

But in the urgency of the moment, I didn't think about that. I keyed Parker. "OK, Jimbo, we're going back in. I'm going to slow down so we can check it out. Be ready with your M-60 because I'm going to see if I can get them to make a move."

Keeping an eye on the tall tree, I decelerated and slid the ship into a hover on its right side just over the top branches. Then I looked down the tree trunk to see if the four brown faces were still there. They were, and obviously more frustrated this time by my second interruption to their scheduled morning activities. All four whipped up their AKs and opened up. Parker's M-60 chattered back instantly. I saw his rounds hit and people fall.

Then fire erupted from the entire rubber plantation. It looked like a hundred or more muzzle flashes, all aimed at me. So that's where all the people from those boats were.

I jerked the Loach up again. It was a wonder I didn't yank the collective right out of its socket. As the little bird instantly responded, I shouted to Sinor, "We're taking fire from directly beneath us . . . from our six o'clock now, mark, mark. They're in the rubber . . . hit the rubber. Shit! . . . there must be a hundred or more in there . . . hit the rubber!"

"Saw you kick it, One Six. We're rolling," Sinor answered.

I looked over my right shoulder to see if Parker was OK. He was hanging outside the aircraft, shooting his M-60 down under the tail boom. Then I looked for the Cobra. Sinor had already completed his first run on the target and was peeling away from the rubber to come around again for another pass.

He came back on the radio, "How many people down there, One Six? Are you hit? Are you OK?"

"I can't tell if we took any hits, so we must be OK. There are at least fifty to a hundred bad guys down there in the rubber."

"We concur, One Six," Three One came back. "We saw at least that many muzzle flashes."

"You know what I'm thinking, Thirty-one? We've got an awful lot of unfriendly people down there, and I think we better put a cap on them to keep them from moving any farther north. I'll bet they're heading on up to pay a little surprise visit on Mahone."

"Roger that," Sinor acknowledged. "If we don't put a collar on 'em, they'll didi the area."

"Right, Thirty-one. We need to hold them in the rubber until the ARPs can get on the ground; otherwise, we'll never find them all together again."

"OK, One Six," Sinor said, "I'll call the guys at Mahone and tell them that they've got some uninvited guests coming up on 'em from the south. I suspect my rockets have already woken them up."

Putting a cap on the area meant that the scout got down as low as he could, repeating fast orbits, and doing all he could to not allow the enemy to slip out of the noose. As I started that tactic, I heard Sinor radio FSB Mahone to bring them up to speed on what we had found.

"Fearless Seven Seven," he called, "this is Darkhorse Three One. You've got an estimated fifty to one hundred enemy troops in the rubber to your southeast, presumably moving northwest on your location. Do you have observation posts or ambush patrols out in that area? If not, we're calling in Dau Tieng arty to do some shooting in the plantation."

"OK, Darkhorse Three One, this is Fearless Seven Seven. We have no friendlies in the rubber . . . no friendlies outside the base in that area. It's a go on Delta Tango arty."

With that, we headed for altitude and Sinor radioed Red Leg to line up division artillery for the fire mission. It wasn't long before 105mm HE rounds began thundering into the rubber area, and continued pounding for almost fifteen minutes.

When the smoke and debris began to clear, I headed down again to make an assessment. At the same time, I overheard the radio conversations of the slicks that were getting off from Phu Loi—the ARPs would be on station soon.

Back down at treetop level, I saw the results of the heavy tube artillery barrage. Dirt, debris, and dust covered everything. The artillery rounds had uprooted trees, splintered the wood, and left gaping shell holes and general devastation throughout the rubber. I wondered if many enemy troops had lived through that. Some of them apparently did, because I could see numerous blood trails and drag marks through the artillery dust.

Following one of the trails, I came upon three of the enemy moving slowly through the rubber. They were dragging a couple of bodies. Although dazed from the bombardment, they raised their weapons as our ship came into view. Parker shortstopped the threat by quickly cutting them down with one sustained burst from his M-60.

I was now running low on fuel, so I radioed Sinor to scramble another scout team from Phu Loi. I had just enough gas to hang on until we got the ARPs down. They arrived a few minutes later and I put them down into an LZ about two hundred yards from the enemy boats.

Bob Davis (One Three) was my replacement scout and he came on the scene just after the ARPs landed. He fell in on my six o'clock and we flew over the area while I briefed him on the situation. That freed me up to head on over to Dau Tieng for fuel and rearming.

That refueling trip was only the first of the day. I gassed, rearmed, went back to the rubber and relieved Davis. Then he did the same. Back and forth, back and forth we went, trying to keep a tight lid on the contact area and prevent the enemy troops from escaping.

Finally, the day lapsed into very late afternoon. It was Davis's turn back at Dau Tieng while I orbited over the ARPs, covering their return to the LZ. They had assaulted

and secured the enemy boats, and the slicks were waiting
to take them back to home plate.

Suddenly on one of my circles I caught a glimpse of
movement over on the ARP's right flank. I immediately
flared that way to see what had caught my attention. It was
a group of about fifteen enemy soldiers, about forty yards
out from the ARPs and moving laterally with our rifle
platoon. They were obviously trying to make an unde-
tected escape from the rubber by moving along with the
ARPs.

The enemy hadn't seen me yet. I had moved in right on
top of the trees and was looking at them at an angle
through the treetops. I slowed, turned the ship, and
dropped the nose to put my minigun square on their column. I pulled the trigger—on through the first detent to a
full four thousand rounds a minute—and cut the full burst
right across them. Many of the soldiers were blasted down
instantly. Others dropped as I turned the Loach so
Parker's M-60 could open up.

But we weren't the only ones shooting! When we
opened up, so did about a dozen enemy right beneath us.
There were obviously more enemy soldiers in that neck of
the woods. I could feel and hear the ship taking numerous
solid hits.

As I reacted to get the ship out of there, a red flash of
light from the right side of the instrument panel caught
my eye. It was the engine-out visible warning light.
Then I heard the W-H-O-O-P . . . W-H-O-O-P . . .
W-H-O-O-P of the low RPM audio warning signal in my
headphones. That, I knew, was word from the final authority that I had lost all power in the engine. At that moment
I was about forty feet off the ground and doing maybe fifty
knots. I had just enough time to get on the radio and
shout, "One Six is hit. I've lost my engine. I'm going down
. . . I'm going down!"

My next moves were automatic. I dumped the collective
all the way to the floor, pulled the cyclic back as far as it

would go, and managed to cyclic climb to about 150 feet. With that little extra altitude I was able to enter autorotation and hope that I could get the ship down without splattering us all over the countryside.

I yelled to Parker, "Get your feet in, Jimbo, we're going down!"

Seeing an open space ahead, I aimed the ship toward an old Rome-plow cut. It was located just to the east side of Highway 14 and about three hundred yards to the southeast of fire support base Mahone. I was coming in from the north, right down the long north–south plow cut.

Quickly losing what altitude I had left, I dropped the ship down. We landed hard, but the skids took the punch; from what I could tell right away, we didn't do any more damage to the aircraft.

I sat there in the cockpit for a fleeting second, thankful that we were down. The engine was completely dead and, as I looked up through the bubble, I noticed that the rotors were hardly moving. They were dead, too.

Popping my seat belt loose, I radioed Sinor. "We're down, Three One. We're OK . . . we're exiting the aircraft."

"Roger, One Six, I'm getting the other team," came right back.

I reached down, flipped off the battery switch, and started to jump out of the aircraft. But I had forgotten to take off my helmet, let alone unplug my headset. My head jerked as I started to roll out of the ship, and the communications plug broke off the helmet.

Parker jumped out right behind me, his M-60 in hand. He trailed a long belt of ammo behind him as we ran for a little berm that had been pushed up by the Rome plow. It was only about ten feet away from the ship and offered some protection from the tree line we were facing on the east.

Dropping down behind the dirt pile, we took a quick look around. It was beginning to get dark, and that con-

cerned me. I was suddenly struck with the fear that if the
ARPs didn't get to us before dark, the bad guys might grab
us before our people could find us.

I told Parker to set up his machine gun so he could
cover the jungle in front of us, and to blast anything that
moved. I knew that the ARPs couldn't be very close to us
yet, whereas the bad guys we had just shot at were only
about sixty yards away.

Then I remembered the M-79 in the back cabin of the
bird. That would give us a little heavier firepower if the
enemy decided to rush us. I ran back to the ship and
grabbed the grenade launcher and a bandolier of ammunition. No sooner did I get back to the dirt pile when I heard
a burst of AK-47 fire coming from my left front at about
sixty to eighty yards. The rounds cracked as they went over
our heads and we both ducked, almost burying our faces in
the reddish earth.

The bad guys obviously knew we were down and could
see our aircraft. But they probably weren't sure where the
crew was. The AK fire seemed to be aimed at our ship.

My first response was to get on my PRC-10 survival
radio and call Sinor. "Hey, Three One, we got bad guys
shooting at us down here. I know about where they are,
and I'm going to put some M-79 on 'em. Let me know
when you see the smoke from my rounds, then hit the
smoke with rockets."

"Roger," Sinor answered. "We got the ARPs moving
your way. Put some M-79 on Charlie and I'll roll on your
smoke."

I laid in several rounds of 40mm in the direction I
thought the enemy fire had come from. On their detona-
tion Sinor rolled in from the east, put down rockets, and
broke to roll in again. He blasted the target area two more
times before the ARPs got close. Then he told me that I
could expect to see their slicks hovering in right at our six
o'clock on Highway 14 at any moment.

By now it was almost completely dark. I could see the

interior lights of the slicks coming up the highway. Then the rifle platoon was on the ground. They moved right on through our dirt pile position and set up a defensive perimeter in front of us.

I was thinking about what a long day this was turning out to be, when Bob Harris walked up. "How bad is the ship, One Six?"

"Not too bad," I answered. "I got a round through the engine, but if Three One can get Pipe Smoke in here, we can still get the ship out of here tonight. I sure as hell don't want to spend the night out here!"

While we were waiting for the maintenance chopper, Parker popped the Loach's blades and we took all our gear out of the ship.

In about thirty minutes the aircraft recovery unit from the maintenance unit came hovering in. It was a Huey, which had enough muscle power to lift out a scout bird. As the Huey hovered over the Loach, a rigger was dropped to put a canvas rigging around the top of the aircraft. Then the rigger hooked the OH-6 onto the end of a cable and motioned for the Huey to lift the little bird up and out.

With our ship gone, Parker and I loaded aboard one of the slicks for the ride back to Phu Loi. On the way back, my head bobbed as I fought off exhaustion. I realized that we had ended the day in the dark. The guys back at the base are probably wondering what happened to us, I thought.

When we landed back at Phu Loi, I stopped in at operations. I found out that the last sixteen hours had been worth it. We had jumped a battalion-sized force in the rubber, and they had come in by boats for the specific purpose of launching a surprise attack on the southern flank of FSB Mahone. But the enemy had been contained, Mahone had been alerted in time to react, and Charlie's whole show was flushed down the tube.

I was feeling pretty good as I finished up in ops and walked over to the hootch. When I pushed open the door,

I expected someone to say, "Hey, man. How in the hell ya' doin? We were beginning to worry about you."

Instead, I found my hootch mates huddled together, playing poker. They hardly glanced up. One of them, between reaching for his pack of cigarettes and dealing the cards, finally looked over at me. "Hey, boss, hear you screwed up another Loach today!"

CHAPTER 12

HOTDOGGIN' IT

During July, August, and September, the Outcasts were training some new Loach pilots from B Company of the 1st Aviation Battalion. Their outfit was located across the base area from us at Phu Loi.

The Bravo Company guys operated a platoon of attack helicopters called the Rebels, used primarily in general support of the division; a platoon of Hueys called the Longhorns, which provided the division's command and control aircraft work; and a platoon of OH-6s called the Ponies, which flew the division ATO on liaison missions. The 1st Aviation Battalion commander, Colonel Allen, had the idea that in order to maximize use of all the helicopters in B Company beyond just general divisional support, he would get their crews trained to act also as hunter-killer teams like those in D Troop.

That's where the Outcasts came in. It became our duty to take the Pony pilots and train them as scouts. The first one we worked with was Pony One Six, their platoon leader.

Colonel Allen's idea of getting more air cavalry assets in the field was a good one for several reasons. The first was that Outcast scout crews were flying 130 or more combat hours a month and were still not covering all the ground.

Plus, our scout platoon was never up to its full complement of pilots. So the prospect of having more qualified
aeroscouts in the air was welcomed. Bravo Company had
pilots who had already been in country for six to eight
months, they were flying the same types of aircraft we had
in D Troop, and they were operating over much the same
Vietnam countryside. We all, therefore, were enthusiastic
about the cross-training of 1st Aviation Battalion pilots to
Darkhorse tactics. Creation of a new mini-cav "Light-
horse" organization promised to put even more pressure
on the enemy in the field.

Overall, the scout pilot training went fine. There were a
few areas of disagreement, however. Even though their
pilots were experienced in the OH-6 aircraft, normal liaison missions for the 1st Aviation Battalion were generally
flown at altitude, fifteen hundred feet or more. Pony pilots
simply weren't used to flying on the deck, down low and
slow, where the working aeroscout spent most of his time.
And there was sometimes a reluctance from the guys from
B Company to accept our combat scout tactics.

For instance, while out on recon, if a Pony pilot discovered a ground object, such as a bunker, he would rein up,
hover in circles around the point of interest, and study the
situation. It was not even uncommon for him to come to a
dead hover over the scene while he examined his find. Of
course, an experienced scout knew that that kind of flying
could get you killed . . . in a hurry.

On every occasion, we tried to impress on the Pony pilots—DON'T hover, DON'T return to the target area
twice from the same direction or at the same speed, and
DON'T give Charlie the chance to anticipate your movement, or lack of it, or he will set you and shoot you out of
the sky. That advice came from the aeroscout school of
hard knocks.

Either forgetting or choosing not to follow that advice,
Pony One Six took a dose of enemy AK medicine and was
shot down on 23 August 1969. "Red" Hayes, one of our

experienced Outcast crew chiefs, was flying with Pony One
Six that day. Phil Carriss (Darkhorse Three Eight), a very
experienced Cobra driver, was his gun. While searching an
area that showed some fresh traffic, Pony One Six became
more or less fixated on a particular detail that he was
studying below. Hayes became concerned and spoke to his
pilot over the intercom. "Sir, don't slow down. We're getting too slow, sir . . . we're getting too slow."

Pony One Six's scouting technique, however, had not
developed enough at that point to quickly identify what he
had on the ground. So he felt that he must slow down and
stay in the area long enough to read the signs. It was his
misfortune. His slow, lazy, easy-to-figure-out circles made
him an easy target for the enemy gunners. Charlie's
rounds came up in a fury.

The Pony platoon leader took one bullet through the
leg. Another enemy round bit into the fuel line of his
OH-6. The engine quit and the Loach went down in a
sheet of flames fed by the spewing jet fuel.

Carriss, in the Cobra above, was shocked to see his
scout suddenly engulfed in flames and heading for impact
in a tree line below. He called Phu Loi for assistance, then
went down dangerously low to circle the area and try to
determine if the crew had survived.

Three Eight couldn't tell whether anybody in the burning wreck was still alive, so he had a real dilemma: wait for
the scrambled scout team to arrive and get to the wreck,
or take the terrible risk of landing his own Cobra. One
thing was for sure: somebody had to get to the downed
Loach in a hurry. If the crew didn't get out within seconds,
the flames would have them.

Realizing that the scrambled scout team from Phu Loi
was still ten to fifteen minutes away, Carriss made a quick
and gutsy decision. He decided to put his Cobra down in a
rice paddy near the crash and send his front-seater, Jon
Gregory, through the tree line to try and get the scout

crew out of the ship and bring any survivors back to the clearing, where they could be extracted.

Carriss eased his big, heavy bird down into the water of the rice paddy. As the Cobra's skids settled onto the bottom, Jon threw back his front canopy and jumped down into the foul water. He immediately went ass-deep into the muck, while Carriss's rotor wash drove him like a nail even deeper.

With his pistol held above his head to keep it dry, Gregory struggled through the rice paddy water. By the time he reached the bank of the paddy and hauled himself ashore near the tree line, Carriss had lifted off again to cover the people on the ground. With the front seat now vacant, all Carriss could do was throw the override switch for the M-28 gun turret, lock it into a straight-ahead position, and make low-level firing passes to deter any enemy drawn to the crash site.

As anybody in his right mind would have been, Gregory was scared. Cobra crews didn't make a practice of being out of their aircraft and alone on the ground in hostile territory. But as he ran through the trees, slowed by his wet and foul-smelling flight suit, his thoughts were on getting to the burning wreck and helping Hayes and Pony One Six.

When he got there, the ship was still flaming, but the crew was nowhere to be seen. "Thank God," Gregory mumbled to himself. "But where in the hell are they?"

Then he spotted Hayes about fifty feet away—on his feet but doubled over and holding his groin. Pony One Six was on the ground trying to nurse his wounded leg. Hayes was obviously in pain. When the Loach hit the ground at about 2 g's, the impact had shoved the shoulder stock extension of his M-60 machine gun up into his crotch.

Finally, Gregory was able to lead both injured men back to the edge of the clearing to await assistance.

At that moment, Carriss was still trying to cover the friendlies on the ground with his firing runs, but he had no idea how Gregory was faring or whether he had found anybody alive in the crash.

Just then, the scrambled scout team arrived on the scene. The new Cobra went to work shooting with Carriss while Joe Vad (Nine) dropped his Loach down to the tree line to look for Gregory. Niner soon spotted the three men waiting at the edge of the clearing. He could see that the Pony platoon leader was wounded and that Hayes was bent over in agony. Gregory was frantically waving and jumping up and down to make sure that Vad saw them.

What to do next was answered rather quickly. Both Koranda (Three Nine) and Carriss had begun to take ground fire on their firing passes. They had to get back up to altitude fast or risk the danger of having their Cobras shot out from under them. Besides, a snake didn't have room to carry anybody except a pilot and gunner. This meant that Joe Vad, in his scout ship, would have to go in and pick up Gregory, Hayes, and Pony One Six.

For a split second, Vad pondered the fact that there were three men on the ground and two already in his bird. Besides all that potential weight, he was just fresh out of base and was still carrying a full load of fuel and ammo. Another impossible job for the incredible little OH-6.

In order to quickly lighten his ship, Vad hovered directly over the guys on the ground and began to expend minigun ammunition. He kicked left and right pedal and arbitrarily sprayed fifteen hundred rounds of 7.62 into the countryside. Niner's crew chief began emptying his box of belts with long, chattering bursts from his M-60. He couldn't just dump his machine gun ammunition out the door because the enemy looked for that kind of stuff, and when they found it they cleaned it up and shot it right back at you.

With the weight of the minigun and M-60 ammo gone, Vad dropped down into the rice paddy and the three men jumped into the water and started wading toward the ship. Two of the guys climbed into the back cabin with the crew chief, the other in the front left with Vad. With the additional weight, the skinny, thin-skidded scout bird began to settle fast into the slimy mud of the rice paddy.

Wanting to haul ass before the Loach sank in too far, Vad poured on the coal. But the ship didn't move; it was held down tight by the suction of the mud.

Thinking much clearer than I had when faced with the same problem just days before, Vad immediately yelled for everybody to throw their chicken plate armor and everything else possible out of the aircraft. Then he pulled an armpit full of collective, which immediately freed the plane and sent it to a hover a good fifty feet above the surface of the rice paddy.

When everybody was back at the base, the score was added up. Pony One Six was only lightly wounded and soon recovered. Hayes limped around the area for a few days, favoring that part of his body that took the full impact of the M-60 shoulder stock. Jon Gregory earned and received the Bronze Star with "V" device for his ground actions. Phil Carriss and Joe Vad were each awarded the Distinguished Flying Cross as the key players in the rescue.

I was proud of the way the Darkhorse guys reacted to the situation and were able to successfully extract the people on the ground. It was a dangerous area flush with enemy troops.

But I must admit that I was less than happy with Pony One Six. He had, in my estimation, pretty much brought the situation on himself. Obviously, every scout ran the risk of getting shot down every time he took off on a combat mission. But he should always do everything he could to try and avoid it. That was the bone I had to pick with the Pony platoon leader.

After finding out that his leg wound was minor and that he was feeling OK, I went to talk to him. I didn't pull any punches. I strongly emphasized what the experienced Darkhorse scouts had been telling them all along: You just cannot hover. You cannot make a lot of slow orbits over a target just looking! The *experienced* pilots who do those things are hanging it out; the *inexperienced* pilots who do those things are asking to get themselves, and their crew chiefs, killed.

"You've got to impress on your people to start fast, stay fast, and come back in from different directions and at different speeds," I told him. "As your ability to read sign improves, you'll begin to discover that you won't have to make so many orbits over a target. You'll see more in a single fast pass than you will in three or four slow orbits. But if you don't live to reach that degree of maturity, it's not going to make any difference to you anyway. Do you read?"

The place to let off a little steam—in fact, the total social life for the officers in D Troop—was the officers' mess, or the O club, as we called it. We took our lunch and supper there, drank there, saw movies there, played "Liar's Dice" there, and shot a lot of bullshit there.

Social activities usually got started at about 1600 or 1700, when everybody began to gather for some drinks and a few throws of the dice. Then we'd sit down for a usual night's dinner of roast beef, wax beans, and Jell-O (which was sometimes laced with pimiento bits and diced raw onion).

Following supper, it was generally back to the bar for another drink and a few more rounds of Liar's Dice while we waited for dark and the movie to begin. Then, after the movie, somewhere around 2100, most of the guys went back to their hootches and hit the sack. Those 0330 calls to get ready for first light VRs separated the social from the hard drinkers. Those who stayed after the movie for more drinks usually closed up the club at midnight.

One evening a few of us decided to socialize for a while after the movie. We were soon joined by a couple of new lieutenants from the 82d Airborne. Just south of us and across a ditch from our base was the 82d Airborne Division Replacement Station. New 82d troops came here before going to the field, and those in the field came back here for stand-down and R and R.

The 82d guys would sometimes come over into our area to do a little hell raising—fire their weapons at our buildings, throw CS gas grenades into our showers, disrupt our movies. We took their horseplay in a friendly spirit, mainly because some of our guys occasionally made "shopping" trips over to the 82d side of the ditch. It was funny how some of the things desperately needed in D Troop were in abundant supply over in the 82d. So we got along swell, and even welcomed 82d Airborne officers to our O club to socialize.

On this night a couple of young, new, in-country 82d officers walked into the club and sat down at the bar between Bill Jones (One Eight) and me. After a few minutes, Jones (as drunk as I ever saw him) and I began getting on these two lieutenants because they were decked out as though they were ready to stand a stateside general inspection. They were all dressed up in their greens and jump boots, with a second lieutenant bar shining like a beacon on each shoulder. They had Airborne and Ranger patches all neatly sewn on. In short, they were a sight to behold at a combat base in the middle of Vietnam.

About that time, Joe Vad wandered by. He took one look at these two bright and shiny objects and decided they deserved a friendly verbal shot across the bow.

"My God," he said to them, "you guys look like real snake-eating killers. Do you airborne soldiers really eat live snakes?"

To which one of the lieutenants replied, "You're damned right! We're airborne Rangers, and one of the lesser things we do is eat real live snakes."

That kind of bantering kept going back and forth, with our two airborne guests extolling how tough and combatwise they both were. We egged them on, knowing that neither of them had ever been out of the replacement station.

While this was going on, Bill Jones just sat there on his barstool, drinking away. Vad and I didn't even think he was paying attention, because his eyes would close once in a while, his head would nod, and his elbow would periodically slip off the bar.

Then suddenly old One Eight came to life. He quietly slid off the barstool and disappeared out the front door of the club. We thought he had reached his limit and was heading back to the hootch to hit the sack.

In about five minutes, however, Jones was back. He remounted his barstool, turned to the two green lieutenants, and slurred, "Are you guys really snake-eaters? I mean, do you fierce, hard-hearted airborne soldiers really eat live snakes?"

They smirked at each other. "You got it, man. You're fuckin' A we do!"

"Well then," Jones mumbled, "I couldn't find a snake, but what about this toad frog? Can you eat this poor, little ole toad frog, caught fresh just now out in the perimeter of Vietnam's famous Quarter Cav aeroscouts?"

Jones pulled a huge toad out of his fatigue jacket and plopped the bug-eyed, wiggling thing down on top of the bar. Vad broke into a crazy laugh, and I just sat there staring at that struggling mass of croaking warts and ugliness. Apparently, Jones, rousing himself from his alcoholic lethargy, was determined to put our two airborne lieutenants to the acid test.

Eyeing the by-now ill-humored toad, the two hot RLOs (real live officers) saw their masculinity threatened. Even so, they didn't want anything to do with the kicking creature that Jones was holding down on the bar. After a couple of quick glances at each other and at the toad, they began to allow that maybe they really weren't snake-eaters, that they didn't have to put up with that kind of chicken shit.

By then, however, all the Darkhorse warrants still in the club had gathered around the bar and weren't going to let those two hotshot RLOs off the hook.

The taunting went on until one of the lieutenants, finally feeling that he had to defend the honor of the airborne, grabbed the toad and began trying to get it into his mouth. The lieutenant closed his eyes, opened his mouth as big as he could, and tried to stuff the creature down his throat. The toad was kicking and croaking and making a hell of a fuss.

Every time the lieutenant would just about get the toad's body inside his mouth, he'd gag and retch and throw the thing back up on the bar. We'd grab the regurgitated toad and christen it "airborne qualified" by lifting it up to arm's length and dropping it back on the bar. Then, pouring some beer on the bartop, we'd slide the toad along through the foam and duly pronounce the poor thing "carrier qualified."

After all this foolishness, I finally said to the lieutenants, "You guys can quit trying to shit us now. You obviously can't hack it!"

That inspired one of the jump troopers to try again to get the now-slimy toad down his throat. He had gotten it about halfway down when the toad hitched his legs and let out a thunderous croak. Back out it came, with the bewildered lieutenant leaning against the bar dry-heaving.

Now Bill Jones, in his obviously inebriated state, shifted himself on his barstool, looked the lieutenants in the eyes, and announced: "You know, I don't think you guys are snake-eaters at all. Let me show you what a real Darkhorse aeroscout can do."

With that, Jones picked up the toad, threw back his head, dropped in the creature and, in one gargantuan gulp, swallowed it down whole!

The two lieutenants looked at each other in total disbelief. They began to turn green. Then they both raced out the front door and began heaving.

Jones's eyes were bugged out and he had a funny look on his face. As soon as the two lieutenants were out the front door, he immediately took off for the back door. Once outside, he began making violent groaning noises. Then he coughed, gagged, and retched until, finally, he heaved up the still-struggling toad. As the dazed toad limped away, our equally dazed aeroscout returned to the bar and ordered up another drink. We never saw the two airborne lieutenants again.

Wednesday, 26 August, was the start of a three-day series of events that culminated with a most unusual combat engagement.

During that time most of our scouting operations were concentrated in the western Trapezoid—a hotbed of enemy activity. Enemy soldiers and supplies were almost constantly infiltrating south into the area from their sanctuaries behind the Cambodian border and from their intermediate staging area in a string of low mountains called the Razorbacks.

On 26 August, while looking for trails and other signs of these infiltrators, a Darkhorse scout team out on routine VR made an enemy contact up near FSB Kien. The contact appeared heavy enough that Darkhorse ops decided to alert elements of 2d Battalion, 2d Mechanized Infantry Regiment, which were then located at FSB Kien.

When the infantry (call sign Dracula) moved out to where the aeroscout had made his initial contact, our troops ran into the outskirts of a huge bunker area. At that point I went up to the contact area with my gunship to help coordinate operations.

As soon as I moved in over the enemy base camp, about four AK-47s let go at me. Things were really hot down there! Dracula had advanced to the base camp perimeter and run into a veritable buzz saw.

What we needed, and fast, was for some tac air to get fast movers and heavy stuff in there to bust up the bunkers

so our friendlies could break into the area and clean it out.
I immediately went up on the net for our FAC, who turned
out to be our Australian OV-10 driver, Sidewinder One
Five. We gave him the target information and asked specifically for any heavy stuff he might have around.

It wasn't long before Sidewinder had a brace of Martin
B-57 Canberras loaded with five-hundred-pound bombs
vectored into the area. Guided by Sidewinder's Willie Pete
rockets, they gave the base camp a hell of an iron bomb
shellacking!

When Sidewinder's jets were finally winchester, he
asked that a little bird be put back down for a BDA. I
dropped back down when the smoke and dust started to
clear. The Canberras had raised a lot of hell down there.
The bombs had blown away all the overlying jungle vegetation and I could clearly see the square outlines of the
bunker structures. It was immediately obvious that this
was a very large base camp with many bunkers, connecting
trench lines, and doughnut positions for .50-caliber anti-
aircraft guns.

I reported in as I circled the base area. "We have three
bunkers, five by five, partially destroyed. There are two
bunkers, five by seven. Looks like about 50 percent destroyed. We've got two bunkers, probably eight by eight.
One bunker ten by ten. We'll call those destroyed—the
roofs are caved in. We've got numerous small arms and
equipment spread in the area. We've got about forty feet
of trench line, looks like four, negative . . . make that
five bodies KBA. They're in the trench line."

With the BDA, we had to break station. It was beginning to get dark and fuel was low. All the time we were
doing the BDA, Drac had been moving in closer to base
camp. We wondered how much more trouble they would
run into that night.

As I climbed away, I contacted them on FM. "Dracula,
this is Darkhorse One Six. We are breaking station because of fuel and darkness. The base area has been hit

good and is pretty well opened up. You do have some KBA bodies down there. Good luck to you tonight. We'll be back on top of you first thing tomorrow morning."

We were back out at first light on 27 August. As we came up on the enemy base camp, my gun, Paul Fishman (Three Four), radioed the friendlies on the ground to report our presence and tell them we were ready to go back to work.

"Drac Three Two, this is Darkhorse Three Four. We're overhead with a hunter-killer team and I'm going to put the little bird down to do a VR for you. Is there any particular area that you want him to work?"

Dracula came back. "Negative, Darkhorse. We fought an engagement here last night until about 2400. The enemy backed off about then and we're going to try to reestablish contact this morning. So let the scout go whatever direction he wants and keep us posted on what you find. We had light casualties but we got to Charlie pretty good. Their KIA are unknown, however, because they dragged away all the bodies during the night."

As I listened to the conversation, I was looking down at Drac's night defensive position. I could see ACAVs and some supporting M-48 tanks all loggered up in a wagon wheel situation. I figured that right over them was the best place for me to go down low level; then, if I had any problem, I could put the bird down in the middle of friendlies. I dropped down to the treetop altitude and pulled a hard right-hand turn to bring me right on top of the NDP. I intended to start working concentric circles outward from our position.

As I rolled around and started outbound, I caught a glimpse of an enemy soldier's body lying on the ground face up, not more than forty yards from the tanks and ACAVs. I went back for another look. It looked like an NVA soldier in a dark, electric blue uniform, no sandals, no headgear. His brown eyes were wide open and staring right up at me. An AK-47 was beside him on the ground and he had the weapon's ammunition pouch on his chest. He had obviously been hit because I could see some wound damage to his leg and quite a bit of blood on the pant leg of his uniform.

I wondered what the heck he was doing lying out here. Why hadn't he been dragged off with the rest of the enemy wounded and dead during the night?

I got on FM and dialed up our friendlies. "Drac Three Two, this is Darkhorse One Six. Have you swept your perimeter since the firefight last night?"

"Darkhorse, this is Dracula Three Two. Roger. We have done some sweeping. Why? Have you found something?"

"Roger, Drac. I've got an enemy soldier down here. He's lying on the ground about forty yards off the backside of one of your ACAVs. Do you see where I'm circling?"

There was a moment's delay while he looked, then he came back. "Roger, Darkhorse, I see you. How about dropping a smoke on the body and we'll police it up later."

"That's negative, Dracula. This is *not* a body. This is one live NVA soldier. Looks like he's been hit in the leg but his eyes are wide open and the little son of a bitch is staring straight up at me!"

Drac must have thought that I was seeing things. "Darkhorse One Six, this is Dracula Three Two. *Confirm* the enemy soldier in our vicinity is *alive.*"

"Roger, Drac Three Two. He's alive. He's watching me. His head is moving and he looks like he's trying to wave. He appears injured and he *does* have a weapon. If you can send somebody over here on foot, I'll cover your man. Over."

"Roger, Darkhorse," Drac responded. "We'll be right there."

I came to about a forty-foot hover over the trees and keyed the intercom to Parker. "Watch that guy, Jimbo. If he moves toward his weapon, if he even *looks* like he's goin' for that weapon, blast him with the 60. We've got troops coming over here from the NDP, so watch for them, but if that bad guy moves, blast him!"

In a few minutes, an ACAV came rumbling up and a couple of our friendlies jumped out of the back. The two American troopers didn't look as though they were quite ready for combat that morning. They had on jungle fatigue pants, boots, and T-shirts. They were carrying their M-16s but didn't have any web gear on. One of our soldiers appeared to be an NCO and the other a specialist.

Because of the vegetation they couldn't see exactly where the enemy soldier was, but they could see me hovering over the trees nearby. The guys didn't have a radio, so I told Parker that I was going to guide them in with hand signals. I put the Loach over on her right side so I could see beneath me and hovered to a spot directly over the wounded enemy soldier. I steadied the collective with my knee, flew with my left hand on the cyclic, and started motioning with my right hand.

The two infantrymen finally got close enough to see the NVA lying on the jungle floor. They crept toward him, covering each other with their M-16s. I backed away to get the rotor wash and noise off them while they took him prisoner.

As I continued on with my VR, I began to hear reports on the radio about the NVA soldier. Though wounded badly by one of our .50-caliber machine guns—his leg was shattered and just barely hanging onto his body—he was hustled back to Dau Tieng for medical attention and interrogation by the 3d Brigade's S-2. The S-2 learned from the unusually cooperative prisoner that he was a member of the infamous and elusive Dong Nai Regiment. He had moved out of the Fishhook area in Cambodia with the regiment, gone on into the Michelin rubber plantation, then on down into the western Trapezoid.

The 1st Division had more bones to pick with the Dong Nai Regiment than a dog had fleas. We had been looking for that unit: We wanted desperately to know where it was, what it was doing, and what its tactical intentions were. This was the first good link to the Dong Nai's recent whereabouts and activities—an intelligence windfall. The wounded POW turned out to be a noncommissioned officer. Because of his rank, he was privy to a lot of planning and, during his debriefing, revealed considerable information about the movements and activities of the Dong Nai. Afterward, the prisoner indicated strong willingness to join our Hoi Chon program and convert to one of our Kit Carson scouts.

Back at Phu Loi that evening, I was given a mission for the next morning to fly up to 3d Brigade HQ at Dau Tieng. I was to attend a briefing by the brigade S-3 on what the POW had said, then plan some scout team VRs in the sectors that the prisoner had designated as Dong Nai Regiment operational areas.

From Phu Loi, it was a straight-shot flight up northwest to 3d Brigade HQ. The route—without artillery firing path deviations—would normally take us up over the heart of the Iron Triangle, on to the north of the Mushroom, then right on across the western edge of the Trapezoid to Dau Tieng. From my standpoint, staying at altitude always made for a boring flight, so before we got started that morning I asked my snake driver, Paul Fishman (Three Four), if he had any objection to me going down low for the course of the flight instead of camping on his wing at fifteen hundred feet. Realizing that with his scout down on the deck, there was always the chance of scaring up a little enemy activity, Fishman had no problem with my plan.

As soon as we cleared the base boundary, I flipped my weapons system to "arm" and the fire selector switch to "fire norm," then settled in for the flight at an altitude of about twenty feet off the ground. After a couple of minutes I heard Three Four check in with Lai Khe artillery. They reported that they were firing 105s into the northern area of the Iron Triangle, meaning that we would have to either detour up north around Lai Khe or head south to the Saigon River and follow it on up to Dau Tieng. Rather than go north, which was farther out of our way, Paul gave me a heading for the river. We turned west, picked up the Saigon River, and started following its general course around the southwestern edge of the Iron Triangle. I was cruising along right on top of the trees and holding airspeed at a consistent ninety knots.

I was relaxed. So was Parker. He was sitting on his little jump seat just watching the scenery go by. The collective control was resting on my left knee; I had hold of the cyclic and was flying the airplane with my left hand. With my right hand I was leisurely puffing on a cigarette. My right foot was dangling outside the cockpit door. It was another beautiful morning in sunny Vietnam.

We came up on the vicinity of our FSB Kien. It was just a few more minutes from there to Dau Tieng, and I was having so much fun that I thought I would play a little "pop-up" for the rest of the way. I dropped the bird down to an altitude of about two feet and moved the airspeed up to a hundred knots, then up to one hundred and ten. As we ripped along, I would yank back on the cyclic, which tilted the rotor disk to the rear, and pop the bird up and over the rice dikes and tree lines. Then I'd shove the cyclic stick forward again, which tilted the blades sharply forward and pushed the nose down, and drop to two feet. I was just plain hotdoggin' it, and I loved it!

My antics didn't escape my gun pilot, however. As always, Paul was carefully watching me. "Hey, One Six, what the hell are you doing down there?"

"I'm having a ball," I answered. Then I warned Parker to hang on for the next pop-up as yet another tree line loomed ahead through my bubble.

It was still early in the morning, and the semidarkness made it difficult for me to see really well. But the approaching tree line looked clear of obstacles on the other side, making it a piece of cake to pop up over the trees and then right back down again without missing a beat. I could just barely make out a rice paddy on the other side with a dike going through the middle of it. No sweat.

I closed in fast on the tree line, waited until the very last split second, then jerked back a chest full of cyclic stick. The little OH-6 jumped straight up about forty feet as though she had suddenly been kicked in the tail boom by a Missouri mule.

As we leapt up to the crest of the trees and the OH-6's nose depressed for the letdown on the other side, I looked forward through the bubble. Spread out across my front from left to right was a string of thirty NVA soldiers in column, walking on the paddy dike, taking their own sweet time.

I was moving very fast and very low, so the sound of my engine and blades was muffled by the vegetation, and my Cobra was high and too far behind me to be seen or heard. The enemy was taken completely by surprise.

When I popped up over that tree line, doing more than a hundred knots and less than thirty to forty yards off their left flank, those poor bastards were thunderstruck.

I could tell as soon as I saw the column that these guys were NVA regulars. Unlike guerrillas, they were loaded down with equipment, such as mortars, SGMs, radios, and web gear. It looked like an NVA heavy weapons platoon. They had probably scouted the open ground ahead, satisfied themselves that there was no potential danger, then started to move the whole platoon across. And at that very instant, up I bounced over the tree line, catching them bare-assed in the open with no cover and no place to run.

Snapping back from my initial shock at seeing a whole column of enemy soldiers strung out across my front, I started to look at them more carefully. My eyes focused on their point man. He was no more than thirty yards in front of me, frozen in place, staring right at me. Then he started to jerk up his weapon.

I hit my radio transmit switch and yelled, "Dinks! Dinks! They're right under me!" Then I squeezed the minigun trigger to two thousand rounds a minute. My initial blast caught the wide-eyed point man square across his belt line and literally cut him in half.

I kicked hard right pedal, held the bird's nose down, and spun around in order to bring the minigun to bear on the rest of the column. Squeezing the minigun trigger again—this time all the way back to four thousand rounds per minute—my second burst raked through the next four men. The bullets slammed them to the ground in a cloud of dust, debris, and body parts.

The paddy dike now seemed to explode as the NVA soldiers shot back at me, running every which way trying to find cover. I again broke hard right in order to bring Parker's M-60 to bear on the maze of trapped enemy in the clearing below.

He ripped off a three- to four-second burst, then keyed his intercom button. "Level out, sir. Level it out!" he yelled at me.

The right turn I was executing was so sharp that Parker couldn't fire without the risk of hitting the bird's tilted rotor blades. I slammed the cyclic stick to center, leveling out the aircraft, and instantly heard Parker's M-60 go to full bore. He had caught a group of three NVA soldiers trying to make it out of the clearing and back to the jungle. He dropped them all in their tracks.

I was pulling the ship around for another circle over the mass of enemy confusion when Three Four's voice suddenly erupted in my earphones. He was shouting, "One Six, One Six, what the hell's going on down there? What have you got? What have you got down there, One Six?"

"Dinks . . . I got dinks, lots of dinks," I blurted. "We've got 'em trapped. They're running all over the place!"

I didn't hear his reply because Parker was going crazy with his 60. Besides, I had just spotted an NVA with an AK-47 rifle running toward the jungle. Another soldier

was running in front of him and they were both hell-bent
for election.

Determined not to lose them, I pulled the bird hard
around to come up on their rear. It was then that I noticed
all the shooting that was coming up at us from the ground.
There was a constant stream of AK-47 fire, and I could
hear rounds beginning to impact the aircraft. But I was
still not going to let those two soldiers make it back into
the jungle. I pulled up to about forty yards behind them.
They knew I was on their tail and they were running for
their lives.

As I raced up the trail behind them, I noticed that one
of the soldiers had a large black rice cooking pot strapped
to the back of his pack. It was the size of a large wash
bucket and was bouncing furiously up and down as he ran.
I pulled the nose down a little, watching the bottom of the
cooking pot come into view through the cross hairs grease-
penciled in front of me on the bubble's Plexiglas. I
touched a shade of right pedal, then I pulled off a short
minigun burst.

My rounds walked right up the trail behind the last man,
then tore into the bottom of the rice pot. The man pitched
forward to the ground. So did the soldier running in front
of him. My bullets had apparently gone through the last
man and hit the soldier in front, killing them both. There
were nine enemy down in less than a minute of battle.

I jerked the bird around in a hard right turn to get back
over the main group of trapped enemy soldiers. Again,
intense ground fire poured up. We offered a pretty choice
target at only five to seven feet off the ground, and I could
hear bullets ripping and snapping all through the aircraft.
I was trying to bring my minigun to bear on Charlie again,
and Jimbo's 60 was firing in long, sustained bursts.

Things were so frantic that it took me a while to realize
that Three Four was yelling at me through the headset.
"Get out of there, One Six . . . get the hell out of there
and let me in!"

I snapped back to reality. "Roger, Three Four. One Six is out to the west."

As soon as Paul saw my tail kick up, he was rolling in and firing rockets. I could see his 2.75s impacting the rice paddy and the nearby jungle. The last pair of rockets that he fired into the swarming enemy soldiers in the clearing contained nail flechettes. From my circling position nearby, I saw the puffs of red dye explode as the nail flechette canisters blew open and saturated the whole area with thousands of naillike metal spears.

As Three Four broke from his last firing pass and headed back to altitude, I punched my transmit button: "One Six is back in from the east on BDA." I pulled back into the clearing from the east, made a couple of fast turns over the area, and discovered that there were still plenty of people moving around. They were still shooting at me, and Parker opened up again with his M-60 on everything he saw moving. I could hear more of Charlie's rounds impacting the aircraft, and I wondered how much more punishment the OH-6 could take.

Coming around again, I engaged two more enemy soldiers with the minigun and knocked them down. Continuing the turn I saw Parker's rounds splatter up the dust around two more, then slam them both to the ground.

Out of the right corner of my eye, I saw another NVA jump up from the ground and start to run toward the center of the clearing. Just as I was coming around I saw him dive into some bushes. It was a small vegetated spot, out there all by itself—the only piece of cover in the clearing.

I hit the intercom and told Parker, "Shoot into the bushes. An NVA just jumped in there. Spray the bushes . . . he's got no place to go. Get 'im!"

Parker yelled back, "I can't, sir, I'm out of ammo!"

I could hardly believe it. In several minutes, Jim had gone through thirty-two hundred rounds of M-60 ammo. "OK," I said, "I'll pull around and take him with the mini. Hang on!"

I whipped around, zeroed out airspeed, eased the nose down, and squeezed the minigun trigger back all the way to the stick. Nothing happened. It didn't shoot. All I heard was the gun motor running. I was out of ammo for the minigun.

I punched the intercom again. "I'm dry on the minigun, too, Jimbo. Do me a Willie Pete."

Parker yanked a dark lime green canister off the bulkhead wire, pulled the pin, and held the grenade outside the aircraft, ready to drop on my command.

As I came up on the man's hiding place, I keyed the intercom again. "Ready . . . drop!" The grenade sailed down right into the center of the bushes. I accelerated away just as the explosion erupted in the vegetation, sending up arms of hot-burning white phosphorus.

I called the gun immediately. "OK, Three Four, target my Willie Pete. Hit my mark, hit my mark! One Six is out."

As I headed out I glanced back at the little vegetated area. The man was running frantically out the other side of the scrub. Patches of his clothing were burning fiercely where fragments of the white phosphorus had landed on him.

He had taken about five steps when Three Four's first rockets came in. They were the last he ever took. One of Fishman's rockets impacted directly between the man's legs.

As Three Four rolled out and away from his firing pass, I got on UHF. "Good rocks, Three Four. One Six is back in. You better scramble the ARPs because I've still got *beaucoup* people moving on the ground and lots of equipment lying out in the open all over the place."

Of course, the guys back at the troop had been monitoring our transmissions, so Three Four's request was almost after the fact. The next thing I heard over the radio was, "OK, Three Four, this is Darkhorse Three. Stand by over the target area. ARPs are saddled up and about to be under way, and I've scrambled another hunter-killer team to relieve you. Stand by."

As I arced back down over the clearing, more enemy rounds came up at the airplane. I jigged and jogged, trying to keep the remaining bad guys corralled and to convince them that I still had ammunition. Parker had resorted to a backup M-16, which he promptly emptied on anything that moved. Then he hauled out a twelve-gauge Ithaca pump shotgun that he had stashed under his jump seat and shot it point-blank until it was dry.

I followed his lead and pulled my Colt .357 Python out of the shoulder holster. I was able to shoot the big revolver out the cockpit door by hooking the collective stick on top of my left leg, holding the cyclic with my right hand, while resting my left elbow on my right forearm and firing with my left hand. I'm sure I didn't hit a damned thing with the Colt, but I may have scared a few NVA to death. Every time I fired that .357, which had Super Vel Magnum cartridges in it, flames shot about a foot and a half out the muzzle and it barked like a howitzer.

As I emptied the last .357 round, I got a call from Bob Davis (One Three) telling me that he and his gun were now on station. While I was taking him on a high-speed pass of the battle area, I heard him say, "Damn!"

"What's the matter, One Three?" I jumped back at him. "What have you got . . . what the hell have you got?"

"Damn, One Six, I've got nothin', and that's the trouble. I count about twenty-two bodies down there and you guys didn't leave a thing for us!"

On the way back to Phu Loi (I never did make the meeting in Dau Tieng) I keyed the intercom and told Parker, "Let's get a red smoke rigged on your M-60 so we can let the boys back home know that we stung Charlie today."

I heard him chuckle. "Sir, the red smoke is already there." I glanced back and saw it already wired to the muzzle of his machine gun.

We made our traditional pass of the base trailing a stream of billowing red smoke. The field personnel waved and cheered us on. Hundreds of people worked on the base, and when the hunter-killer teams came back home trailing red smoke, you could hear them slapping each other on the back and yelling, "Hey, our guys did good today!"

It was a morale booster for us, too. We knew we were doing the job that we had been sent to Vietnam to do. Maybe, just maybe, we had shortened the war a few minutes or hours.

As quiet and reserved as Jim Parker was, his emotions showed as we came back into base and settled the bird down near the revetment. My emotions probably showed, too.

I cut the battery switch, then twisted around in my seat to look back at my crew chief through the open panel in the bulkhead. Jimbo broke into a broad grin and shot me a big thumbs-up. That said to me, You did good, sir. We stuck it to Charlie pretty hard today.

I nodded and smiled back, then gave him a thumbs-up. That was my way of saying, Good job yourself, Georgia farm boy. I wouldn't have survived that engagement today with any lesser man in the crew chief's cabin.

By that time, Paul Fishman had walked over to the ship. He clapped his arm around my shoulder as we walked together toward the ops bunker. "Goddamnit, Mills," he said, "you scare the shit out of me! If you don't quit mixing it up down there for as long as you have a tendency to do, you're going to get your ass shot full of holes. And I'll just be sitting up there at fifteen hundred feet watching it happen!"

I told him the truth when I answered, "I scare the shit out of myself sometimes, Pauly, and this was one of those days that I nearly scared myself to death!"

The base maintenance guys went over my OH-6 after we got back, and their report scared me even more. Altogether, about twenty to twenty-five enemy rounds had impacted the airplane. My airspeed indicator had been shot out. The altimeter had a round through it, smashing it to pieces. The armor plate under Parker's seat had been hit twice. The armor around my pilot's seat had been hit several times from the rear, indicating that enemy bullets had gone through the crew chief's compartment, missing Parker but smashing into the back of my seat armor before ricocheting somewhere else in the ship.

Also, Parker's M-60 door gun itself had caught an AK-47 round near the front sight, right between the barrel and the gas operating tube. The almost impossible hit put a neat half-moon gouge in the bottom of the barrel and blew the gas cylinder right off the gun.

Then there were four or five NVA bullet holes in the Plexiglas of the bubble, a couple more in the tail boom of the aircraft, and at least three through the rotor blades. For good measure, one AK slug had gone into one side of the engine compartment and exited on the other—completely missing any engine vital, without which we would have gone down into the middle of those thirty or so bad guys.

The way I figured it, between the NVA and our Loach, in just the 120 seconds of that battle, somewhere between eight thousand and ten thousand rounds of ammunition had been fired in a jungle clearing no bigger than half a football field. And through it all, that miraculous little OH-6 kept flying. Even more miraculous was the fact that neither Parker nor I was hit. Man . . . we both must have been living right!

That same day when the ARPs got back from their ground sweep, we found out just how much havoc we had actually caused those enemy soldiers we caught on the paddy dike. We learned that there were two POWs and twenty-six KIA—four more dead than the twenty-two bodies Bob Davis had quickly counted from the air when he relieved me. Also, ARP leader Bob Harris brought back a load of enemy weapons and equipment that his platoon had found strewn around on the ground after the fight was over. Among the recovered items were numerous late-issue AK-47 assault rifles, a 60mm mortar, a skid-mounted SGM machine gun, and two Russian handguns.

But, to me, the most interesting piece in the lot was the rice cooking pot that was strapped to the back of the soldier I caught running off into the jungle. The ARPs had found it on the jungle trail, took it off the body, and brought it back to show me the twenty-four minigun slug holes right up through the bottom of the pot!

I hit the sack that night having already been told that, for the day's action, Parker and I had been written up for the Silver Star medal (my second such award). That was a good feeling, but not half as good as also knowing that the aeroscouts had finally discovered a fair-sized element of the elusive Dong Nai Regiment.

The enemy unit that we jumped in the clearing had definitely been identified as a heavy-weapons platoon belonging to the Dong Nai. We had been hunting those bastards for a long time. Now we had found them, and stirred them up pretty good by destroying one of their crucial subunits in that jungle clearing.

After rehashing the morning's activities, I finally dropped off to sleep, knowing that I was going to be back out at first light the next morning looking to find the Dong Nai again. I wanted to help deliver the coup de grace.

CHAPTER 13

BAD DAY FOR THE ARPS

The next morning, 29 August, we went back out and searched and searched. Nothing. It looked as though, after a day of scouring, we were going to go home empty-handed. It was getting late and we had found absolutely no evidence of recent enemy activity, let alone any traces of the Dong Nai Regiment itself.

It got to be last light and I finally keyed the intercom. "It looks like a dry run, Jimbo. We've lost 'em again."

I decided to make one more run before heading home, so I pulled in low over a strip of trees that ran from southeast to northwest right near FSB Kien. Watching intently in the fading light along the edge of the tree line, I suddenly spotted people.

Coming into view low, out my right door, was a group of what could only be enemy soldiers, lying on the ground at the base of a couple of trees. They were being perfectly still, weapons resting across their chests, and they were looking straight up at me. They apparently thought that if they didn't move, I'd pass them by unseen. But they looked ready to shoot if they had to.

I punched the intercom to Parker. "Don't move a muscle . . . don't do anything. We've got *beaucoup* bad guys right below us . . . right below us in the tree line."

"I see them, Lieutenant," he came back calmly. "Looking up at us like they're waiting for us to make a move."

I jumped on Uniform to Sinor in the Cobra. "Three One, I got dinks, out my right door in the tree line now. Mark, mark. When I break, you roll."

Sinor answered, "Roger, One Six, on your right break."

."Breaking . . . NOW!" I jerked the ship hard over on her right side to get out of Sinor's way. In the split second that I put the ship into the turn, the enemy opened up on me with everything they had.

Sinor was back on Victor to me instantly. "You're taking fire, One Six . . . heavy fire, heavy fire! Break left . . . break left now."

Just as he finished his transmission, I heard a loud impact on the aircraft, and felt a sharp burning, stinging sensation in my right hip. I bent forward to look down at the cockpit floor. I didn't see anything that looked like a bullet hole. But leaning forward was painful as hell.

I continued my turn out for about five to seven seconds before I noticed that my seat was beginning to fill up with blood. "Ah, son of a bitch!" I groaned. "If I had only flown right on by them instead of making a break and settin' them off."

Then it became obvious that my body just didn't feel right from the waist down. I keyed the intercom. "Hey, Jimbo, I'm bleedin' like a stuck hog. I've been hit."

"Do you want me up front to help?" he asked.

"No," I answered, "just hang on tight. I can still fly this thing, but I don't know for how much longer. I'm going to try to put her down at Contigny."

Thank God I was close to that fire support base, because I was beginning to feel woozy. Contigny had a small helicopter landing area within the wire near the center of the complex, and I managed to put the bird down in that spot. Parker jumped out of the back, stuck his head in the cockpit, and calmly asked, "Whatcha got, Lieutenant?"

"What I got, Jimbo," I said, looking for bullet holes and rubbing my hip, "is an AK round in my ass!"

"I see what happened, sir," Parker said as he pointed to the instrument panel. There was the bullet hole I had been looking for. An AK round had come up through the instrument panel, hit the inner side plate of my seat armor, and ricocheted into my hip. After going through both cheeks of my backside, the bullet then hit the other side of my seat armor, ricocheted again, and flew back out of the airplane through the floor of the ship!

Just then a young soldier came running up to the helicopter. "What can we do for you, Lieutenant?"

"Have you got a surgeon here?" I asked.

"Yes, we do, sir. What do you need?"

I very tenderly lifted myself out of the cockpit and stood —a little wobbly—outside the aircraft. "Well, buddy, I've been shot in the butt."

A smile broke across the young infantryman's face. "But, sir, that's not a very dignified place for an officer to get shot."

"Be that as it may, Private," I fired back, "I'm still shot in the ass, and would appreciate it all to hell if you would please get the surgeon!"

The battalion surgeon just happened to be at the fire base, and it wasn't long before he came out to the helicopter carrying his little aid bag.

"Can you walk?" he asked.

"Yes," I replied, "if I don't have to move double-time anywhere."

He grabbed my arm. "Well, then, come on back over here to the aid bunker and we'll take a look at you."

Parker wanted to stay with the airplane, and I noticed that quite a little crowd of soldiers was beginning to gather around him and the ship. They were interested in looking over the OH-6 and asking Parker questions about it, but in typical Loach crew chief manner, Parker shrugged off their queries. I overhead him tell one man, "Keep your hands off . . . don't touch the fuckin' helicopter!"

But when the doctor got me over to the aid bunker and dropped my flight suit, the crowd wandered over, seeking some new entertainment. As my posterior came into open view and the doc began his examination, I began to hear a lot of one-liners followed by muffled yuks and snickers. By that time my fanny hurt so bad I didn't care.

Finally, after probing and sending spears of pain through my punctured buttocks, the doctor said, "You're awfully lucky, Lieutenant. No bones were hit. It's a through-and-through flesh wound, but you'll have a beautiful scar to show off."

Finally the doctor told me I could lift my flight suit back up, and a Dustoff was ordered to take me into Doctor Delta.

"But I don't want a Dustoff," I said. "I've got an aircraft out there on the pad and I've got to get it home. I'm sure as hell not going to leave it out here all night."

The battalion doctor stiffened at my response. "No, you're not flying! We'll take care of your gunner here tonight while Dustoff gets you to the hospital, so just go on out there and secure your helicopter."

When I told Parker what the doctor had said, his eyes got as big as dishes, then his boyish face screwed down into a hard frown. "Oh, no you don't, sir," he said to me. "If you think I'm staying out here at a fire base in these boonies, you're crazy.

"And furthermore, Lieutenant Mills," Parker continued, "I'd be awful pleased if, right now, you'd get your ass —shot up as it is—back into this airplane and take me home!"

I knew Parker was right. I turned to the medic who had helped me walk back out to the ship. "Tell the doctor thanks, but I'm going on back home to Phu Loi. I feel fine, and I'm not going to leave my crew chief and airplane out here overnight."

It was about a twenty-minute flight back to Phu Loi. The only way I made it was to roll over in the pilot's seat so I was resting on my left hip. Also, Parker sat up front with me and I let him fly to take the strain off.

But God, my ass did burn and hurt. I didn't know why it was throbbing so badly, but I *did* know what the burning was. The doc had told me that the AK-47 round that passed through my buttock was a tracer!

A few minutes out of Phu Loi I radioed ahead and made the mistake of telling operations, "I'm coming in. One Six is hit. I have been treated at FSB Contigny, but I'm going to need help getting in off the flight line. Get me some help off the line when I get down."

Unfortunately my help was Davis and Willis. I could hear Willis laughing even before I got the aircraft shut down.

"Tell me it's not true," he kept saying. "Tell me it's not true that you've been shot in the ass!"

"OK, OK, you miserable bastard," I answered. "I'm shot in the ass. Now help me get the hell out of this aircraft!"

"My God," Willis went on, "get an ambulance, call in a specialist. This is severe, this is crass. Our fearless leader has been shot in the ass!"

The next day, our troop first sergeant, Martin L. Laurent, came over to the hootch and announced, "Well, Lieutenant, you got your first Purple Heart, and the flight surgeon has grounded you for the next several days."

I realized my wound was minor, just a scrape compared to the wounds that so many other guys suffered. I was lucky. Even so, every nerve ending in my tail screamed for the next several days, reminding me that a .30-caliber tracer round through the fanny was not as much fun as Willis tried to make it.

The month of September began with Charlie getting more and more aggressive. The enemy was using the Razorback area as the staging point for their offensives, not only into the Michelin and western Trapezoid, but also to renew their attacks on our supply convoys moving up and down Thunder Road between Lai Khe and An Loc–Quan Loi.

On 4 September, Rod Willis and I were asked to fly up to Lai Khe for a G-2 briefing. It was a routine briefing to bring us up to date on what the enemy was doing in the general area of Thunder Road. We left Phu Loi for an early morning flight to Lai Khe. Our flight of two scouts and no Cobra formed a "white team."

As we passed over an open area just to the south of Lai Khe, I caught a glimpse of movement below. We were no more than three-quarters of a mile out of Lai Khe; I was surprised an enemy soldier would be messing around so close.

I radioed One Seven. "Come right on my wing. I think I've got a dink underneath me."

Willis and I skidded into a tight right-hand turning maneuver over the spot where I thought I saw movement. Sure enough, there was an enemy soldier prone on the ground, amidst a few three-foot-high bushes that made up the only possible cover in this otherwise open area. When he saw us overhead, he made the mistake of jumping up and heading toward some other nearby scrub, firing his AK-47 at us from the hip as he ran. But in this relatively open area, he really didn't have anywhere to hide.

With Rod tight on my wing, we swooped down over him at about eight to ten feet off the ground, firing short bursts from our miniguns. The enemy soldier dropped dead in his tracks.

As we headed in to Lai Khe, I got on the radio to an ARVN force that was headquartered just to the south in the village of Ben Cat. I told them about our enemy soldier and suggested that they mount a recon party with their adviser and sweep the area.

When we got the ARVN recon report later that day,

Willis and I were surprised to learn that they didn't find just one enemy soldier, but three more KIA. From the information gathered by the ARVNs at the scene, it became apparent that a group of four enemy scouts had been observing and reconning around the division fire base at Lai Khe. I saw only one of them, but the other three were nearby, and when our minigun rounds dropped the one, we got the other three without even knowing it.

The next day we were scheduled to work Thunder Road in support of the supply convoys that were running hot and heavy between Lai Khe and Quan Loi. We had learned in the briefing that enemy forces were deployed along a line from the Razorbacks north to the Parrot's Beak, with the presumed intention of moving east and hitting our Thunder I, II, III, and IV fire bases to disrupt our supply convoys.

Before first light on the fifth, and before we were even near take off time from Phu Loi for our early morning VR, just such an enemy attack was thrown against Thunder III. The fire base was located about ten kilometers north on Highway 13 from Lai Khe and was occupied by our 2/2 Mechanized Infantry soldiers. The enemy attack was very well planned and executed, and was launched at first light. Charlie was obviously aware that our aeroscouts, who probably would have detected their movement, didn't fly in the dark.

The fighting was nearly hand to hand. The situation at the base got so bad at one point that the enemy actually got through the perimeter wire and was headed with satchel charges directly for the operations bunker. The only thing that stopped him was our Zippo tracks (M113s with flamethrowers), which formed the base's interior defensive line. Zippos were not stationed on the outer perimeter of bases because they were susceptible to Charlie's RPG fire. But as the inner defense, they were devastating. And they were on this night. The sappers running for the ops bunker were burned alive as they charged directly into the nozzles spraying flaming jellied gasoline.

With the work of Cobra gunships and the 2/2 guys in the fire base, the attack was repelled. A sweep of the base the next morning found twenty-three NVA dead inside the perimeter wire. All indications were that a hundred or more had been killed trying to get to the wire, but all those enemy bodies had been dragged away by their comrades.

Even in the teeth of his Thunder III defeat, Charlie wasn't through for that Saturday, 6 September. He struck again later in the day a mile north of Thunder III. There, a battalion-sized enemy force attacked U.S. armored personnel carriers that were moving a small reconnaissance party down Highway 13. A couple of hours after that, and just another mile up the highway, an outposted unit of Bravo Troop, 1st of the 4th Cav (our sister ground troop), was hit.

The enemy didn't seem to care that they were engaging us in broad daylight, and along a two-mile stretch of our main supply route, where we had massed armor and mechanized forces. The determined Charlie didn't seem to care, either, about the manpower losses he was taking in such attempts to cut Thunder Road.

In one day, on that little stretch of highway, in those two blatant attacks, the enemy lost more than sixty soldiers. Add those to his losses in the abortive attack on Thunder III, and it became apparent how badly the enemy wanted to stop our flow of supplies north.

The next day, in his continuing battle for Thunder Road, Charlie gave us the surprise of our lives. He not only made our G-2 information look bad, but he slapped us back hard while taking a terrible toll on Darkhorse troop.

Early on that day, Chuck Davison, an Outcast scout pilot, was heading from Phu Loi up to FSB Thunder I to relieve me and Rod Willis on our VR operation. As Davison passed over the same spot where Rod and I had killed four enemy troops a couple of days earlier, he spotted another NVA. Seeing an enemy soldier that close to division HQ shocked him, and he was unable to get a shot before the man quickly dropped out of sight into a spider hole. Not knowing what to think, Davison continued to circle around the area where he thought the hole was. His crew chief, Clinton "Red" Hayes, dropped hand grenades and sprayed a little 60, but failed to see any other enemy.

Then, just as Davison was about to abandon the search and head on to Lai Khe, the enemy soldier popped back out of the hole and emptied an entire magazine of a U.S. M-16 rifle on full automatic right into the cockpit of Davison's Loach. Bullets crashed through the aircraft and into both of Chuck Davison's arms, instantly disabling him. Davison crashed practically on top of the spot where he had seen the enemy soldier.

Though painfully hurt in the crash—he was rammed in the kidneys by the butt of his M-60—Hayes crawled out of the wreck and pulled Davison out with him.

Davison's accompanying Cobra, of course, rolled and fired, but he couldn't get close with his rockets because he had no contact with his downed scout. An emergency radio was in Davison's survival vest, but it had dropped out somewhere when Hayes pulled him out of the Loach.

The gun's next reaction was to immediately call back to the troop and scramble the ARPs to the scene. Willis and I heard the transmission, and we flew off at flank speed to put a cover over the crash area. As we hit 120 knots down the road toward the scene, we could see Davison's Cobra circling over the area. I radioed him and asked what the situation was.

The gun came back: "The scout is down, the crew is out of the aircraft, and they've got enemy all around them."

Our first responsibility was to locate and cap the crew. We went straight to the crash site, pulled a skidding right turn, and found Hayes and Davison immediately. We could see that Davison was badly injured. Hayes was obvi-

ously scared and looked to be in pain himself. As Willis
and I took up station right over them, Hayes looked up
and gave us a weak thumbs-up.

Within minutes, the slicks bearing the ARPs showed up.
Rod left to put them down into a nearby LZ. Shortly
thereafter, the aerorifle platoon (now led by infantry Lt.
Doug Veitch) was at the crash and tending to the crew.

As a medevac came in to get Davison and Hayes, Major
Moore in his C and C ship suddenly appeared on the
scene. Apparently he wanted to discuss the situation with
his new ARP platoon leader.

As I circled overhead, a tactical conference was going
on. Major Moore, Doug Veitch, and the rest of the ARP
platoon were all standing around talking as though they
were out on a training camp maneuver.

Suddenly VC popped up out of holes all around the
gathered group and began firing RPGs and automatic
rifles, and throwing grenades. The enemy fire came so
quickly and with such intensity that no one had a chance
to shoot back. All they could do was hit the ground and
hope they didn't get cut in two by the barrage of fire that
had seemingly come out of nowhere.

Major Moore and the entire ARP platoon were standing on top of a major underground enemy tunnel system,
located just a few thousand yards from our 1st Division
field headquarters in Lai Khe. The enemy's cunning was
perfect. We'd expect their tunnels to be located in more
remote jungle areas, or in hillier spots. But right under our
noses within a stone's throw of our division HQ? Right
under a wide-open field with only scrub brush to provide
cover for the entryway spider holes? Never! But there it
was.

After incapacitating over fifty percent of the ARP platoon, the enemy disappeared back down into their spider
holes. With no bad guys to shoot at, my first concern was
to put a cap over the ARPs while they attempted to re-
store order. Then it took about forty minutes to shepherd

the hard-hit unit away from the ambush site and back to the LZ, where slicks returned them to base.

For us to learn of this enemy tunnel network cost us the following casualties:

Maj. Charles L. Moore, troop CO—hurt as he hit the ground diving for cover.

Lt. Douglas S. Veitch, ARP platoon leader—frag wounds in chin, hands, both thighs and legs.

WO Charles W. Davison, scout pilot—multiple bullet wounds in both the right and left upper arms.

Sfc. Harold R. Goatcher, ARP—shrapnel wounds in the right hand.

S.Sgt. James A. Broach, ARP—shrapnel wounds in the neck.

Sgt. Louis J. Baer, ARP—shrapnel wounds to the left knee.

Sgt. Russell H. Clark, Jr., ARP—deep shrapnel cut on his back.

Sgt. Thomas A. Maklary, ARP—frag wounds in both legs.

Sp. Robert A. Hawkins, aid man—shrapnel wounds on his left side.

Sp4. Clinton T. "Red" Hayes, scout crew chief—multiple cuts and bruises on the shoulder and right hip.

Pfc. Daryl J. Fisher, ARP—shrapnel wound of the left knee.

Pfc. Ronald C. Head, ARP—right leg broken, left arm broken, multiple frag wounds in legs and arms.

Pfc. Clarence Holloway, Jr., ARP—broken eardrum, frag wounds in the neck and right arm.

Pfc. Terry D. Houck, ARP—frag wounds in right arm, left leg, and thighs.

Pfc. Jerry F. Kolasinski, ARP—left leg broken and multiple frag wounds in the lower body.

Pfc. Robert A. Krehley, ARP—shrapnel wound in the stomach.

Pfc. David L. Littlefield, ARP—frag wounds in the left leg and right arm.

Pfc. Daniel P. Morrison, ARP—frag wounds in upper back.

Pfc. Larry W. Roop, ARP—frag wounds in left arm and leg.

Ho Van Tau, Kit Carson scout—multiple frag wounds in the back.

Hoang Van Nguyen, ARVN interpreter—frag wounds in the left thumb.

Nguyen Van Chinh, Kit Carson scout—bullet wounds in the head and stomach.

7 September 1969, a bad day for the ARPs and the entire Darkhorse troop.

CHAPTER 14

THE RAZORBACKS

Though the division G-2 didn't have the faintest idea that a highly complex network of enemy tunnels existed in the backyard of his headquarters, he certainly was right about the Razorback Mountains. They were a thorn in our side.

The Razorbacks was our name; the name for them on the map was Nui Tha La. The Razorbacks were the perfectly located staging area for enemy troops coming down into Vietnam from Cambodia. Their supply trails wound from the Fishhook, the Parrot's Beak, and the Angel's Wing through the hills and jungle to this string of low mountains that lay at the northwestern corner of the Michelin rubber plantation. They provided excellent ingress into the Michelin, Trapezoid, and target points to the east, such as Thunder Road; in addition, the southwestern tip was less than a kilometer from the Saigon River above our base at Dau Tieng. That's where all the enemy sampan traffic was coming from.

Because of the growing strategic importance of the Razorbacks, Darkhorse began to work the area on a regular basis, and we learned a couple of things really fast.

First, the area was indeed a major supply point for enemy forces: The high ground around the southeastern edge of the Razorbacks was the main base for enemy troops that were working out of there into the Michelin, the Trap, and points east.

It didn't take us long, either, to learn that the Razor-back area was hard to scout because of the many natural hiding places for the enemy, and that the whole damned place was hotter than a firecracker as far as enemy activity was concerned.

On early Thursday morning, 11 September, I was sitting in the operations bunker listening to the radios and having a cup of coffee. I was there because I was the designated Scramble 1. Besides that, the ops coffee was a lot better than the stuff they called coffee over at the mess hall.

My old scout mentor and toad-swallowing friend, Bill Jones (One Eight), was the scout pilot out on VR-1 that morning, and he and his Cobra were just arriving at their working area for the day at the Razorbacks. Jones had a new crew chief with him, a sergeant by the name of James R. Potter. Jones's gun was Mike Woods (Three-Five), and Mike's front-seater was Tom Chambers, a hootch mate of mine.

That's the team I was listening to on the radios as I sipped my first coffee of the day in the ops bunker. Jones and Woods had just begun working their routine VR-1 scouting patterns down near the southern end of the Ra-zorbacks.

As I listened to them work, I couldn't hear what Jones was saying, just what the Cobra was transmitting. When a scout was down low, his signal wasn't strong enough to get out very far, and the Cobra relayed anything important that the scout was saying.

After just a couple of minutes, Chambers came up on troop net to the ops radio watch and very matter-of-factly reported: "One Eight believes that he has spotted move-ment below. He's going to swing back around and make another pass to confirm."

The next thing we heard in the bunker was Chambers yelling into the radio, "One Eight is taking fire, taking heavy AK-47 fire. He's going down. One Eight is hit and going down!"

I jumped to my feet and clunked down the coffee cup. Reaching for my CAR-15, I headed for the door without even waiting for the scramble alert.

As I reached the bunker doorway, I heard the rest of Chambers's radio transmission. "My God!" he said, "when One Eight hit the ground, his bird exploded and burst into flames. The Loach is burning and there's a pillar of smoke and flame shooting up out of the trees. My God, my God! He's burning up!"

Those words stopped me cold for an instant. Loaches didn't explode on impact. I had never heard of an OH-6 exploding and burning on impact. It simply never happened.

I rushed toward my aircraft, yelling to Parker, who was busy cleaning and polishing the bird's bubble, "Scramble, Jimbo. We're scrambling north. Let's get the hell out of here!"

As I approached the ship, the scramble siren began to whine. People exploded out of their hootches—pilots, door gunners, ARP infantrymen all headed for their ships and a full troop scramble north.

In the case of a downed aircrew, both Scramble 1 and Scramble 2 scout-Cobra teams got off immediately to get to the scene and put an aerial cap on the crash site. Willis was my Scramble 2, and his crew chief was Ken Stormer (like Willis, from Texas). We were both cranked and off in less than a minute, leaving our Cobras behind to catch up. It took a while for their heavily armed and fueled machines to get wound up and airborne. But once in the air, their big engine and blades gave them up to 165 knots of speed, and they caught up and passed the scouts in short order.

I had no more than cleared the Phu Loi perimeter when my VHF radio came to life. It was Tom Chambers calling in to troop operations. I was dumbfounded to hear him

say: "Darkhorse Control, this is Darkhorse Three Five.
We've got movement out of the wreck. It's one of the crew
members—pilot or crew chief, don't know which. We're
putting down!"

What the hell's he doing? I thought. Three Five must be
making a low pass because he sure as hell can't be thinking
of putting that Cobra down on the ground!

Woods then proceeded to drop his big bird down to
about five hundred feet. He could see that the man stag-
gering around the burning Loach was Bill Jones. He
looked dazed and was burned all around his head and
shoulders. There was no sign of Potter. They concluded
that the crew chief must still be in the aircraft.

Three Five got as low as he could to take a better look.
But there was heavy jungle all around the area, and thick
black smoke was pouring up out of the little clearing
where the Loach was still burning furiously.

Then Woods made a daring decision. He had spotted a
small open piece of ground about seventy-five yards south
of where Jones's ship had gone in. Knowing that it would
take crucial minutes for help from the troop to arrive, and
assuming that Sergeant Potter was still inside the burning
Loach, Woods didn't falter for a second. He proceeded to
put his Cobra down on the small LZ.

Once down, Woods left the aircraft engine running and
told Tom Chambers to grab the portable fire extinguisher
and go try to find Jones. Chambers left his canopy open,
jumped out of the cockpit with the fire extinguisher in his
hand, and took off through the jungle.

Woods stayed in the ship and, not knowing if he would
be attacked by enemy soldiers, locked the nose turret in
the forward-only firing position. Woods could then fire the
front turret straight ahead by just aiming the helicopter.

After Chambers had been gone a couple of minutes,
Woods began to get concerned. He realized that Chambers couldn't get both Jones and Potter back to the LZ
without somebody to help him. So, leaving the Cobra en-

gine running, Three Five jumped out of the airplane and raced through the jungle after Chambers.

By the time they both reached Jones, they could tell that he was very badly hurt. His neck and shoulders were deeply burned. The top of his Nomex flight suit had been completely burned off, exposing charred and blackened flesh.

Knowing that Jones might not be coherent, Woods tried anyway. "Jonesy, it's Mike. Where's your crew chief? Where's Sergeant Potter?"

Somehow in his agony, Jones was able to mutter, "He . . . he's still in the ship . . . he . . . he didn't get out."

Chambers rushed over to the still-burning Loach. He aimed his little five-pound cockpit fire extinguisher at the searing flames fed by the ship's leaking JP-4, but it was like pissing on a roaring forest fire. Then Chambers looked into the ship. On the floor of the burning crew chief's compartment was Potter's body, now fairly well consumed by fire. Knowing that it wasn't going to make any difference, he emptied his pitiful little extinguisher into the ship anyway. Then, in disgust, he slammed it into the ground. There was no way anybody could help Sergeant Potter.

Chambers turned back to Woods. "So what do we do now?"

Three Five was struggling to keep Jones's limp body upright. "We gotta get him back to the ship. Come on, help me carry him."

Supporting One Eight under each burned shoulder, Woods and Chambers half-carried and half-dragged the pain-stricken pilot back through the jungle toward their still-running gunship.

As they approached the Cobra, Chambers asked, "What are we going to do when we get him to the bird? How are we going to get him out of here?" The Cobra had only two in-tandem cockpit spaces, and no place to put a third man inside the aircraft.

"He isn't going to last if we don't get him to a hospital

right away." Woods puffed. "We can't wait for a Dustoff.
We'll just have to get him in the ship some way and take
him ourselves."

Chambers had an idea. "The ammo bay door—we can
drop the ammunition compartment door and lay him on
that."

Struggling with the then totally unconscious Bill Jones,
Woods and Chambers finally reached the helicopter. As
they were trying to get Jones in the Cobra, a CH-47 Chinook helicopter arrived at the scene, having heard the
transmissions about the downed aircraft. The "hook"
hovered over the airmen and lowered its cable with a jungle penetrator for hoisting personnel. With Tom holding
Jones, they were both winched upward into the belly of
the Chinook. Woods climbed back into the Cobra and
roared into the sky, following the rescue ship to Dau
Tieng. He advised operations that they were safe and approaching Delta Tango, but that the crew chief had not
been recovered and was believed to be KIA.

Willis and I overheard this message just as we reined in
over the site of Jones's crashed Loach. Given the situation, our first mission responsibility was to get down out of
altitude and put an aerial cap on the area surrounding the
crash.

I keyed the intercom to Parker, "OK, Jimbo, we're going lima lima. Watch your ass. We just lost a scout down
here so we're going to have bad guys. You're clear to fire
. . . anything that moves, take 'em out!"

"Gun is hot, sir. I'm ready!"

I saw him tense up and lean farther out into the slipstream as he set his M-60.

With Willis tight on my tail, I went into a descending
right-hand turn that would put me down about a hundred
yards from the smoke of Jones's downed bird. Then I
made a fast ninety-knot pass over the wreck to check it out
before taking up a scouting orbit around the site.

A feeling of surprise and shock shot through me as I

swept over the still-smoldering OH-6. I just couldn't believe that Jones's Loach had burned on impact. That was
the surprise. The shock came when I saw what the fire had
done to the ship. The interior of the bird was pretty much
burned out. The tail boom had separated and was lying on
the ground. The blades were off and also on the ground.
The cabin section around the engine and fuel cell was
completely burned away, and the front of the bubble was
broken and largely melted down onto the ground.

Then my eye picked up the worst of all: Potter's arm
and helmeted head hanging out of what used to be the
back cabin of the airplane. "Shit," I whispered, and my
face involuntarily grimaced. "My God . . . no!"

Not attracting any ground fire on the first fast pass, I
told Willis to stay on my tail for another run over the
crash, this time lower and slower.

We came around again and headed back into the clearing at about forty knots and maybe ten feet off the ground.
Just as we neared Jones's smoldering ship, some of the
ordnance on board began exploding. There were sharp
cracks from some of the M-60 rounds. Then a big burst
from one of the Willie Pete grenades went up right in
front of my bubble.

Damn, I scolded myself, what a dumb shit I am not to
remember that there was live ammo on board! With no
alternative, I flew right through the billowing white phos-
phorous smoke while yelling over the radio to Willis.
"Veer off, One Seven! Take it out wide! We've got ordnance going off in the wreck!"

Rod's reaction was instantaneous. He peeled his OH-6
off my tail and whipped around the wreck. He obviously
didn't want his next shootdown to be the result of getting
hit by our own bullets.

Then I hit UHF again for a report to my gun, Dean
Sinor. "Three One, this is One Six. One Eight's bird is still
burning, and there's some ordnance going off out of the
back cabin. We confirm Charlie Echo KIA. The Loach is

pretty much burned up. We've got no sign of enemy contact. The area is cold at this time."

Sinor's "Roger, One Six" was practically smothered by the unexpected voice of the troop CO, Major Moore. He was apparently nearby in his C and C ship.

"One Six," he bellowed, "this is Six. What's it like down there? Can you pin the bastards down?"

"Six, this is One Six. We've got the aircraft capped. The pilot is out. Charlie Echo is KIA. No current activity . . . no sign of enemy activity at this time. The area is cold."

"OK, One Six, find a place to put the ARPs down. They'll be coming up on the contact area right away."

Acknowledging the Old Man's request, I went over to take a look at the LZ where Woods had put down to recover Jones. It looked fine. There was no sign of the enemy, so I had Parker pop a smoke in the clearing to mark the LZ. Then I began orbits around the landing zone to see if the smoke attracted attention from any enemy who might be nearby.

Still nothing. I began to think that whoever clobbered Jones must have departed in a hurry. The area seemed completely free of any sign of enemy troops.

My radio came up again, just as I saw the slicks carrying the ARPs come in over the trees and begin their run into the LZ.

"OK, One Six." It was Major Moore again. "This is Six. I'm going on the ground to supervise recovery operations."

Well, I'll be damned, I said to myself, I *thought* I saw five Hueys instead of just four drop down into that LZ. The Old Man must have ordered his C and C ship to slip in with the four ARP birds when they went into the landing zone. What in the hell is the major doing? All this to "supervise" the recovery of one friendly KIA?

The ARPs had hardly deployed out of their Hueys when Major Moore's voice came over the radio. In a very matter-of-fact way he said, "One Six, this is Six. I've got movement, and they're all around us."

Déjà vu! I thought. They're surrounded again, and the Old Man—again—is down there in the middle of it! I hadn't seen anybody or anything hostile around that area, and I had been orbiting over it for the last ten to fifteen minutes.

Well, we looked and looked. We fired all kinds of miniguns and rockets. The ARPs shot off their weapons like crazy. But nothing. We never did find anything that could have caused Major Moore to think he was being attacked. And thank God for that. We sure didn't need a repeat of the recent ARP disaster at the Lai Khe tunnels.

By noon that day the ARPs had done all they could do on the ground. With Sergeant Potter's body finally recovered from the wreck, I put my bird down in the clearing for a couple of minutes so the ARPs could transfer some of Jones's gear to my ship to take back to the base. There was Jones's fire-blackened chicken plate, his charred helmet, and codebook. The way that stuff was burned I couldn't imagine what Jones must have looked like.

The ARPs had also pulled the fire-damaged minigun off the bird and dragged it back to the LZ. They put it aboard one of the Hueys to take back to Phu Loi to keep it from possibly falling into enemy hands.

But the burned, twisted hulk of One Eight's ship was left in the jungle. There was no way that mess of scorched and melted junk could ever be put back together to fly again.

As I lifted back out of the jungle to head home, I took a long last look at Jones's wrecked aircraft. Was Jones hit by hostile ground fire, or could something else, such as impacting a tree, have brought him down? As I tried to think of an explanation, the radio broke my spell. It was Bob Harris, and he solved the mystery of Jones's crash.

"Hey, One Six," he called, "this is Four Six. When we removed the Charlie Echo's body, we found that he had

been shot in the head with an AK-47 round. He was probably KIA before the bird ever hit the ground."

That settled that. Jones *had* received enemy ground fire
and was shot out of the air, eliminating the prospect that
he might have hit a tree or gone into a "Hughes tailspin"
(an OH-6 design characteristic that might force the bird to
become uncontrollable and spin into the ground under
certain conditions when a right, decelerating turn was
made at low speed).

Four Six continued. "And we found out why One
Eight's Loach burned. When it went into the ground, it hit
a tree stump that impacted the right rear belly of the ship.
It impaled the fuel cell, split it open, and allowed burning
JP-4 to flow forward over the bulkhead and down One
Eight's shoulders and neck."

"My God," I cringed, "so that's how it happened!" That
explained, also, the areas of Jones's body that were burned
so horribly—his head, neck, and upper body.

The ARPs had hardly gotten back to base from the
crash when the troop scramble siren wailed again.

I had arrived back at Phu Loi just ahead of the rifle
platoon, grabbed some lunch, and settled in at the ops
bunker to monitor the radios. When I was not out flying
myself, I often checked in at the ops bunker to listen to
the scouts work. This afternoon we had a couple of afternoon VR teams out reconning in the vicinity of the western Trapezoid. It was still Thursday, 11 September, although the tragedy of the morning made it feel as though
the day was already a month long.

I had just taken my first sip of coffee when the voice of
one of our crew chiefs broke out over the air. Crew chiefs
normally did not transmit outside the ship, but apparently
Red Hayes, in his excitement, had keyed his transmitter
instead of just the intercom as he talked to his pilot, Pony
One Six.

"Sir! I've got dinks underneath me. They're all over!"
Then there were the sharp reports of Hayes's M-60.

Over the rattle of Hayes's machine gun, Pony One Six's voice came through: "OK, I'm coming around to the right in a three-sixty."

Not again, I thought. Pony One Six had just made what I considered a bad tactical mistake for a scout pilot in combat. To pull an immediate right three-sixty before his OH-6 was out of the line of sight of the enemy ground troops would bring the Pony Loach right back over the same track in which the enemy contact had been initially made. I silently hoped that it wouldn't cost him.

Then Hayes talked to his pilot again. "Lieutenant," he said, "I've got a red smoke ready to drop, but you're too far off to the side of the contact point. Come around . . . come around again."

Even though the Darkhorse scout pilots had told him many times to never—never EVER—come back into an enemy contact point the same way, in a predictable flight pattern, Pony One Six immediately hauled another hard right 360-degree turn. Again, right over the watching enemy's head.

As I bent forward intently listening—but unable to do a damned thing to help—I heard Hayes scream back at his pilot, "No, Lieutenant, break left . . . break *left. LEFT,* sir!"

Pony One Six apparently then jerked a hard left to get the ship over the contact point and allow Hayes to throw the smoke. But the smoke still wasn't where Hayes wanted it, and Pony pulled another hard left turn—making the third time he had brought the ship in from northwest to southeast right in the enemy's clear line of sight. That's all Charlie needed. The enemy immediately sent up a barrage of AK-47 fire that pounded into the little OH-6.

To his horror, Hayes suddenly saw Pony stiffen in his cockpit seat, slam his head back into the bulkhead that separated the pilot from his crew chief, then slump forward in his seat, dropping his hands from the plane's controls. The next thing Hayes remembered was awakening in

the wrecked ship on the ground, with excruciating pain in
his leg . . . and the almost deafening quiet of the jungle.

Without even hearing Pony One Six's gunship call back
to ops control for a full troop scramble, the siren screamed
and we all ran for our ships again. Helping another
downed scout was our highest response priority.

Scout Bob Calloway (One Zero) happened to be working another VR near the spot where Pony One Six and
Hayes had gone down. One Zero was vectored in to put an
immediate cap over the crash scene until the rest of the
troop could mount up and fly to the site. What Calloway
saw when he arrived over the crash was Red Hayes sitting
on the ground near the wrecked plane attempting to ease
an obvious leg wound and cradling the limp body of his
pilot across his lap.

When the Loach crashed, it had hit the trees, fallen to
the ground, and nosed over, leaving the helicopter upside
down. When Hayes regained consciousness, he realized
that his knee and ankle were seriously hurt, but he suc-
ceeded in cutting Pony's seat belt and shoulder harness so
he could get the pilot out of the ship in case of fire.

As Calloway circled over the wreck, he realized that
Hayes did not have a survival radio and could not talk
from the ground. But it was obvious that the crew chief
and pilot were hurt. Minutes later, the ARPs were put
down on a nearby road and moved over to the wreck site.
They secured the area, determined that Pony One Six was
KIA, and executed the evacuation of the downed crew.

Pony One Six's ship had taken an AK-47 armor-piercing
round up through the cockpit floor. The projectile entered
the pilot's left thigh, tore through the femoral artery, and
traversed up through the stomach, lungs, and finally into
his heart, where the bullet fragmented. The Pony platoon
leader was dead the instant Hayes saw him stiffen in his
seat.

Just three weeks earlier, Pony One Six had been shot
down after becoming fixated over a contact area and pre-

senting his airplane as a target the enemy could not miss. Red Hayes was Pony's crew chief that day also, and he had tried desperately to warn the pilot that he needed to speed up and get out of the enemy's line of sight. But, for some reason, Pony wouldn't take Hayes's advice—on either occasion.

All of us in Darkhorse felt the loss of the Pony platoon leader. It made it worse to realize that his death might have been avoided if he had just given more credence to the scouting lessons that combat experience had taught the Darkhorse scout pilots.

If there was a bright note for that ugly day, it came that evening when we all got back to base. We learned that Bill Jones, though in dangerous condition with second and third degree burns over his upper body, was still alive and had been transferred from Dau Tieng to the evac hospital in Long Binh.

A day or so later I decided that I couldn't wait any longer to go down to see Bill Jones. Willis, Davis, and I piled into my bird and headed down to Long Binh. When we arrived at the hospital we asked directions to the intensive care unit, shushing Willis as he remarked rather loudly on the notable physical assets of several of the nurses.

Finally finding the ICU, I walked up to the nurses' station. "I'm Lieutenant Mills from the Quarter Cav, and we're here to check on one of my pilots. He was brought in here two days ago with burns. His name is William Jones."

"Yes," she said, "Warrant Officer Jones is down in the last bed on the right."

With Davis behind me—Willis was lagging back at the nurses' station—I walked down to where the nurse had directed me. I looked at the person in the bed and immediately said out loud, "No, that's not Bill Jones."

The guy didn't look anything like Jones. His head was

twice again as big, and so was his body. Besides, the man
in the bed was black.

I went back to the nurses' station. "Ma'am, you made a
mistake. The man in the bed down there is not Warrant
Officer Jones."

"Well, Lieutenant," she answered, "that *is* Warrant Officer Bill Jones from Delta Troop of the Quarter Cav, and
he was brought in here two days ago with burns."

"But, ma'am," I argued, "Bill Jones is a skinny little guy,
and besides that, he's *white*!"

It was obvious that I had tried her patience. "You don't
seem to understand, Lieutenant, what second and third
degree burns can do to a person. You go on back down
there; you'll find out that's Mr. Jones."

Back at his bedside, I studied the person for a moment.
The blazing jet fuel that spilled over his upper body had
burned away most of the right side of his neck, as well as
the right shoulder. The burned areas were charred and
had swollen up to monstrous proportions. The distortion
was so bad it made the man look twice the size.

I leaned down close and said, "Bill, can you hear me?"

In a very labored whisper he responded, "Yes, who is
it?"

"It's Mills, Jonesy. How are you doing?"

"I feel like shit," he answered.

Trying to keep it light I retorted, "Well, Bill, you really
look like shit. What happened?"

He couldn't even smile. He was obviously in incredible
pain. But he did move his head ever so slightly, and then
slowly whispered, "I saw movement . . . and when I
came around, I saw people. I don't know what hit me."

"OK, Jonesy," I said quietly, "we'll talk about it later.
Look, ol' friend, there isn't much that any of us can do for
you right now, but the guys are thinking about you and
wanted to see how you were doing."

His eyes opened a little bit. "Who's that with you . . .
is that Fox Bravo?"

"Yes, it's Davis, and he's as full of BS as ever."

"Who else is with you?" he whispered.

"Rod's with us, too."

"Bet he's chasing nurses, right?"

"Well, yes," I stammered. "He's back at the nurses' station talking to some girl from Texas.

"We're going to take off now, Bill, and let you get some sack time. We'll catch you later and see how you're doin', OK?"

"OK, you guys," he said, as though he was already drifting off. "I'll just see you . . . later."

By that time, Willis had made it down to Bill's bed. I had never seen him look so solemn. Rod reached down and gently patted the bed sheet. I knew he felt the same way Davis and I did—that we would probably never see Bill Jones again.

Flying back to Phu Loi, not a word was said. All three of us were deep in our own thoughts. We all realized that what had happened to Bill Jones could have happened to us. It could happen to any one of us, any day of the week. Every day, Charlie had his chance to send any one of us back in a body bag.

In a moment of honesty, I think every scout would have admitted that fear was with us constantly. Our ability to fly, in my opinion, came from our ability to recognize that we *were* afraid, to understand why we were afraid, and to continue to work through the fear.

Scout pilots understood their own mortality. The figures were there: If you were a pilot in the air cav and you were killed, you were probably a *scout* pilot. That's the way it was. Sometimes it was a slick pilot. Very rarely a Cobra pilot. Usually a scout pilot.

The key was that we never thought about the odds. We dealt with the prospect of getting shot, getting burned, dying, but never allowing ourselves to think about the consequences. Instead, we rationalized, we immersed ourselves in our own illusions of immortality. Like Bob Davis,

who used his sense of humor to wrestle with his own de-
mons. Like Bill Jones, who drank more than he should
have.

I had come to the conclusion that when it was time for
me to chuck it in, there wouldn't be a damned thing I
could do about it. So I took the pragmatic view that I
wasn't going to worry about something I couldn't control
or influence. I never did totally crazy things, however; I
never abandoned reason. But I felt that if I dwelled on the
potential of getting hurt or killed, I would start getting too
cautious. And when people get too cautious, they make
mistakes—mistakes that get themselves and other people
hurt. But if I ever wavered from my pragmatism, it was in
those moments after seeing Bill Jones that day at the hospital.

We had lost Jim Ameigh. We had lost Chuck Davison.
We had lost Pony One Six. We had lost two gallant crew
chiefs. And I couldn't even recognize Bill Jones—my toad-
swallowing bar buddy, my scout teacher, my good friend.

But tomorrow was another day, and I was VR-1.

CHAPTER 15

BUT ROD WAS ROD

The rest of September passed in a blur. It was one of the hottest months we had in terms of flying hours and sustained enemy activity. The scout platoon was shorthanded because of the casualties we had taken. The rest of us flew more hours to make up the difference. I logged more than 138 combat flying hours in September, and the other scouts did much the same. It was a hectic and tiring pace.

October started out the same way. I ended up taking a few days off, however, during the first part of the month, but not because I planned it that way.

On 2 October, Rod Willis and I were working the early morning VRs out of Dau Tieng. We flew two hunter-killer teams up to Delta Tango, then took turns reconning the area around the western Trapezoid.

Willis (One Seven) was up first and started his VR along the east bank of the Saigon River heading south out of Dau Tieng. I stayed on the pad monitoring his radio transmissions and waiting for my turn to relieve him on station.

It wasn't long before I heard that Willis had picked up some fish traps in a little tributary (Suoi Don) that headed off north and east of the Big Blue about three kilometers above our FSB Kien. Spotting the fish traps, Rod pulled in over the riverbank adjacent to them to see if there were

footprints around. There were prints of sandals around
the bank, and a trail showing recent moderate traffic.
Dropping down to a couple of feet above the trail, One
Seven determined that the latest foot tracks led away from
the river and off through the jungle.

Willis followed the foot trail for four to five klicks into
the jungle, where he discovered that it ended in the middle
of an NVA base camp. He could see the outlines of the
bunkers, the freshly washed clothes hanging on lines, the
equipment and weapons leaning against trees. If those
clues didn't tell One Seven that the base camp was occupied, the bursts of enemy ground fire that suddenly
erupted were conclusive.

The instant I heard Willis yell to his gun that he was
taking fire, I cranked, took off out of Dau Tieng with my
gun (Mike Woods—Three Five), and headed to the point
of contact. It was less than ten kilometers down to where
Willis was. I stayed down on top of the trees to get there
fast.

About halfway to the point of contact, I called One
Seven on Uniform to ask him what he had run into.

Willis answered, "I followed a foot trail up from the Big
Blue and found myself in the middle of a hot NVA base
camp. Several of the little sons a bitches tried to didi out
the back door, and we got a couple of them with the door
gun. Now they're holed up in their bunkers and I've got
Taxi on the way to blast 'em out." Taxi was an armored
group out of FSB Kien. "They're about three hundred
yards out now. In the meantime, I'm taking a heavy load
of ground fire."

"Have you got anybody out in the open now, One
Seven?" I asked.

"That's a negative. They're all in the bunkers. I'm trying
to blast 'em out, but my minigun just jammed and I can't
shoot. I've got to break station for Delta Tango and get my
minigun cleared."

A few seconds later I was on the scene, fell in on One

Seven, and hit the radio again. "OK, One Seven, One Six is on your tail. What you got?"

"They're getting a little skittish down there," Rod said. "They can hear the armor coming and know they're going to get their asses blown off, so they're trying to knock the scout down to cut off our observation and keep us from guiding the armor guys in."

"That's a roger," I came back. "I'll try to keep their heads down while you go back to Delta Tango and get your minigun unjammed."

Rod peeled off and I went into the bunker area in a slow hover to see if I could catch anybody in the open. Nothing doing. Not a soul showed his face as I made several slow passes with the mini and door guns blazing. Apparently Charlie felt safer at the moment in the bunker.

"Screw this, Jimbo," I finally said to my crew chief. "Heat me up a CS. We'll try and pop a gas down their chimney."

Parker pulled the pin on a gas grenade and held it out the door as I skidded to a low-level quick stop over one of the bunkers. Just as I slid over the bunker entryway, Parker released the gas canister. "Well, I'll be damned—bull's-eye!" I hollered. Parker had pitched the gas canister squarely down into the bunker entrance.

Knowing that this would really piss off the bad guys, I immediately swung wide. I wanted to come around again for a minigun pass to dispatch anybody who stuck his head out for a breath of fresh air.

As I came back into the bunker area for the gun run, I miscalculated the wind direction and flew through some of the CS gas grenade residue. Parker and I both got our eyes full. Catching a snoot full of our own gas happened once in a while, so I knew what to do. I kicked left pedal and swung the cyclic to the right rear to throw the Loach out of trim. That brought the nose left and immediately forced slipstream air into the right side of the aircraft. Then I leaned out my door and let the rushing air blow the gas out of my eyes.

That got rid of the gas all right, but it also took my eyes off the enemy bunker for just a fleeting second. That's all it took for Charlie to pop up out of his hole and let go with an AK-47.

I heard the rounds leave the muzzle, then heard the bullets ripping into the helicopter's fuselage. Parker's M-60 hammered back a reply.

At the same time, there was blinding pain in my head and for an instant my vision exploded into orange. I felt a slamming impact to my body, and then a strange numbness below my waist.

"God!" I gasped. I looked down at my body and couldn't see my right leg. My first, horrible impression was that my leg had been shot off at the knee. But I didn't see any blood.

Shock, pain, and confusion tore at me. I was trying desperately to control the helicopter and keep away from the ground fire that was still coming up at us from the enemy bunker.

I stole another look down in an effort to get my throbbing brain to acknowledge the fact that one of my legs had just been blown away. Is this the way this war is gonna end for me? I thought.

Suddenly it dawned on me that most of the pain that was surging through me seemed to be coming from the heel of my right foot. I cradled the collective under my left knee, grabbed the cyclic with my left hand, and used the other hand to investigate my leg. I patted my right thigh and knee, then rubbed my hand over my lower leg. I still had it! It had been there all the time, bent back under me and hanging outside the aircraft on the right door frame. At altitude, I often flew with my leg hanging there.

Lifting and tugging with one hand, I managed to drag the leg back into the cockpit. I couldn't see anything wrong, except there was no heel on my boot. Then, blood began running out of the pant leg of my flight suit and, as the wind caught it, the blood splattered on me and all over the inside of the cockpit.

Realizing I had been shot someplace, I pushed the intercom to Parker and yelled, "Jimbo, I'm hit. My leg's screwed up!"

"Can you fly, Lieutenant?"

"I think so. I'm going to head for Kien and try to put 'er down, but I just don't know how much control I've got over my leg."

It was then that my nerve endings all realized at the same time that something had violated my body and that they weren't going to stand for it. The pain became almost unbearable.

A voice over the VHF radio distracted me momentarily from my agony. It was Mike Woods. "Hey, One Six, you're wobbling a little. You OK down there?"

"We're OK, Three Five," I gasped, "but we've taken hits . . . I'm hit. I think I can make it to Kien. I think I can make it that far."

As I finished talking to the Cobra, I heard some rustling noises in the back cabin. Looking over my left shoulder I saw that Parker had unstrapped from his seat, unplugged his helmet, and was beginning to crawl out the left rear door of the aircraft. We were about fifty feet off the trees and doing seventy knots, and there was Parker out of the aircraft, climbing up front to get in the cockpit with me.

Fighting the rushing slipstream and holding on tightly to the ship's door frames, Jim planted a foot on top of the minigun, then swung himself into the left front seat beside me. I wasn't hurting so badly that I didn't realize what a gutsy thing he had just done.

Parker quickly buckled himself to the seat and plugged in his helmet. "Can I help you on the controls?"

"I can handle them OK," I said, "but my leg is hurting pretty bad and I may need some help on the pedals."

Jim put his hands gently down on the collective and

cyclic, then positioned his feet on the pedals. He was essentially flying the airplane along with me.

Though crew chiefs were not pilots, they were familiar with the basics. They could fly the ship on a straight and level course, and could even land it in some emergency situations.

As Parker gradually took over the controls and flew on toward Kien, I used my free hands to pat over my body and try to find out exactly what had happened. With my feet now off the pedals, I felt around on my right leg and discovered that a bullet had gone completely through my calf. But that wasn't the only place I was hurt. Blood was also beginning to puddle up in the pilot's seat, and my backside was burning like fire.

Together, Parker and I pieced together what had happened. The enemy AK round had come up through the floor near the pedals. The bullet struck and carried away the heel of my right boot, went through the calf of my leg, and literally blew my leg to the side and out the cabin door. The round then apparently hit the fire extinguisher stowed to the right of my seat, and ricocheted up into my seat and through my thigh. Then it evidently kept going right on out of the aircraft.

We were so busy looking around the cockpit that we nearly overflew Kien. I got back on the controls to help Parker land the ship, and we set her down right at the front gate of the fire base.

I was so groggy by the time we touched down that I bypassed most of the engine shutdown procedures. I went right through the idle stop to full off on the throttle, switched off the battery, then tried to get out of the ship. But I couldn't. All I could do was sit there in the seat that was, by that time, full of blood.

I didn't remember him doing it, but Three Five had radioed ahead for a medevac Huey to pick me up at the fire base. It landed just shortly after Parker and I did and made immediate preparations to load me up and take me to the Second Surgical Hospital at Lai Khe.

Before that, however, I was helped over to the battalion surgeon's tent, where they checked me over and put some bandages on my leg and backside. I just barely remember the corpsman from the medevac ship getting me aboard Dustoff before the morphine took over and the lights went out.

I phased in and out of consciousness during a brief stop at Second Surge in Lai Khe. I was awake enough to recognize the hospital building as the same place where I had watched Jim Ameigh die on the operating table. It was an ugly thought. I closed my eyes and turned my head away. Then I was back in Dustoff and headed to the field hospital in Long Binh, where I had been just a couple of weeks before to visit Bill Jones.

They kept me at Long Binh for three days. My wounds turned out to be minor—much messier than devastating. I guess I wasn't exactly a model patient. By the third day in the hospital, I was fit to be tied. We were shorthanded in the platoon before I left. Now I knew that the scouts were having to double up on missions. With Willis running the outfit, the only thing I could think was, God help us all!

I used the landline telephone to call back to Phu Loi and ask if the troop supply ship could come down to Long Binh to get me. I was back in the platoon that same day, sporting a row of stitches in my thigh, as well as a cane to help me gimp around.

A few days later, the troop officers were invited across the runway to a party that battalion was throwing. There was a change of battalion commanders and the party had been scheduled to mark the event. The only problem was the dress—the invitation called for attendees to be in khaki uniform, and wearing all ribbons and regalia.

I hadn't worn a set of khakis for at least ten months. Neither had most of the other guys. But, in the military, an invitation was really a polite demand that you be present, and in the uniform prescribed!

Most of us had forgotten even the basics, such as which breast pocket your name tag went over, and on which side of the collar went the rank versus the branch insignia. Or, even more perplexing, what ribbons we were entitled to wear, and in what order they were put on the uniform.

So, it was off to see troop 1st Sgt. Martin L. Laurent. The first question generally was, "Check my file, will you, Top, and see what ribbons I'm entitled to wear." Then, ". . . and what order do they go in on the rack?"

Thank God First Sergeant Laurent was a tolerant man. Not only did he have to shepherd all the new soldiers and young NCOs, but also a troop full of young warrants and officers. In our final inspection before leaving that night for the party, I remember the first sergeant saying to one of our number, "Young warrant officer, hold on there just a minute. I can readily understand that you are duly proud of that Army Commendation Ribbon with 'V' that you're wearing, but damnit all, son, it goes *behind* your Silver Star. The Silver Star ribbon goes in front! Now, will you please fix that before you go parading into the party for the battalion commander?"

Decked out in our starched and pressed khakis, spit-shined low quarters, and overseas caps, we all took off across the runway to the 1st Aviation club.

We had to hand it to them, those battalion guys really knew how to throw a party. They had a floor show with Filipino performers and an open bar with plenty of booze. The place was fairly well rockin' right along.

We had so much fun that we stayed late. At about 10:30 or 11 P.M. we noticed that one of the majors from the battalion staff was taking a fancy to one of the female performers. That was all Rod Willis needed. He sure as hell wasn't going to let a major get the best of him, not when it came to a member of the fairer sex. So every time the major left to get another drink or go to the rest room,

Willis tried to snake this young lady. Both men were more than just a little inebriated, and we all knew that sooner or later there was going to be trouble.

The next time the major went to the john, he came back to find Willis sitting at the lady's table with his arm snugly around her shoulder. The good major stomped back over to the table, struck a very majorly demeanor, and yelled, "What the hell do you think you're doing? *I'm* talking to this lady. She didn't invite you to this table, and you need to get the hell away from here!"

Rod remembered, thank God, that the man was a major. So, showing unexpected and uncommon respect for the gold oak leaf on the major's collar, Rod very politely excused himself from the young lady's presence and walked over to the bar where I was standing.

Then the lady, evidently having had enough of the bickering, got up and left. Instead of that breaking the chain of events, her leaving served only to further infuriate the major. His face turned beet red. He clamped his hands on his hips, stomped over to Willis, and stuck a forefinger into Rod's face. "All right, Lieutenant," he fumed, "I want your goddamned name and unit!"

Rod got this shit-eatin' grin on his face. He continued drinking his beer but didn't say a word in reply.

"You're the sorriest excuse for an officer of the United States Army that I ever saw," the major raved on. "Your conduct was unbecoming an officer, and an insult to every man who wears an officer's uniform. That young lady was *my* girl and you shouldn't have been messin' around with her. Do you hear that, Lieutenant?"

I was proud of Rod. Though he kept grinning, he didn't say a word back to the major.

With a few more stabs of his finger into Rod's now-blissful face, the major ended his tirade with the threat, ". . . and don't you forget it!" Then he stormed off, still hurling expletives over his shoulder.

With the major's final departure, Rod let go with one of

the most heinous giggles I've ever heard. Nothing sounded very funny to me. "For Christ sakes!" I told him. "For a guy who just got his ass chewed out from one end to the other by a ranking battalion staff officer, I don't understand what in the hell you're laughing about."

"Well," Rod replied, "do you know that for the last thirty-five seconds that he was rantin' and ravin' I was actually pissin' all over the major's left leg, and he was so fuckin' busy reading me off that the son of a bitch didn't even know it! How do you like that, One Six, for a little piece of low and slow aeroscout response to an enemy action?"

Willis had unzipped himself during the height of the staff officer's berating diatribe, and surreptitiously urinated all over the major's leg and shoe! I knew it would be only a matter of seconds until the good major realized what had happened. I grabbed Rod, who was still giggling and watching the wet-legged officer across the room. "Let's all get the hell out of here while we can still save our skins!"

It was so late by then that no jeeps were available to take us from the club back to the troop. But wanting to didi the area with no further delay, we started half-walking, half-staggering back across the centerline runway ramps toward our hootches.

With the amount of booze we had in our tanks, some celebrators encountered navigational difficulties and didn't make it back to the troop at all. They were discovered the next morning sound asleep in a low spot on the tarmac runway. Thank God Phu Loi didn't have many nighttime flight operations.

Somehow, and thank goodness, we never heard any more about One Seven's dramatic drenching of the staff major's leg. But Rod was Rod, and he was developing a singular reputation. Since coming to the scouts a few months back, Rod Willis had already become known around the troop for flying with what might be called "a touch of wild abandon." He routinely returned to the base from scouting missions with sprigs of foliage, whole tree limbs, and sometimes even pieces of livestock impaled or otherwise hanging off his aircraft.

On at least four occasions, Rod didn't even make it back to Phu Loi in his own aircraft. He had either hit something, or something had hit him, hard enough to bring down his Loach—with Willis and his crew chief always walking away unhurt from the wrecked airplane. I was never quite sure whether Willis was simply a bad pilot, or couldn't see where in the hell he was going, or just didn't give a damn.

On this particular day, Willis and I were wingmen on the early morning VR of the Thi Tinh River valley from approximately Ben Cat north to the area of the Michelin rubber plantation. There were two hunter-killer teams with Sinor (Three One) and me working VR-1, and Phil "Combat" Carriss (Three Eight) and Rod Willis to relieve us on VR-2.

At first light both teams took off from Phu Loi and headed directly up to Lai Khe. The VR-2 team would land and shut down at Lai Khe while VR-1 went right on to the mission area; we'd relieve each other about every two hours. After a while, we'd move the operations base from Lai Khe to Dau Tieng, as our search pattern progressed farther northwest.

While working one of my patterns near the Ben Cat–Tri Tam province line, I spotted a foot trail that ran east and west across the river valley. As I dropped down closer on it, I could tell that it had had some recent light foot traffic. Swinging the Loach around, I followed the trail west into the jungle for about seven hundred to eight hundred yards. Just as I stalked around a sharp turn in the path, I saw ten to twelve VC soldiers below me walking in column.

I banked hard and hollered to Sinor, "I've got dinks!

VC on the trail, mark, mark. VC on the trail right below me!"

Parker opened up on the column and his M-60 immediately dropped four VC out of the middle of the group. The rest scattered into the jungle, trying to escape Parker's red-hot fire.

I pulled the Loach into another hard right and came around 180 degrees. Parker was still firing out his door as I cut loose with the minigun. I kept kicking left and right pedal to spray both sides of the trail with 7.62.

After making that run, I came back in again and asked Parker to pop a smoke. "It's already out, sir," he said. "It went out on the first pass."

When I saw the red smoke beginning to come up from the jungle floor, I accelerated eastbound back toward the Thi Tinh and came up to Sinor. "OK, Three One, smoke is out. Hit the red smoke now. I'm clear, One Six is clear to the east."

I no sooner got the words out of my mouth when Sinor rolled on the smoke and worked his rocks and minigun all the way down the trail.

Watching him hose down the area almost made me forget that I was getting low on fuel and ammo. So I came up to Sinor again. "When you get a chance, Three One, crank the other team in here and I'll hold for One Seven to brief him on the contact area when he gets here."

Willis's Cobra (Carriss), being much faster than the OH-6, got to the scene first and pulled into an orbit behind Sinor. A few minutes later, along came Willis. He was down very low, scraping the landscape as he cruised in leisurely from the west. He had apparently flown up to the contact point right down on the deck, all the way from Dau Tieng. That was Romeo Whiskey for you.

Once on the scene, Willis pulled up to where I was orbiting at about eight hundred feet, then we both headed back down low again with One Seven tight on my tail. I started briefing Willis as soon as we bottomed out over the area where we first discovered and hit the column. "OK, One Seven," I said, "you see the east–west trail? It's just on the west side of the Thi Tinh where Thirty-one's rocks have impacted."

Willis gave me back two short squelches on his transmit button, so I continued: "OK, you'll want to work in this area east to west along the trail. This is where we hit ten to twelve Victor Charlies westbound on the trail. Door gunner engaged with mike 60. I engaged with minigun, Cobra engaged with rocks. Negative knowledge of results, no return fire."

Willis rogered again and then I said, "We're bingo on fuel, One Seven. I'm going to cut a chogie on over to Delta Tango to refuel and rearm, then I'll be back out to join you. See ya." Sinor elected to stay over the contact area with Carriss since his snake was not low on fuel or ammo.

Parker and I had just landed at Dau Tieng and taken on some fuel. Parker was out of the airplane getting ammo. As I sat waiting in the idling Loach with radios up, Sinor's voice suddenly popped on UHF. "I'm in hot, One Seven . . . I'm in hot!"

Realizing that enemy contact had apparently been reestablished back on the Thi Tinh, I motioned to Parker to haul ass and get back on board ASAP. I asked the tower for clearance and we were on our way.

As I cleared the Dau Tieng fence and rearmed the minigun, I flipped the radio back to troop Uniform so I could hear all the transmissions from the guys at the Thi Tinh.

The first thing I heard was Carriss yelling, "Turn left, turn left, One Seven . . . now straight ahead . . . straight ahead . . . there's an open area straight in front of you. Straight ahead of you, One Seven."

I immediately switched to Victor and transmitted to Sinor. "Three One, this is One Six. I'm just off Delta Tango. What's happening?"

"One Six, Three One. Bust your ass, bust your ass back here. One Seven is going down. One Seven's been hit and is going down!"

I was flying down so low that I couldn't pick up all of the conversations, but I did hear Willis say, "I think I can make it to the open area." That was the last thing I heard from him.

I climbed up to about five hundred feet and headed straight for the Cobra, just in time to hear Sinor say, "OK, he's down. The crew's out of the little bird and they both look OK. Looks like they both made it down OK."

I needed to get on top of Willis as quickly as I could to cover him. "OK, Three One, One Six is in hot. I'm on the trees. Have you got me in sight?"

Sinor rogered. "OK, One Six, I've got you coming in from the northwest. Crew looks OK, but I don't know how they're fixed for Victor Charlies."

I keyed Parker on the intercom. "Keep your eyes peeled, Jimbo, we've got a crew down. Stormer and Willis are on the ground. Watch your gun so you don't accidentally shoot our friendlies."

I made a low pass, turned right, and did a three-sixty on top of the crash site. I could see Willis and Stormer lying flat on the ground looking up at me. Willis had his PRC-90 emergency radio in his hand and I cranked in on the emergency Uniform frequency just in time to hear him say, "One Six, this is One Seven. How do you hear me?"

"OK, One Seven," I answered. "I've got you loud and clear. Are you OK, buddy?"

"Yea, man," he came back, "I'm OK, but the bastards are right over there. They're right over there, man." Willis pointed to the tree line over to his west. "They shot the hell out of me, Hubie!"

I hated it when anybody called me Hubie, but I guessed that this wasn't a good time to discuss it with Rod.

"Are you hurt?" I asked again.

"Negative," Willis answered. "Stormer's back hurts, but

he's OK. The dinks are real close, One Six. I can hear them. They're real close, I shit you not!"

I thought for a second, "OK, One Seven, put your head down. I'm going to come around hot and hose down that tree line on your west. You and Stormer keep your heads down."

I pulled the Loach around to the west, ran my gun stop to four thousand rounds per minute, and kept kicking right and left pedal, spraying minigun all the way down the tree line.

As I turned back to make another pass, I told Parker to get out a red smoke and let it fly. Then I came up to Sinor in the Cobra. "Hey, Three One, we've got a covey of bad guys in the tree line on the west side of the downed bird. When you see the red smoke, hit it! Don't worry about me, I'll be clear to the east."

"OK, you guys," I said to Willis, "stay low to the ground and keep your heads down. Rockets are on the way. You copy?" Then I jerked my tail up and accelerated eastbound.

Both Carriss and Sinor hit the tree line, and I could hear their rockets as I beat it out of the area. After about three gun passes I went back in to check things out. I circled around and hovered directly over Willis, Stormer, and the shot-up bird. At about thirty feet off the ground, I could look right into Willis's face. Normally, no matter what, Willis was always grinning. But there wasn't any grin on his face now. I think, for the first time since I had known him, he was actually scared shitless.

I could understand why. An aircrew downed in the middle of nowhere, with an enemy firefight going on, is totally out of its element. A scout pilot and gunner are used to having the advantage of height—being able to look down to see and shoot an enemy. They were not prepared to be in the middle of elephant grass over their heads, not able to see more than a couple of feet.

As I orbited tightly on top of them, I asked Willis, "What's it looking like down there now, One Seven?"

Rod looked up at me as he spoke back over his emergency radio. "Looks rough, One Six. There are bad guys all around us. I got gook chatter all around, a lot of voices on the west . . . no . . . on the east . . . ah, shit, I don't know . . . maybe on the south of us, too. They're shooting the hell out of things. Get us out of here, One Six!"

I got on Uniform to Sinor. "Hey, Thirty-one, Charlie's throwing everything but the kitchen step stool at One Seven. What's the ETA on the ARPs?"

"They're loading up now," Sinor came back. "They were on strip alert for another mission. It'll be another ten to fifteen minutes before they can make it up here."

I moved my bird out of the fire zone and thought for a second. "OK, Three One, they're hearing bad people all around them down there. We don't have time to wait. Have we got anybody in the neighborhood who can get in here now and pick up the crew?"

"Negative," Sinor came back. "I've been up on Guard, but no response. Nobody but us chickens around until we get the ARPs in here."

"OK," I answered, "why don't you and Three Eight cover us on both flanks, one on the left and one on the right. I'll make my run in between you from north to south. I'm going in and pick up the crew before those guys get blown away."

I rolled around and headed in directly toward the downed bird. "One Seven, this is One Six. I'm coming in to get you while the guns try to keep Charlie's head down on the flanks. You need to mark me a place where I can set down."

I studied the ground as I steered directly for One Seven's ship. It was fairly open, obviously the site of an old fire base right there near the Thi Tinh River. The high,

thick grass would make it hard as hell to see anything at
ground level.

As I reached the area, I arched slightly off to the side of
Willis's ship so I could land right beside it. I wanted it to
be a short run for Rod and Stormer, so we could get back
out of there in a hurry.

Sinor and Carriss rolled in and put rockets down on
both sides of the trees. Willis jumped up out of the grass,
holding his CAR-15 in both hands about chest high, parallel to the ground. He was rotating the weapon toward him,
signaling me to land.

I kept my eyes riveted on Rod while Parker watched out
the side for any trouble that might be coming from his
direction. I got right on top of Willis and decelerated to
almost zero at about four feet off the ground.

My rotor wash blew Rod's hair flat on his head. It also
parted the elephant grass around the site and laid it level
against the ground, almost like a giant's foot had stomped
on it and mashed it down.

Then, suddenly, as I began to let down the last few feet,
to my absolute horror I saw below me what appeared to be
about a ten-foot section of rolled-up concertina wire. As if
brought to life by my rotor wash, the barbwire roll began
to uncoil out of the elephant grass. It was almost like
watching a slow-motion movie.

Like a long, writhing serpent, that damned ugly section
of wire unfurled and came right up off the ground. It flut-
tered up over Willis's head, past the cockpit door, and was
sucked right on into my tail and main rotor blades.

In the instant it took to happen, there was nothing I
could do to stop the stuff from choking down my engine.
But before it did, the ship spun uncontrollably in two or
three violent revolutions before finally slamming down
hard into the ground, right beside Willis.

I immediately chopped the throttle, jerked up the fuel
shutoff knob, cut the master battery switch, and rolled out
the cabin door. Parker, unhurt in the slam-down, jumped

out of his backseat. We both looked up at the grisly strands of barbed concertina wire wound tightly around the Loach's main rotor system. The tail rotor was gone altogether, having separated completely from the aircraft.

"Ah-h-h SHIT, sir!" Parker spat.

"AH-h-h shit isn't the half of it," I sputtered. "Wait till I get my hands on that goddamned Willis!"

The enemy soldiers were going crazy with this new development—they now had two Loach crews down in their playpen. Bullets were flying everywhere around us, and I was madder than hell!

By this time, Willis was back up off the ground where he had thrown himself when he saw me spin in. He jumped into my face and hollered, "You stupid son of a bitch! What the hell are you doing crashing your stupid airplane into the goddamned concertina wire? You're supposed to be rescuing me. Now you break up *your* aircraft, and here we both are with no way to get our asses out of this mess!"

I shoved my face right back into his. *"You* stupid son of a bitch. If you had picked a better landing zone we'd *both* be out of here by now and not standing around with two busted-up airplanes in the middle of a goddamned firefight!"

Rod burst out laughing. I started to grin. Then both of us were laughing hysterically over the sheer insanity of the situation.

Our crew chiefs, however, failed to see the humor. Stormer, with an ugly cut on the side of his head, had set up his M-60 and gone prone on one side of Willis and me. Parker had done the same on the other side. They were ready to chop down anything that moved toward us through the grass.

Stormer looked around over his shoulder at us. "Jesus Christ, sir, can we get the hell out of here? Come on, Lieutenant Willis, we need to get out of here before Charlie decides to come and get us!"

That snapped us back to reality. Rod and I hit the prone

position and I grabbed Willis's radio. "Hey, Three One," I yelled, "One Six is now down with One Seven."

"So I see, One Six," Sinor came back. "Are you OK?"

"Both crews are OK," I answered, "but I've got a main and tail rotor strike. We've got to get out of here. Gooks are close by. Keep the ARPs coming. We'll sit tight till they get here. You copy?" He rogered.

Glued to the ground, we began to notice that hostile fire from the tree lines on both sides of us had stopped. The VC must have figured they had either gotten us or perhaps we had created so damned much fuss and confusion in cracking up two helicopters that Charlie had used the diversion to escape the area.

It was just a few minutes later that we began to hear the distant whop, whop, whop of Huey rotors. It was the ARPs coming inbound to get us.

I got on the emergency radio to Wayne McAdoo, who I knew would be in the lead slick. "Watch out, Two Six, we're in an old fire base here. There's an old tank run beside us. Set down on that road, because there's all kinds of crud lying around in the elephant grass. I had a rotor strike from concertina wire in here."

He rogered and moments later brought the ARPs flight of four slicks in on the old tank road about twenty yards away from us. The appearance of four more helicopter targets started the unfriendlies firing again, and they promptly drilled several AK-47 holes in McAdoo's tail boom. As we raised our heads, trying to see through the elephant grass, the ARPs off-loaded and made their way over to us, sighting on the downed helicopters. The point man and his backups flared out around us and kept making their way toward the enemy tree line.

Then Bob Harris, whose headquarters element was always back in the middle of the platoon, came sauntering up. Obviously feeling that the enemy had gone, Four Six had his CAR-15 drooped over his shoulder, his helmet off (as usual), his bright red hair and freckled complexion shining like a mirror in the sun.

He walked over to Willis's ship and took his time looking over the shot-up bird. "One Seven, what happened to you?"

"Damnit, Four Six, can't you see that I got the holy heck shot out of me?"

Harris smiled, stroked his chin, and then asked me, "So-o-o, One Six, what in the hell are *you* doing here?"

"I just listened to Willis," I answered, but before I could elaborate, Rod cut in.

"Come on, guys, cut the crap. I *would* like to go home!"

CHAPTER 16

TIT FOR TAT

A couple of weeks later, we had the opportunity to worry about Rod Willis again. This time, however, he was hovering over an old French fort in the bush, rather than over a young Filipino lady in the 1st Aviation club.

On 25 October, Rod and I took our VR-1 and VR-2 teams up to Dau Tieng to scout the eastern side of the Michelin rubber plantation. It was an area where Charlie was always up to something.

Rod took the VR-1 slot that day and I stayed at Delta Tango to relieve him on station with the VR-2 team. I was monitoring the radios back at Dau Tieng as One Seven reached the eastern side of the plantation and dropped down low level to start his patterns.

I listened more closely when I heard that Rod had found a recently trafficked foot trail that was leading him over toward one of the French forts left over from the Indochina war. Those old forts were readily identifiable by their unusual construction. They were made mostly out of earth that had been mounded up in either a diamond or triangle shape; inside the walls was a little parade ground with a flagpole, living quarters, and fighting chambers. These vacant fortifications were relics of the past, and no-body ever seemed to bother them or occupy them. That was why my ears perked up when I heard Rod say that he had seen movement inside.

I heard One Seven say to his gun, "I'm going around again to see if a party is going on down there that we weren't invited to."

Willis pulled his OH-6 into a hard right turn and rolled the ship so he could look straight down into the fort. I heard him again, "Damn, I just corralled myself a couple of Victor Charlies inside this old pile of dirt. I'm going to come around again and lay some 60 on them."

As Rod spoke, in the background I could hear One Seven's crew chief, Ken Stormer, let go with his door gun. Willis yelled, "I'm turning again. The dinks are running for cover in the wall, but Charlie Echo's on 'em with the 60. Shit! They just dove in a hole. We'll get these two. Stand by, we'll put some CS down on 'em. Stand by, stand by. Son of a bitch, we've got a jam on the 60. Stand by."

Willis apparently was hovering at the side of the entrance where the two enemy soldiers had disappeared into the fort's wall area. The crew chief was shooting into the opening when his M-60 jammed.

It just happened that on that particular day, Stormer had brought along another weapon he had wanted to test-fire. It was a CHICOM RPD, the Communist China version of the Russian PK .30-caliber machine gun. A quick glance at this weapon reminded you of the old U.S. Browning automatic rifle (BAR). It was a big, sturdy shooter with a bipod, but ammunition was fed to it through a drum magazine instead of a twenty-round box magazine as in the BAR. In an earlier action, Stormer had killed an enemy soldier who had been carrying the weapon, and the ARPs had liberated the RPD and brought it back to Stormer as a souvenir.

In the seconds that it took Stormer to shove his jammed M-60 aside and reach for his RPD, the two VC popped out of their concealment and threw a couple of hard AK-47 bursts at Willis's hovering helicopter. The crew chief's CHICOM went off in return, then we heard One Seven's voice, about two octaves higher: "Taking fire, we're taking fire. Hauling ass!"

There was a moment of dead silence on the radio. Then Ken Stormer's frantic voice. "One Seven is hit," he yelled. "We need some help!"

Stormer was intentionally transmitting outside the Loach. It was a good thing I could hear him because it was obvious that something had happened to the aircraft, or Willis, or both.

I quickly called my crew chief, Jim Parker, and my gun pilot, Dean Sinor (Three One), then announced a scramble to the Dau Tieng control tower and took off across the treetops of the Michelin.

The old French fort was located near the Boundary Road where it cut into the eastern side of the rubber plantation, about ten to twelve kilometers from Dau Tieng. I had been over it a number of times.

As I crossed the Michelin, I could see the Cobra circling in the distance. The gun pilot saw me and immediately gave me some assistance. "OK, One Six, I've got you coming off of Delta Tango. Turn left one zero degrees. One Seven will be at your twelve o'clock at two hundred yards."

When I turned left the ten degrees, I saw Rod's ship just as it was passing behind a bunch of trees. I poured on more coal. When I pulled in on Rod's right wing, the first thing I noticed was Stormer hanging out of his door as though he was trying to reach up front to his pilot.

I could see Willis in the cockpit. He was moving, so I figured he was still able to fly the aircraft. But a couple of things were totally out of synch with Rod's normal flying behavior. First, he was sitting upright, almost at attention, in his seat. That was unusual because Rod normally looked half-asleep as he flew: He slouched down in the pilot's seat with the cyclic between his legs, and worked the stick with barely discernible wrist movements.

That was the other thing that seemed so wrong: Willis was going berserk with wild, exaggerated moves on the cyclic stick. His arms were jerking all over the cockpit as he violently threw the stick forward, then back into his gut, then to the right and back to the left. I could see that he was getting lateral movement on the ship with the wild left and right swings of the cyclic, but his frantic fore and aft movements were producing no longitudinal change. He couldn't get the nose to go up or down and he couldn't get lift or descent.

I tried to raise Willis on Uniform. "One Seven, are you hurt? Are you OK, One Seven? What the hell is going on with your bird?" All I got back was a series of hisses and sucking and gargling noises.

"Come on, One Seven," I pleaded. "I'm right here on your wing . . . talk to me. Are you hit? Can you fly 'er down?"

Again, nothing came back over my radio but a faint hissing sound, like escaping air, and more god-awful gargling noises. It sent chills down my spine. I thought I had the answer: He had been hit in the chest and his lungs were collapsing. No way was he going to get the ship down.

I couldn't, however, explain why the cyclic wouldn't control his ship. There are controls on the top of the OH-6 that translate the cockpit movements of the cyclic pitch stick to the rotor head and blades of the aircraft. The stick is linked to push-pull rods through valvelike mixers that end up tilting the rotor head in the direction you want the aircraft to go. Thinking that I might be able to see if something was wrong with the rotor swash plate, I kicked my ship closer to Rod's and a little higher.

Some parts around the hub seemed to be moving in an odd way, but I couldn't tell what was causing the pitch problem. One thing was obvious, however—Rod was going to have to get his ship down.

As I kept up my one-way conversation—"Hang with it,

One Seven, you're OK. Try to slow it down. OK, One Seven, try to slow 'er down . . ."—I was frantically looking for a hole in the jungle where Willis could put the bird down.

I radioed the Cobras. "Look, we're in deep trouble down here. Better get Dustoff rollin' because it looks like One Seven is going to crash this thing."

Just then I looked up over the trees, and coming right up on our nose was an open area that looked about two hundred yards wide and maybe three hundred yards long. I practically pushed the transmit switch all the way through the stick and hollered, "Rod! Twelve o'clock, twelve o'clock. Take her down. Put it down, Rod . . . right at your twelve o'clock. Set 'er down!"

He must have heard me. I saw his arms and elbows flailing wildly trying to fight the controls, trying to get the aircraft to descend. Finally his nose started to come up a little, but that seemed to start his tail swinging.

I inched in closer on his right wing and tried to talk him down. "You're OK," I said. "Come on down, One Seven. You're doing OK now, drop her down. Take her on down, Rod."

I knew he was talking back to me because I could see his lips moving behind his mike. But I still couldn't hear anything except those terrible noises. I tried to see if he showed any other evidence of being shot. I didn't see any blood. Though he looked scared as hell, he didn't appear to be in great physical pain, as he would if he had a bullet through his chest.

Then his nose dropped. What he apparently had done, in desperation, was chop his throttle. That seemed to slow him down enough to do a hovering autorotation, which was enough to put his bird down in the open field before he overflew it.

As Willis's ship sank down, hit the ground, and jolted to a stop, Rod and Stormer exploded out of the helicopter and hit the ground running toward my bird like a couple of cheetahs pursuing their evening meal! As I landed close by, both pilot and crew chief jumped into my aircraft— Rod in front with me and Ken Stormer in the back. I yanked pitch and off we went, straight out of that unfriendly jungle.

Rolling out of the clearing, I had my first chance to look at Willis closely. Rod's face was pale and, for once, he wasn't wearing a silly grin. As soon as he got himself strapped in and his headset connected, I keyed the intercom. "Are you OK? What in the hell happened to you back there?"

Again, I saw his lips moving, but all I heard were the now-routine hissing, gurgling, sucking noises. Willis didn't look to me as though he'd been hit in the chest. If he had been, how could he have run the way he did, out of his ship into mine? And what about his chicken plate? I didn't see any evidence of bullet damage to that.

Then his helmet caught my eye. I punched the intercom. "How about your head—you hit in the head? Did one of the AK rounds hit you in the head?"

He nodded his head back to me . . . no.

I cradled the collective on my knee and reached over to Willis with my left hand. Then I twisted my finger into a small, ragged hole in the right side of Rod's helmet. "Son of a gun! Here I am thinking that you were all shot up and next to dead, and you haven't even been hit!"

What had happened, I surmised, was that a round had gone up through the side of Willis's flight helmet, splitting some of the electrical components in his headset, which caused all that sucking and hissing noise. His "gurgling chest wound" was plain old radio static.

When we got back on the ground in Phu Loi, it was interesting to observe how differently Ken Stormer and Rod Willis reacted to the harrowing experience they had just been through. Stormer jumped out of the back of the ship, a very concerned look on his face. He was obviously worried about the condition of his pilot. He was also mad because, in the couple of seconds it took him to reach for his RPD, Stormer thought his pilot and his aircraft had been hit by enemy ground fire. The only saving grace was that he himself hadn't been hit or hurt in the forced landing.

As soon as he discovered that Willis hadn't been hit, and that the downed OH-6 was going to be recovered from the jungle—with all his gear still in it—Stormer was a new man. He hit the hootch telling everybody what a fantastic job his lieutenant had done in landing the damaged airplane. After that, he couldn't stop talking about what a great weapon his RPD was, always adding, "Oh, by the way, if I cut the flash suppressor off the barrel, I'll betcha I can get at least a three-foot flame out of the end of that thing."

Rod was a different story. He was visibly shaken by his experience—quite a departure from his usual demeanor. This time Rod wasn't grinning. This time he was scared to death. The fact that an enemy bullet had gone through his helmet, not a fraction of an inch from his skull, didn't bother him a bit. But the fact that he wasn't able to control his aircraft nearly paralyzed him.

When Willis's aircraft was recovered from the jungle and inspected by maintenance, it was found that he had taken AK rounds through the push-pull tubes and the pitch change links on the rotor head. This was what I saw flapping around near the main rotor swash plate when I nudged in close to his ship.

A pilot, in order to fly his aircraft, must have instant reaction from his control input. With the damage Willis had sustained to his controls, he suddenly discovered that he couldn't get a nose up–down reaction when he pushed the cyclic forward and back. With a forward input of the stick, the nose, instead of going down, rolled to the right. Everything was about ninety degrees off its plane of reaction, and it took one hell of a piece of flying to keep that thing in the air. It would be like driving your car down a football field at a hundred miles an hour, with the field covered in a solid sheet of ice, then trying to turn left and stop your car at the same time.

It took a few days for Willis's "pucker factor" to finally relax. ("Pucker factor" is best defined as the reaction to a desperate flying situation, when your butt puckers to the point of almost sucking the seat cushion right up your backside. Unless you've experienced it, you couldn't really understand.)

Three days later, I had my own experience with the pucker factor. On 28 October, I was up to do an early morning VR of the Saigon River near fire support base Tennessee in the area of the Mushroom. Dean Sinor (Three One) was my gun and Jim Parker was my crew chief.

The Mushroom was a particularly hot area along the Saigon; it was a major dropping-off point for enemy troops and supplies destined for the Iron Triangle. They would hit the river up at the Razorbacks, their staging area, and bring their loaded sampans down to the western stem of the Mushroom. They'd get off the river there, march overland across the stem of the Mushroom, cross the river again on the eastern edge of the stem, then march on into the Iron T.

With the curfews we had imposed on river traffic, Charlie used the dark hours of the night and early dawn to make the trip down. As daylight broke, they'd duck into tributaries or little coves to avoid detection. They knew that anything seen on the river in daylight was fair game for our guys.

When we took off that morning, it was cool and damp. It had rained much of the night and into the early hours of the morning. The mist and fog from all that moisture hung over the river like a blanket, covering the nipa palms and elephant grass along the shoreline.

As soon as we hit the Phu Cuong bridge, I dropped

down as close as I could get to the surface of the river and moved out toward FSB Tennessee. I cranked up my speed because our mission that day was not to provide hard intelligence, but to find and intercept any enemy river traffic that dared to be on the river at first light.

The flight was uneventful all the way up to the Iron Triangle. Parker, in his typical fashion, lounged in the back cabin looking unconcerned, his left hand on the M-60, and one foot cocked up underneath his armor-plated jump seat. As we neared the Iron T, I noticed that there was some artillery coming out of Lai Khe, impacting in the northeastern corner of the Triangle; it didn't affect us as long as we stayed west of the river boundary between the 1st and 25th divisions.

I stayed down on the Big Blue at about ninety knots, flying at about two to three feet above the river surface. Flying was exhilarating, but always with the anticipation that a target could be just around the next corner.

As we skimmed along, I spotted the telltale sign of a cooking fire up ahead. It looked as though it was coming from my left on the 25th Division side of the river, on the western side of the Mushroom stem. Charlie probably thought he could get away with a cooking fire because of the low-hanging fog, which would absorb the smoke.

His logic was OK. My gun pilot couldn't begin to see the smoke from a cooking fire at his altitude—everything looked like one continuous gray blanket of fog. But humming along at river level, I could see that little plume of smoke curling up from about a mile away, before it had a chance to diffuse into the mist.

Not only could I see the campfire smoke, I could smell it. The air was thick with moisture and quick to carry the distinctive charcoal odor along, to be picked up by an aeroscout nose waiting for just such an enemy sign. Burning charcoal in Vietnam smelled just like the smoldering coals of a backyard barbecue at home. The only difference was the kind of food Charlie was cooking. So, from almost a mile away, I knew that we had bad people.

I radioed the gun, "Three One, this is One Six. I've got a cooking fire at ten o'clock long . . . about a mile. Must be a turn in the river up there."

"Ah, roger that, One Six," Sinor came back. "That's right up there in the Mushroom stem."

"All right, Thirty-one, I'm on it. It *is* a cooking fire and it looks like it's right on the river. I'm going straight at it."

Because of the kind of weather that day, I had no reluctance to head right for the fire. I stayed down on the river below the tops of the trees on the bank. I wanted to diffuse the noise of the aircraft and prevent Charlie from seeing us until I got as close as possible. That way I could pop up out of the river and engage the enemy party before any of them could take cover.

I increased power and nudged the Loach up to a hundred knots. I continued straight up the riverbed, flying between the two banks, right on the surface of the water, keeping my eye glued on the plume of smoke.

Getting the distance down to about five hundred yards, I keyed Sinor again. "I know you can't see me very well, but I'm going to make a run. If we've got something we can't handle, I'll put out some smoke."

As we rounded the northeastern edge of the stem of the Mushroom, I was ready with the minigun. Parker was leaning out of the aircraft and ready with his 60.

The enemy cooking fire was beyond the trees ahead of me. I jerked a cyclic climb and popped up out of the river over the trees. As I cleared the nipa palms, the fire was about fifty meters in front of me in a little open area. I snapped a decelerating right-hand skidding turn and looked straight down. There was a large black pot over the fire, and about eight to ten NVA main force troops sitting around waiting for breakfast. Some had weapons lying across their laps; others had them leaning against nearby trees. We had surprised them.

Instantly, Parker opened up with his M-60. I was so momentarily mesmerized watching Jimbo's tracers that I hardly noticed when some of the soldiers jerked their AKs out of their laps and began firing full magazines back at us as they jumped to their feet and ran for cover.

For several seconds, it was AK-47 versus M-60 in a vicious, blazing duel. I couldn't join in the exchange because I was too close to get an angle with the minigun.

We slugged it out for about a minute before I decided it was too hot to stay over the camp site any longer. I punched the intercom and hollered, "Dump a red, Jim!"

Parker, in his usual state of preparedness, already had a red smoke grenade attached to the carry handle of his M-60. He quickly pulled the pin and let the canister go. As I saw the red smoke land in the middle of the campfire area, I dumped the nose, pulled power, and keyed Sinor. "Red smoke is out, Thirty-one. Hit the smoke!" I moved off and watched as the Cobra made its run on the target.

Sinor sent pair after pair of rockets crashing into the camp site in what was becoming known as Three One's "ripple fire maneuver." On a normal Cobra rocket run, it was common for the gun pilot to shoot a couple of pairs of rocks, break at about a thousand feet, then come around on the target again. Since Sinor didn't break off his run until about five hundred feet from the ground, the several pairs of rockets that he could pump into a target created a ripple, or salvo, effect that was absolutely devastating.

Standing off a couple of hundred yards, I saw the enemy camp site literally explode with Sinor's fusillade of 2.75s. Then he broke away very low and punctuated his run with a trail of minigun tracers.

As the smoke and debris cleared, I went back up on Uniform and told Three One to cover me as I went back in for a BDA. In what had been the NVA camp site before Parker and Sinor's blistering fire, twelve enemy soldiers lay dead in a fifty-meter circle.

I keyed Uniform again. "Good shooting, Thirty-one.

Between your good rocks and my crew chief's 60, we've got about a dozen NVA regulars KIA down here."

"Roger, One Six," Sinor answered. "If you've done everything you need to do here, let's head on up the river on the VR. We'll either put the 25th or our ARPs on the KIAs later."

With that, I turned back toward the Saigon River. Just as I started to drop down on top of the Saigon, Parker keyed his mike and said, in his typical low-key way, "Lieutenant, if we've got all those bad guys back there taken care of, how about taking me to the hospital."

Thunderstruck by his calm, matter-of-fact statement, I jerked my head around. "My God!" I gasped. Parker was slumped over in his jump seat, his M-60 lying across his lap. Both of his hands were clasping his neck in a futile effort to stem the sickening squirt of blood that was streaming through his fingers.

I couldn't react fast enough. I punched UHF and told Sinor, "Three One, One Six has a crew chief hit . . . he's bad. Give me a steer to Doctor Delta and I'm en route direct. Clear my way with arty."

I heard Sinor shoot the message right back to Lai Khe artillery. "Red Leg, this is Darkhorse Three One. We've got a helicopter inbound to Doctor Delta with a wounded crew member on board. Shut down all artillery. I say again, need you to shut down all arty in the vicinity of the Iron T."

"Roger, Darkhorse," Lai Khe came back, "artillery is shutting down. However, we do have mortars coming out of fire support base Lorraine going into the northern edge of the Iron T. It will take us a minute to shut them down."

Sinor then keyed me. "OK, One Six, you heard. Lima kilo arty is shutting down, but it will take a minute or so to stop the mortars. Turn right and give me a couple of orbits."

"Negative," I yelled back. "Negative, Three One. I can't

do that. Charlie Echo is hurt too bad. I'm going to take it down on the deck and head straight in!"

I took another fast look at Parker. The blood pumping out of his neck was getting caught up in the slipstream and was splattering all over the gunner's compartment. I didn't have much time!

I took the bird down to ground level and picked up Highway 14. It was Rome-plowed, and the wide-open space gave me some standoff from the jungle as we headed east along the western edge of the Iron Triangle. Then I swung right and cut off over the northern edge of the Iron T directly toward Ben Cat, which was just south of the Lai Khe base. I kept looking back at Parker. The way he was bleeding, I didn't know how I was going to make it in time.

In a couple of minutes, I was closing Lai Khe. I notified Sinor that I was switching off fox mike and going up on Doctor Delta frequency.

"Doctor Delta, Doctor Delta," I called, "this is Darkhorse One Six inbound. I've got a Charlie Echo shot in the neck. I need a surgeon and litter on the pad." I was doing all the ship could give me, 110 to 115 knots, and passing over Ben Cat.

As I got back an affirmative to land at Lai Khe, I remembered to reach down and safe my minigun. Then I spun the Loach around and dropped it down right in the middle of the PSP pad that formed an H adjacent to the hospital emergency building entrance. A group of soldiers was waiting nearby with a litter.

The instant I touched down, I flicked the emergency shutdown switches, unbuckled, and jumped out of the ship. I wanted to help with Parker, but the medics were right there. They already had him out of the airplane and were jogging his litter toward the receiving hut.

I started to follow, but one of the medics called back to me over his shoulder. "Hey, Lieutenant, we need you to move your aircraft because we've got a Huey inbound with a bunch of wounded."

I continued to watch until Parker was out of sight, then climbed back into the Loach and moved the bird over about seventy-five feet. I ran back to the building where they had taken Parker. The emergency room was just inside the door. Moving quietly into the almost too familiar surroundings, I thought of the other times I had been there. Ameigh. Me. Now Parker.

Jimbo's whole upper body was a gory mess from the blood he'd lost. I figured that he must have been hit in the initial exchange when we first swooped in over the camp site—before Sinor made his run, before our BDA. Why hadn't he let me know so I could have gotten him out of there?

My thoughts were interrupted by the unmistakable sound of a Huey landing—the one, I guessed, that I'd had to move my Loach for. The emergency room double doors suddenly slammed open and litters of wounded from the Huey were rushed in. I was numbed anew by the appearance of the wounded men.

There were six of them, all young soldiers from the 82d Airborne who were also based at Phu Loi, just a stone's throw from my hootch. They had been, I heard the medics say, in an APC when the vehicle hit a mine while working near the Iron Triangle. The arriving soldiers were flash-burned, concussion-damaged, shrapnel-riddled. They were all desperately injured, and I knew that this was no place for me to be standing around.

I backed out of the room, still looking at the frantic emergency room scene and wondering how many of the men in there, Parker included, would see the light of the next day.

I waited just outside the emergency room for a while. Someone, I was sure, would let me know as soon as they had some word on Parker. The minutes crawled by like hours, and I kept imagining the life and death struggles that were going on in the next room.

Deciding that a cigarette and a little fresh air might help, I decided to walk down to the ship. In my earlier haste, I had left my pack of Marlboros lying on the console between the two pilot seats.

As I walked across the PSP, my eye caught Parker's bloodied chicken plate. It was lying in the middle of the landing pad, where the medics had tossed it. Almost hesitantly, I picked it up and turned it over in my hands. When I looked at it, it was obvious what had happened. There were five AK hits square on the front piece of the body armor. One of those, most likely an AK-47 armor-piercing round, had apparently deflected off the chicken plate and hit Parker in the throat.

Walking over to the Loach, I carefully laid Parker's chicken plate in the back cabin and just happened to notice that his M-60 wasn't safed. It had an ammo belt in it, with a round probably still in the chamber.

To fix that situation before an accident could happen, I crawled into the gunner's spot and sat down in Parker's jump seat. I lifted the feed tray, took out the belt of ammunition, and let it drop back down into the ammo box on the floor. Then I pulled the bolt back to clear the chamber and put the gun on "safe."

While I was going through those almost automatic motions, I began to look around the cabin interior. The mess was appalling! Blood and pieces of flesh were splattered on the sides and top of the cabin. My mind replayed the fierce exchange of gunfire at the enemy camp site, then Parker's unembellished announcement.

I felt sick to my stomach. I didn't know if it was the thought of Parker being hurt so badly, or the sight of those six young American soldiers brought in after being blown to pieces inside that APC. It didn't matter. I was suddenly violently ill. Gagging and vomiting, I added my own mess to the already defiled gunner's compartment.

The next thing I knew, one of the hospital medics was leaning his head inside the cabin door. "Are you OK, Lieutenant?"

I lifted my head out of my hands and answered in a shaky voice, "No, I really feel like shit."

"Yeah," he said. "We all do once in a while over here."

As the medic turned to walk away, I started to call after him, to tell him what I really felt at that moment. But I kept it to myself. I had just begun to think—for the first time in the ten months I had been in Vietnam—about the futility of it all. I was suddenly struck by the futility of doing the same thing day in and day out—the same kind of flying, the same kind of enemy, the same kind of engagements—only one day the enemy got hurt; the next day it was our own people. It seemed as though the only *real* significance of the war was tit for tat.

"Your door gunner's going to be OK." It was the doc, who had walked out to my parked Loach to give me the news. "He was hurt pretty badly, but it was a clean wound and he's going to make it." He confirmed that the enemy bullet had probably ricocheted into Parker's lower right neck. It just missed the jugular vein, went all the way through, and exited just below the base of his skull.

"If you gotta get shot in the neck," the doc said finally, "he did it the right way, believe me. We'll still have to evac him out of the country for convalescence, and we don't know right now if he'll make it back."

Doc's news that Parker would survive sent a shower of relief over me. But I knew Jimbo was gravely hurt and, at that moment, I couldn't help wondering if I'd ever see him again.

I got back to Phu Loi a little before noon that day and turned my Loach over to maintenance. I couldn't take it out again before it got a thorough check; besides, I didn't have another crew chief available to replace Parker.

So, to finish the VR we had started early that morning, I rode shotgun in Three One's Cobra. With another Cobra covering, we made up a red team and went back up the river to VR the area from the Mushroom on up to Dau Tieng. It was a fast, uneventful flight, but we did have the satisfaction of checking out the rest of the Big Blue leg that we had missed after locating that cooking fire.

I was dead tired when I went to bed that night. Parker was so much in my thoughts that I couldn't sleep. Pictures of the day kept running through my mind, and they all kept coming back to the hospital at Lai Khe. To the torn bodies of those young 82d Airborne soldiers as they were carried into the emergency room, to the doctors working over Parker.

The pictures kept coming: the bullet gouges in Parker's chicken plate . . . safing his 60 . . . getting sick and asking myself what in the hell was the sense of it all.

It all played back. Even my gruesome effort of taking the water hose that the medics had used to clean out the gore in the medevac Huey and hosing out the back of the Loach before flying it back to Phu Loi. Thank God, the blessing of sleep finally came.

Chapter 17

COURAGE

Three days later, the troop took another morale drubbing.

On 1 November, we had a hunter-killer team working up in the Thi Tinh River valley, just south of the Easter Egg. While down low working his pattern, the scout picked up a well-traveled trail that led to several bunkers of an enemy base camp. The scout put down a marker, the gun recorded the grid, and the contact information was radioed back to Darkhorse operations. As a result, the ARPs were scrambled to conduct a ground reconnaissance and find out exactly what enemy activity, if any, existed.

I had been assigned Scramble 2 on that day, so I stationed myself in the ops bunker to monitor the radios. I listened as the Horsemen, the four lift platoon Hueys carrying the ARPs, took off north, cleared the base fence, and headed on out over Dogleg Village.

"Two Six, this is Two Three," the number four Huey called flight lead. "You have a flight of four." Having thus been notified that his fourth Huey was up in trail, the flight leader, Capt. Morgan Roseborough, ordered, "OK, Horsemen, go echelon left at my command. Ready . . . now!"

The four Hueys broke trail, with number two sliding over to the left, number three holding its position, and number four sliding over left in behind number two—into an echelon left formation. Captain Roseborough then rogered number four with a couple of fast squeezes on his radio transmitter trigger.

Flying that day in Chalk One (the lead Huey), in addition to flight leader Captain Roseborough, were pilot Bob Holmes, new ARP platoon leader Lt. Jim Casey, crew chief Spec. 4 Eric Harshbarger, door gunner Danny Free, platoon medic Spec. 4 Mike Smith, and a full squad of ARP riflemen.

As the four Hueys passed over Ben Cat and headed toward the Easter Egg, the aeroscout at the contact point was asked to mark the LZ with a colored smoke. This not only told the Horsemen where to put down, but the flow of the smoke also marked the wind direction. In addition, the colored smoke provided a center sector marker for the Cobra, who would normally roll into the LZ for a couple of antipersonnel gun runs to clear any enemy hiding in the grass before the Hueys dropped in to unload.

Now well into the last leg of their flight to the contact point, the lift Hueys began to drop out of their fifteen-hundred-foot cruising altitude. Reaching about six hundred to seven hundred feet in their descent toward the LZ, Roseborough called for his flight to again go into trail.

Falling back into a straight line, and flying with their main rotor blades not more than ten to fifteen feet apart, the ARP-laden UH-1Hs turned onto final. They were fast descending into the marshy little clearing that had just been swept by the Cobra's several flechette runs.

At two hundred feet of altitude, Two Six came up again: "OK, Horsemen, we're clear to suppress both sides of the landing zone . . . no friendlies . . . suppress at my command."

The eight door gunners, with four machine gunners on each side of the formation, were to commence firing on his order and sweep the LZ on both sides before touchdown.

"Open fire," came Roseborough's command as the

flight of four passed through one hundred feet and steep-
ened its angle downward toward the yellow smoke-marked
landing point.

Suddenly the air was shattered by the sound of eight
machine guns going off all at once. Hundreds of 7.62mm
rounds hammered into the marshy earth with every-fifth-
round tracers spitting out a tongue of fire that streaked
into the wood line surrounding the LZ.

Bob Holmes, at the controls of the lead Huey, decelerated and brought the flight straight in toward the still-
billowing yellow smoke. He had made scores of hostile LZ
landings, and knew that he had to move in fast, touch
down for maybe three seconds to discharge his load of
ARPs, then get out before any trouble developed. Yellow
smoke swirled into Chalk One's windshield. Down . . .
down . . . the big Huey's skid shoes settled to within
inches of the marshy ground.

At the moment of near touchdown, a thunderous, blinding explosion erupted underneath Holmes's aircraft.
Chalk One lurched upward, shuddered in its death throes,
and dropped to the ground.

Following just feet behind, the cockpit crews of Chalk
Two, Three, and Four were horror-stricken by what they
had just witnessed. The Chalk Two pilot, who now became
flight lead, instantly realized that it was imperative to get
the ARPs out of the remaining three Hueys and clear the
LZ. He urgently yelled into his radio to the two ships
behind him, "Get out of here! Chalk One's hit. Door gunners, no suppression, no firing. Lift off and break right
. . . break right. Let's get out of here!"

Right on top of that radio message, the Cobra was directing his scout: "Get in there . . . get in there and
cover the LZ. You can't shoot, there are friendlies on the
ground. Don't know the situation . . . get in there and
advise."

By that time, the ARP platoon sergeant (who always
rode in the trail UH-1, whereas Four Six, the platoon

leader, rode with the flight lead) had run forward to assume command of the remaining three ARP squads and secure the landing zone. Though both painfully wounded, Bob Holmes and Doc Smith somehow emerged from the shattered Huey and began helping others out of the smoking, hopelessly wrecked aircraft.

Later the news came from the crash scene that Chalk One had hit a mine as it was about to touch down. It was thought to be a "tilt rod-actuated" mine, which was hard to see once planted because the body of it was covered with dirt. A fine, wire tilt rod poked up about twelve inches off the ground through the grass like a miniature car radio antenna. When something like the belly of an aircraft came in contact with the rod, the mine was actuated and set off the explosion.

The enemy had apparently realized that the clearing was a likely spot for our helicopters to land and insert troops, so they had planted the mine in advance. It was Chalk One's fate to set down on top of it. The resulting explosion ripped through the belly of the Huey—right under the passenger cabin—and sent fire, shrapnel, and tar-black smoke throughout the interior of the helicopter. Every person in the aircraft was injured in the blast. One man was killed.

Not only was the aircraft and its crew immediately out of action, but one fourth of the ARP platoon's personnel (including its Four Six, Lieutenant Casey) was lost as an effective fighting force. What more could Charlie have hoped for, with just one randomly placed mine?

Five days later, the fragility of a combatant's life in the Vietnam War was brought home again to the men of Darkhorse.

I was in the ops bunker monitoring radios because we still had a hunter-killer team out working a VR. Gun pilot Chuck Koranda (Three Nine) was teamed with aeroscout Joe Vad (Darkhorse Nine), and both were heading home from their reconnaissance area up in the Catcher's Mitt, just north of the Testicles. It was late in the day and they were anxious to get back to base while they still had good light. The Cobra was running a shade over a hundred knots at his usual altitude of fifteen hundred feet; Vad was trailing along about three to four hundred feet below his gun.

As the flight came up on an open field about two and a half miles south of Lai Khe, Vad's crew chief, Jim Downing, suddenly hit the intercom. "Hold it, sir," he yelled. "I've got movement down there in that field. I can't tell if he's friendly or a bad guy. We need to get down lower."

Vad took a fast look below and, apparently seeing something also, got on UHF to Koranda.

"Hey, Three Nine, this is Niner. My Charlie Echo has spotted movement down there in that open field. Why don't you do a left one-eighty while I go down and check the guy out to see if he's a friendly."

Koranda came right back. "OK, Niner, roger. I've got you covered . . . you're cleared down."

Joe Vad was a good scout pilot. He had been in the troop longer than I had, even though I was coming up on my year in country. Joe's scouting experience dictated the way he came in on the contact. He rolled out of altitude and quickly spiraled down to the deck, then he intentionally went low level a good distance away from the field where the individual had been spotted. Once down and out of view, he kicked up his speed, staying right on top of the trees as he steered toward the contact. That way his aircraft sound would be muffled and not give away his presence as he closed on the field. His plan was to push his bird up to about ninety to a hundred knots, pop up over the nipa palms, and drop back down again on top of the spot where the suspect was last seen. It was a quick and dirty tactic designed to surprise and gain a tactical advantage at the same time.

Vad's approach was perfect. With his finger tight on the

minigun trigger, and Downing hanging out of the back cabin door with his 60 at the ready, Darkhorse Nine suddenly dropped down into the clearing.

Sure enough, there he was—just off Vad's right wing, frozen almost in midstep as he walked across the clearing. The man's bulging eyes and terror-stricken face were plainly visible as the OH-6 swept by at nearly a hundred knots.

Downing shouted into the intercom, "VC . . . VC! He's a bad guy. Got a weapons pouch on his chest and some kind of weapon. Come around, sir . . . come around!"

Vad immediately hit his transmit button to Koranda. "I've got one VC in the open, Three Nine. I'm rolling in."

Nine turned hard right to come back around and set up an engagement solution for his minigun. By that time, the enemy soldier was running like a madman across the field, obviously trying to make it to the tree line before the Loach could come around on his tail and bring its guns to bear. After a fast one-eighty, Vad dropped down to about two feet off the ground and twisted on more speed to catch Charlie before he made the trees.

Closing fast, and ready to squeeze back the minigun trigger, Vad was within a millisecond of firing when suddenly the enemy soldier stopped dead in his tracks about a hundred yards in front of Vad's nose. The man whirled, swung his weapon up to his hip, and ripped off a totally blind burst of .30-caliber carbine toward Vad's onrushing bird!

One of those wildly fired enemy rounds crashed through the bubble of the aircraft and struck Joe Vad squarely in the forehead. The pilot lurched, instantly dead in his cockpit seat. Flying at at least eighty-five knots and now suddenly uncontrolled, the Loach rolled right, crazily back left again, then violently flipped over onto its back and into the ground. The aircraft exploded in a horrible, fiery blast, instantly killing crew chief Jim Downing.

Gun pilot Koranda was thunderstruck. Watching his scout like a mother hen from fifteen hundred feet above the clearing, he had seen Vad make a normal, calculated gun run on the enemy soldier in the field. Then, a split second later, he saw his scout lurch wildly, pitch into the ground, and explode in a ball of flame. The VC who had fired the fateful shot? Gone. He had vanished into the jungle.

Three Nine did the only thing he could do. He immediately radioed troop ops and scrambled to the scene what few ARPs the troop had left after recent casualties. When the ARPs arrived, Vad's twisted Loach was still burning. There was nothing they could do except secure the crash site until the fire subsided enough to remove the bodies.

To describe our feelings at the time is impossible. It was an incredible blow to us all. We had lost Sgt. James L. Downing, the courageous soldier who was my crew chief the day we made the blood drop to the ARPs pinned in the bomb crater. And we had lost WO Henry J. Vad, one of our oldest and most experienced scout pilots, a raucous, rowdy man who helped, in his own zany way, take some of the pressure off the rest of the platoon.

The next day, 7 November 1969, the 1st Aviation Battalion chaplain came to the unit to hold a memorial ceremony. Stationed on the table in the front of the room were the somber symbols of our Outcasts lost to enemy action: The steel infantryman's helmet with a fresh, new camouflage cover, an immaculately cleaned and oiled M-16 rifle, and a pair of fully laced, spit-shined boots.

As the chaplain spoke his few brief words, everyone had his own private thoughts of Downing and Vad. I thought of their courage and of their fear. I thought that one surely can't *have* courage without fear. Like all of us, these two men knew that every day they got in their aircraft, the odds were against them. Yet they flew with the confidence that they'd make it through, and they did the best they could do for their country.

CHAPTER 18

I THINK WE WON

I had been hearing that there would be a Christmas drop. In other words, if your tour in Vietnam ended near the first of January, as mine did on 1 January 1970, the army would make an effort to get you out of country in time to be home for Christmas.

The prospect was sounding better to me every day, but I really couldn't let myself think about it. A scout pilot whose concentration was distracted by anything—let alone the prospect of going home for Christmas—was looking to get himself and his crew chief killed.

In any case, I was getting very short in country. My picture in the O club was moving up to the number one position over the bar, and I would be transitioning out of scouts soon and passing on the platoon leadership to my successor.

Charlie, however, was unimpressed. The enemy remained extremely active and was showing himself in the field in even greater numbers. Still, the infamous NVA Dong Nai Regiment remained elusive. These North Vietnamese main force regulars were hitting our 1st Division units with disgusting regularity. Then, almost phantomlike, they would steal away into their sanctuaries, defying our best efforts to find them.

On 10 November, I was flying with a young new crew chief by the name of Bolin (Parker was still out with his neck wound and had, in fact, been sent back to Okinawa for recuperation). We were out on VR in the western Trap, not far from where I was shot down last time near FSB Kien.

I was down low working my patterns when we picked up movement of a single enemy soldier. We jumped him out in the open near a bunker complex. Bolin engaged with his 60 and dropped the man almost where he stood.

That brief encounter suddenly brought about fifteen more enemy soldiers into the fight—more than I could handle with my firepower. So I had Bolin drop a red grenade, and asked my Cobra to hit the smoke.

My gun that day was Bill Church (Three Six). He rolled in immediately and made several passes to hose down the area with rockets and minigun. Then I went back in for a BDA. But the area was still hot—I took so much enemy fire that I had to get back out fast before getting shot to pieces. I realized that we didn't have enough horsepower to neutralize the contact, so I went up on the FAC push and told Sidewinder that we needed him to bring in fast movers and whatever else he had available.

After two heavy air strikes, we inserted the ARPs and found a base camp with five enemy KIA. With the extraction of the ARPs, elements of the 2/2 Mech Inf—call signs Label Eight One and Label Eight Nine—were called in to stay in the area and sweep the base camp.

Since we hadn't known about this enemy base, I flew back out the next day to see if I could pick up anything else around that area. Sure enough, about thirty meters from where Label Eight One was working, we jumped one more enemy soldier. Bolin again quickly dispatched a stream of 60 fire that cut the man down.

Not finding anything more on the ground to warrant their presence, the 2/2 element was extracted on 11 November. We had apparently lost contact with the main enemy force that had occupied the base camp.

Just a week later (17 November), Rod Willis (One Seven), with Sp4 Joe Cook in the back cabin, was working a reconnaissance in the western Trapezoid. I was back at Phu Loi standing by on designated Scramble 1 alert. As usual, I was in the ops bunker monitoring the radios and drinking coffee.

One Seven was working down very low on top of the trees. He was just to the southeast of the Michelin rubber plantation and about four kilometers north and east of FSB Kien. The area was covered by very thick vegetation. The triple-canopy jungle was so dense, in fact, that Willis and his crew chief could catch only fleeting glimpses of the ground as they flew over. At one point, however, the foliage beneath them opened up and they thought they saw evidence of an enemy base camp below.

Rod immediately hauled the OH-6 around to go back for a closer look. As One Seven attempted to hover over the area in question, a fierce explosion suddenly erupted beneath Willis's Loach. The force of the blast violently rocked the scout ship and sent hot fragments flying, with some pieces of shrapnel catching Joe Cook in the left hand.

(Coincidentally, Cook was the second crew chief to be hit in the left hand in the last two weeks. It had also happened to Ken Stormer. This was mainly the result of how Loach door gunners positioned themselves in the ship; when at the ready with their M-60s, their left hands were forward out on the gun and more exposed.)

Willis didn't know what had exploded, but he could see that the explosion had obviously detonated in the top of a tree. The tree had nearly disintegrated, in addition to nearly blowing his aircraft out of the sky.

Though wincing with pain, Cook immediately began to throw M-60 fire into the enemy base camp area. A barrage of enemy weapons burst forth in response.

One Seven increased his speed and his radius of attack, and simultaneously broadcast a request to his Cobra that the ARPs be inserted to find out just what they had stumbled upon.

Major Moore was in the ops bunker at Phu Loi when the request came to scramble the ARPs. He quickly consulted his maps and surmised that the enemy outfit probably would try to make it back up into the Michelin and, ultimately, on into their sanctuary in the Razorbacks. With that thought, Six told One Seven to scout out an LZ to the north of his contact; then, if the enemy tried to make a run for it out the back door, the ARPs would be in position to block their escape.

Within thirty minutes, the ARPs were on the scene, led by the new Four Six, 1st Lt. Stuart J. Harrell, replacing Lieutenant Casey, who was badly wounded in the Hueymine incident. As ordered, Willis had picked an LZ north of where he had been rocked by the tree explosion.

Once the ARPs were down, One Seven established FM contact with the platoon's RTO and set about the task of steering Harrell's infantrymen through the dense jungle toward the enemy base area. Leading their ground movement was the point man, Pfc. William J. Brown. To work point, a man needed a lot of experience and almost a sixth sense to detect impending danger. Unfortunately, Private First Class Brown had very little of either. He had recently arrived in country and had just been transferred into the ARP platoon as a casualty replacement.

Willis shepherded the ARPs closer and closer to the enemy bunker complex. As he did, point man Brown became more and more cautious. Quietly, warily, Brown approached the first bunker.

When he was just a few feet away, Brown prudently moved off to the side and took up a position of cover to study the potential firing lanes of the enemy emplacement. As he crouched for a brief moment to observe his front, a single SKS carbine shot suddenly cracked out of the heavy undergrowth to Brown's flank. The ARP point man crumpled forward onto his face, dead before he hit the ground. The carefully aimed round was fired from another bunker to his left—one he hadn't seen.

The whole jungle area immediately erupted into a thunderous hail of gunfire, as the entire enemy camp opened up with its full complement of machine guns, rifles, frag grenades in layers, and RPG rounds, which seemed to be going off in the trees and everywhere else around the surprised ARP platoon.

In that initial enemy fusillade, six more ARPs went down, including the platoon's new Four Six. Both senior squad leaders, S. Sgt. Mark K. Mathewson and S. Sgt. James A. Jordon, were hit, Mathewson with a frag wound to the right leg and Jordon with a ripping gunshot wound to his left hand. Pfc. Sammy G. Lindsay crumpled to the ground with an enemy bullet piercing his left thigh. A CHICOM grenade went off right in front of Four Six, Stu Harrell, and the fragments shredded his left arm from shoulder to fingers. A Soviet RPG-7 round exploded right at the feet of Sgt. Allen H. Caldwell; he was dead before he hit the ground. Pfc. Robert L. Foster caught shell fragments in the thoracic area and was slammed down onto the blood-spattered jungle floor. The murderous barrage had, in just seconds, put one fourth of the ARP platoon out of action.

Flying right over the ARPs, Willis was enraged. But there was little he could do to help the aeroriflemen.

Aeroscout Bob Davis (One Three) had been sitting with his gun at Dau Tieng waiting to relieve One Seven on station. Davis and his Cobra immediately lifted off and arrived at the contact point in less than five minutes.

With One Three on the scene and briefed to provide cover over the beleaguered ARPs, One Seven beat it back to Phu Loi. Joe Cook, his left hand bleeding badly from Charlie's grenade fragments, needed attention beyond the makeshift bandage he had bound around his fist.

I was leaning over the radios back at the ops bunker listening when the troop commander walked in. Davis's gun, Bruce Foster, was yelling at One Three to get out of the way so he could shoot. Concerned that the ARPs were in over their heads, Six asked me to get cranked and fly up there.

I raced for my aircraft. Jim Parker met me there. Just back from his recuperation, he was scheduled as my Scramble 1 crew chief. Willis was also set to fly out with me. He had gotten Joe Cook to the medics, picked up another crew chief, and was ready to get back over the contact area.

As soon as we arrived at the scene, I dropped down low over the ARPs to get a firsthand report from Stu Harrell. I needed visual contact to assess what the enemy force was doing. Zeroing in on the area where Harrell was down with his RTO, I hit FM. "Four Six, this is One Six. What's your sitrep?"

I could see him take the mike from his RTO. "We're in bad shape, One Six. I've been hit either by a very well initiated L-shaped ambush or by a hell of a heavy and well dug in force."

"What about your people?" I questioned.

Harrell's bloody left arm lay limp at his side and, though his voice was sharp and clear, I could hear that he was in pain. "We're completely covered. We're taking very, very heavy fire . . . machine guns, rockets, grenades. I have at least two KIA, another five or six wou—"

His last words were smothered as the jungle below me opened up again with devastating fire—directed this time not only at Four Six's position but also up at me as I flew just twenty to thirty feet off the ground.

Damn! I thought. We must have stepped on a lot of bad people down there. It must be at least a company plus— or, more likely, a battalion-minus-sized base area. But, whatever, it's full of bad guys. They're mad, and they sure as hell want to fight.

I pulled an armful of collective and moved away until the firing calmed down. But I knew I *had* to get back in there and find out from Four Six where his men were.

I hollered back at Harrell. "Get me a position report on your people. I can't shoot until I know where all of your people are."

I swooped back in again—this time faster—to see if I could get a better picture of Harrell's situation. It was hot down there—like touching a light switch and having the lights come on. When I dropped down, the enemy fire came up. Instantly.

But this time, I got a better lay of the land. There was an old tank bust trail that ran from the southeast to the northwest, which roughly bisected what I could see of the enemy base area. Harrell's ARPs had been inserted in an LZ to the west of the trail. They had started advancing directly east toward the base camp when point man Brown was hit, and all hell broke loose.

The enemy base camp most likely had been alerted to impending trouble when the initial explosion had rocked Willis's ship. Probably reacting to the fact that they had been discovered, Charlie decided to get out of his base area and escape north before the aeroscout brought more firepower down on them. When the ARPs were inserted and headed into the base area from the west, they cut the old tank bust, just as troop commander Moore had foreseen. The tactic had blocked the trail and posed an obstacle to the enemy, who wanted to use it to escape north, back to their established sanctuary in the Razorbacks. The enemy soldiers were obviously getting set to ram the ARP's right flank from the south, bust through their ranks, then head on home up the trail.

With this scenario in mind, I dropped down again on a fast run-by. Looking closer this time, the only people I could see moving around the trail were Four Six and his RTO. I spotted several more of our people who were down and not moving. It didn't look good.

Harrell—typically not wearing his helmet—was crawling on the tank bust, M-16 in his right hand and dragging his shrapnel-riddled left arm beside him. Every few seconds, he'd pull himself up on his knees, brace his rifle on his bloody left arm, and fire off a burst down the trail to his southeast. He had plenty of targets down that way—and they could easily overrun his position and split the ARP blocking force.

It was a frustrating situation. The Cobras had worked up some artillery, and Sidewinder Two Two had been called to the scene to order up some of his fast movers. But we couldn't use any of that muscle until Harrell could get organized and tell us where our friendlies were located on the ground. Time was running out. It didn't look to me as though Four Six could hold much longer against what was surely a very large force hammering against his flank.

There was only one thing I could think of that might help relieve some of the pressure. It was not exactly a happy thought, but it was the only one I had at the moment.

I keyed the intercom to Parker. "OK, Jimbo," I said, "we've been here before. The only thing I know to do is get back in there low and slow, make ourselves enough of a pain in Charlie's ass that he pays more attention to us and leaves Four Six alone long enough to get his people reorganized."

I got back two quick squelches from Parker's intercom. He understood and was ready.

As I hovered back toward the trail, I hit the intercom again. "If you can definitely identify the enemy and can make a positive shot, fire at will, but don't hang it out too far. I'm hanging it out far enough for both of us. Here we go!"

I hovered in toward the contact point at a very low airspeed, fishtailing the boom and rocking the aircraft back and forth as I went. As I figured, the heavy fire was suddenly diverted to us. We began to take hits; we could hear and feel the rounds crashing through the Loach's skin and passing through the open interior of the ship.

I yelled to Harrell on the FM freq. "I'm trying to draw the fire away from you. Get your people into one area. Get yourself reorganized into a position so we know where you are and can shoot."

I could see Four Six trying to drag himself along the trail. His RTO, who had also been hit, was crawling slowly behind his platoon leader, painfully trying to keep up.

Still taking intensive enemy fire, I hovered right in over Harrell and looked him square in the face. He was badly hurt. I could see the anguish in his eyes. His left arm and hand looked like punctured raw meat, covered with blood and red dust from the trail.

He let his RTO catch up with him, then grabbed the radio handset. "We're in deep shit, One Six. I think I've got only about twenty men left to hold them off. They're trying to overrun us. Every time we move, they come at us again."

I empathized with him, but there still wasn't a damned thing more I could do. If the enemy had chosen that very moment to overrun our people down there, we couldn't have fired a single shot for fear of shooting into the midst of our own soldiers.

The stalemate continued for almost another thirty minutes. I would draw away from the trail for a minute or so, then run back in to decoy Charlie's fire. The ship was taking terrific punishment, but neither Parker nor I had been hit. Somehow, that sturdy little OH-6 just kept on flying.

The time was enough, however, for Harrell to get his people consolidated and organized on the trail. His earlier guess was accurate—he had only about twenty ARPs left to try to keep the enemy at bay.

Suddenly Four Six's voice boomed into my phones. "Fire's picking up, One Six. I think they're pushing . . . I think they're coming!"

I looked down. Harrell was standing up in the middle of the trail, pointing his weapon to his southeast and letting go with a full magazine of ammo. All his other ARPs were firing off in the same direction. The lid was obviously coming off.

I yelled at Parker. "Open up. Do what you can . . . fire at will!"

We found ourselves sitting on top of one of the fiercest firefights I had ever seen. We, of course, couldn't see the enemy, or whether Parker's barking 60 was knocking any of them down, but it was obvious that our twenty friendlies were holding off a much larger force . . . and could be overwhelmed at any second.

Four Six finally got enough of a breather to talk to me again, in a calm but noticeably apprehensive voice. "We got a lot of people down here, One Six. I shit you not, we got a *whole lot* of people, and they're trying to flank us. They're moving off the trail and heading northeast on our flank. My God, there's a lot of people down here!"

"Four Six, One Six. How many people *have* you got?"

"More than a hundred," he answered.

I silently mimicked his, my God! This was the largest concentration of enemy troops we had ever jumped in the field. And here we were not able to shoot at them, not even able to *see* them as they prowled around in the jungle.

Harrell came back again. "One Six, they're definitely moving toward the northeast. They're trying to move around me on my east flank and head on up north. What in the hell is up there that they want to get to so bad?"

While airborne, scouts never had the free hands or time to even look at a map, but Harrell's question caused me to reach for mine. I cradled the collective on my knee, then reached around with my left hand to pull the chart out of its pocket, located between the two pilot seats. I probably looked like a juggler in his first talent show as I tried to watch where I was going, handle the controls, and spread out the map.

But I managed it, and my eye quickly went to the grid where the ARPs were located on the tank bust trail. Looking north of that point about two hundred yards, I saw a little stream that apparently carried runoff water down south; at that point, the stream ran mostly east and west through some pretty rough terrain. It looked to me as though the stream formed a natural obstacle that the enemy would have to cross in order to escape north to the Michelin.

I decided that was a fine place to throw in some heavy stuff. Even though it was only a couple of hundred yards from our friendlies, we could blow up everything around the stream at that point and contain the enemy's flight.

I called up the FAC to set the plan in motion. "Sidewinder Two Two, this is Darkhorse One Six. You see where the Little Blue crosses through that low area just north of the ARPs about two hundred yards?"

He answered in his now-familiar Aussie twang. "Roger, One Six. I got it."

"OK, then," I continued, "I've got heavy enemy troops moving that way from the south, probably a hundred or more on the run, trying to flank our friendlies and didi to the rubber. You work up your first set of fast movers and I'll make one pass over and give you a smoke."

Sidewinder rogered, and I headed into a big sweeping right turn over the area just south of the streambed. As I looked down, I saw whole groups of underbrush and bushes, but they were moving! The "bushes" were, in fact, enemy soldiers with camouflage capes across their backs. They were obviously the lead element of enemy troops who had flanked Harrell's ARPs.

No wonder Four Six had his hands full. His little unit of twenty riflemen was all that stood between what must have been a battalion of bad guys and their otherwise open and clear flight path.

As I passed low over the stream, I yelled to Parker. "Smoke . . . drop the smoke . . . now!" and the red smoke canister was on its way.

I keyed Sidewinder. "Hit the smoke . . . red smoke is out. Enemy troops are moving north-northeast."

Sidewinder came right back. "Negative smoke . . . negative smoke!"

I jerked my head around and looked back. Damn. Parker's grenade had dropped in the stream and gone out.

We were catching it from below, taking hit after hit in the aircraft. But there was nothing left to do but pull around and make another run over the stream to put down a good mark for Sidewinder.

This time Parker dropped two grenades to avoid a repeat of the problem. He let the spoons fly and both grenades popped in his hands before he dropped them. Parker's gloves protected his hands as the smoke poured from the ports at the bottom of the canister. Red smoke billowed up at us as we hightailed it back toward the ARP's position.

We stayed down as low as we could, fairly brushing the treetops. I felt myself sucking down into the armor plate and tried to keep my pucker factor from totally eating the seat cushion.

Sidewinder's voice popped back into my phones. "OK, Darkhorse, we've got your marker. Get yourself clear. We're inbound with high-drag snake and nape."

As I pulled back in over the ARPs, the whole northern area exploded into great balls of black smoke and fire. Sidewinder's fast movers had just hung a detour sign on Charlie's back door escape route.

Through the roar of explosions I suddenly heard the troop commander's voice over VHF, advising us that he was overhead in his command Huey and that we'd soon have a supporting infantry company on the scene. The plan was to put about 150 troops on the ground, on the backside of the ARPs, engage the enemy soldiers that had flanked the ARP position, then drive the bad guys back toward their base camp.

About eight minutes later a flight of ten Hueys flew in. They descended below the tree line to my north, then took off again, apparently heading back to Dau Tieng for another load of friendlies.

Moments later, the Cobra broke in on FM. "OK, Four Six, get your heads down. Inserted unit reports fifty to seventy-five, possibly one hundred enemy troops coming your way. They have engaged and turned them around. They're now headed back toward your position on the way into their base area. They're comin' fast!"

I could tell that Harrell had read the Cobra's warning. He was crawling around to his men, checking their ammo and trying to get them better positioned to fight off the next onslaught.

The jungle below me literally exploded again with heavy firing. As predicted, the enemy soldiers were rushing back down the tank bust in full retreat, apparently determined to take down everything that stood in their way.

The ARPs opened up with blistering fire. The enemy surged ahead. The battle became head-to-head and nearly hand-to-hand before the surge of oncoming soldiers veered off the trail to the east, trying to bypass the merciless fire of Harrell's aeroriflemen.

Their move off to Four Six's flank gave me the room I needed to shoot. I dropped down to a hover over Harrell, dumped the nose, and took aim over the heads of the ARPs, pulling the minigun trigger back to the four-thousand-rounds-a-minute stop. Kicking left and right pedals, I hosed out everything I had into the tree line. Parker was leaning out of the right side, spraying down the running enemy soldiers with 7.62.

I suddenly went dry on the minigun. Parker, just seconds later, went dry on the M-60. We had thrown everything we had at them, except for Parker's backup. In desperation, he reached back for his "Thumper" and started pumping out M-79 40mm rounds, followed by a full thirty-round magazine out of his "stowed for last resort" M-16.

As abruptly as the furor had started, it ended. There was almost dead silence, except for the whirring sound of my rotors.

I maneuvered back over the ARP's position, about twenty feet off the ground, and looked down at Harrell. He was sitting on the ground, still without his steel helmet, legs stretched out in front of him. His bleeding, grimy left arm was cradled in his lap and his jungle fatigues were black with sweat. The bolt of his still-smoking CAR-15 was in the open position, indicating that he had expended his last round and was on an empty ammo magazine.

I could hardly tell if he was dead or alive, until he finally turned his sweat-drenched face up toward me. Through his pain and exhaustion, he managed a grin.

As I smiled and waved back, he reached over to his RTO and picked up his radio mike. He looked back up at me and flashed another big, toothy grin. "Goddamnit, One Six, I think we won!"

Chapter 19

FINAL SALUTE

Intelligence gathered from the scene, and from the enemy bodies found in the killing zone after that free-for-all on the tank bust trail, told us several remarkable things. Among them was an explanation of the explosion under Willis's ship, which had started the whole fracas in the first place.

As One Seven suspected, it wasn't a glancing RPG round that had been fired at his aircraft. It was, rather, clever use of a CHICOM mine, the enemy's answer to our claymore antipersonnel mine. These mines looked like big black metal frying pans and were filled with military plastic explosive and metal fragments. The enemy soldiers had jury-rigged one of them in the top branches of a tree, right in the center of their newly constructed, heavily fortified, and well-concealed base camp area. Their idea was that when an aeroscout hovered over the tree trying to look down through the jungle to find an enemy base camp, they'd blow the mine by remote control and get themselves a U.S. chopper.

They almost did. They did succeed in giving Rod's aircraft a hell of a jolt, plus wounding Joe Cook in the hand with one of the mine fragments.

Papers found on enemy bodies told us something else—

something that, even in light of all the casualties taken by the ARPs, was damned happy news for the 1st Division. The newly established enemy base camp belonged to none other than the infamous Dong Nai Regiment—the tough, elusive, hard-core NVA regulars we had been trying to pin down for months.

It was determined to be an enemy force of between one hundred fifty and two hundred troops. On that particular day, they had run up against twenty-eight men of the aero-rifle platoon, and had gotten their noses bloodied in the process.

The ARPs had been outnumbered six to one, and had it not been for the tenacity they exhibited that day, like so many other times before in the field, the Dong Nai would have gone through them "like crap through a goose," as General Patton supposedly said during World War II. The ARP casualties were extremely heavy, and came right on the heels of their terrible losses in the Huey LZ mine incident just days before. But these twenty-eight men, with an effective fighting force of only about twenty, prevailed against the toughest regular North Vietnamese Army outfit we knew about.

The 1st Division was anxious to deliver the coup de grace. We had hurt the Dong Nai badly up on the tank bust trail, but they were still a viable force. We wanted to put them out of commission for good.

Hoping to catch the rest of the regiment at home in their bunkers, division set up an Arc Light to hit a suspected jungle base area just south of the Michelin. The target for the B-52 strike was a grid "box" on the ground, two kilometers wide by five and a half kilometers long. We knew that this area contained a number of bunkers, connecting trenches, antiaircraft machine guns, and—we hoped—the remnants of the Dong Nai.

The "Big Belly" B-52 Stratofortresses were equipped with multiple ejector racks capable of carrying up to forty-two iron bombs, each weighing 750 pounds. The airplanes were to fly in from their base in Guam, unload their explosives into our designated box of eleven square kilometers, then head back home.

We had a hunter-killer team waiting at FSB Kien to do a BDA of the area just as soon as the B-52s finished their business. I was the designated scout, Parker was my Charlie Echo, and Bruce Foster was my gun.

At the precise stipulated moment, the Arc Light rained down. The three B-52s, so high that they were invisible from the ground, had been guided into our little grid box by radar. The explosions, even from our distance at Kien, were tremendous, almost as if we were standing right next to a rapid-firing 105. I thought about what it must have been like to be in that box, then put the idea quickly out of my mind.

With word that the last bomb was down, we headed out to take a look. I dropped low and looked down at the smoldering ruins through the gray dust that still hung heavily in the air. I was quickly convinced that absolutely nothing could have lived through that holocaust.

We saw nothing but huge bomb craters, stripped and shredded trees, and the remains of enemy bunkers that had either been blown sky-high or collapsed inward by the blasts. Any form of life surely had been pulverized.

I concluded that an Arc Light strike was the most terrifying sight a man could observe in war. Grimacing from the sight, I was ready to pull the plug and get out of there, leaving that awful grisliness behind. Then, suddenly . . . almost inconceivably . . . we began taking AK-47 fire.

I jerked my head left and right, looking for the source. My God, I thought, I don't believe this. There they were—muzzle flashes coming from a partially caved-in bunker that had incredibly missed being totally destroyed by the bombs. Whoever was on the other end of that assault rifle was mad as hell, and determined to take me down. His fire was sustained and accurate.

As I swung around to meet his challenge, the man broke

from the bunker ruins and dove into one of the B-52 bomb
craters, with Parker's rounds hot on his tail. He was barechested except for his ammo pouch and was carrying his
AK-47.

I keyed Foster. "Believe it or not, I've got one *live* enemy soldier down here. He was in one of the blasted-out
bunkers and has now ducked into a crater. We're going to
take him out and then I'll be right back with you."

Foster rogered, figuring that I couldn't expect much
trouble from one bomb-blasted enemy soldier hiding in an
open B-52 crater.

I swung around over the caved-in bunker, which was at
the edge of the crater. As I came in over the lip of the
crater, the soldier started shooting again. He was putting
out more fire on me than I was giving him back. This guy
was going to put up a fight.

Every time I hovered over the crater to get him, he'd
fire a long, point-blank burst, then disappear back into the
crater. I couldn't tell where he was going.

I backed off again, and decided to make a fast pass over
the crater so I could look for his hiding place. He managed to let me have another burst, and some of his rounds
hit the aircraft. But I was able to spot a hole in the side of
the crater, right underneath the rim. After the soldier
ripped off shots at me, he was jumping back into that little
hole where I couldn't see him.

"Damn it, Jimbo," I said to Parker, "get him. When he
sticks his head out, *get* him, before he gets us with one of
those bursts."

I made three more passes. Again, we exchanged rounds
with the little fighter. He hit us with a couple of shots and
we missed him completely.

In desperation, I keyed Parker again. "Goddamnit, give
me a gas grenade. We'll gas his ass out of there!"

Parker pulled the pin on a CS grenade and let it fly,
right into the center of the crater.

I backed off long enough for the crater to fill with

fumes, then eased the Loach in for what I thought would be my last pass. As I gently nosed over the lip, I was once again greeted by a sustained burst of AK fire. The guy now had me frustrated beyond belief.

The next time I came around on the crater, the enemy soldier was out of his hole. He obviously had a snoot full of CS and was having trouble breathing. But that didn't deter him. As I passed by, he raised his weapon and got off two rounds at me.

Then, nothing. He had either run out of ammo or had a jam. Now I had him. The source of my frustrating little hide-and-seek game . . . I finally had him cold! He was standing in the base of the crater, and I had no reason in the world not to take him out.

With a little bit of left and aft cyclic, I stopped my right-hand slide and came to a hover. I was fifteen feet over him, and we were looking at each other face-to-face. I dropped my nose a fraction. My finger tightened on the minigun trigger. But I didn't fire.

In the back of my mind was a clear picture of an enemy soldier in a trench, with his weapon aimed squarely at my head as I hovered over Bob Harris's ARPs in a similar crater. That guy didn't shoot . . . and he had me cold.

I snapped back to reality and looked at the enemy soldier in this crater. Still holding his weapon, he was looking at me with a question in his eyes—why don't you shoot?

This soldier had endured all that we could throw at him, and he had survived and persevered. His determination and stamina, and that of his countrymen, had sustained him so long, against so many adversaries. To kill this man would have meant nothing, and to kill an unarmed man would have been unforgivable. I said to myself, Let it go, let it go. This bastard deserves to walk out of here.

I hovered in again and looked him in the face. There was no expression. We were eyeball to eyeball for one last moment. Then I nodded my head at him in a salute of respect, dumped the nose, and pulled away.

We would both go home that day. It was my last mission of my first tour in Vietnam.

POSTSCRIPT

Vietnam in 1969 was a place where America's young people went because their country asked them to. While there, they did their jobs the best way they knew how, then looked forward to going home to their friends, families, schools, jobs. Hopefully, also, to the welcome and general approval of the American public.

As a new helicopter pilot, I felt fortunate to be assigned to D Troop (Air), 1st Squadron, 4th Cavalry, and the 1st Division's crack hunter-killer teams. I was proud to be a member of that unit then, and the years since have only deepened that feeling of regard.

In writing *Low Level Hell*, I have been fortunate to locate and talk to a number of the other young men who were in the troop with me in 1969. They were most supportive. First, for urging me to accomplish this task. But, more importantly, for their gentle prods to tell it the way it really happened, and to avoid making a "war" story out of it. I have done my best to do that.

It was my intent from the start to use real people, real names. To also—as nearly as I could—recount real situations happening under the circumstances and conditions that existed at the time. To do anything less seemed unfair to those I served with in the troop.

My sincere thanks go to all my comrades for reaching back in their memories, to help sharpen my recalling and recounting the events of 1969. Thanks, especially, to former Four Six, Bob Harris. He took the time, and the special effort, to give me his vivid reflections of that horrendous 28 July day that found him in a bomb crater, and me hovering over it with a box of medical supplies.

My appreciation, also, to Marianne Thornton of Morrison, Colorado. The hours she so willingly spent transcribing many of my audiotapes contributed greatly to keeping the creative process on track. Sandra Irelan and Jan Allgire spent a great deal of their own time typing and retyping drafts of the manuscript. Their gentle prodding kept me on course for nearly five years.

When basing a writing on fact, one obviously tries very hard to be as accurate as possible in all things. If inaccuracies have worked their way into this narrative, be sure that they are not there as the result of any intent on my part to misrepresent the facts. Of course, memory and records do not document the precise words spoken in casual conversations, radio transmissions, and other verbal exchanges. Much of the dialogue that I have written in this story, therefore, has been extrapolated from what the actual words spoken may have been. The reason, while always trying to keep the words in character with the person speaking them, was simply to make the dialogue more understandable and meaningful to the reader.

To further refresh my memory, and to maintain as high a degree of accuracy as possible, I have referred to numerous printed works, primarily operational and casualty reports of the units concerned.

In September 1971, I would return to Vietnam as a Cobra pilot for C Troop, 3d Squadron, 5th Cavalry working from Quang Tri airfield in I Corps, ranging from the A Shau Valley to the string of fire bases along the DMZ. When the unit deployed to the United States in February 1972, I elected to remain in-country and look for another cav troop. I was a single captain and intended to make the service my career. I was ultimately assigned to C Troop, 16th Cavalry operating out of Can Tho in the IV Corps tactical area. To my surprise this was again Darkhorse. The troop had remained in country in 1971 when the Big Red One went home to Fort Riley, Kansas, and had been redesignated as an independent troop of the 164th Combat Aviation Group.

My new position was aeroscout platoon leader—Darkhorse One Six—and asleep on my new bunk on the day I arrived was my new wingman, Captain Rod Willis.

> Hugh L. Mills, Jr.
> LTC, Aviation, U.S. Army

Shortly after his first tour in Vietnam, Hugh Mills jotted down the following thought: "Many volumes have been and will be written on the Vietnam conflict, for Vietnam was the environment in which doctrine for the employment of the helicopter in airmobile and air cavalry operations was written. This doctrine was written not by the major commanders in the Pentagon, but by the young officers and enlisted men in their daily struggle to complete the mission of combat."

As one of the army helicopter scout pilots who helped significantly in the writing of that doctrine, Hugh Mills flew over 2,000 combat hours in Vietnam, most of them logged in his near idolized OH-6A Loaches. He believed that going to Vietnam was just another chapter in his army career. But while he was there, he was going to carry the point of the bayonet to the enemy's throat every way he could, every time he could. Not for the glory, but in the honest hope that U.S. servicemen and women could soon go home victorious, and that the people of Vietnam could, after being ravaged by war for so long, reclaim their country and live in peace.

Though it is not in Hugh Mills's disposition to speak of

the honors that came to him flying scouts in Vietnam, one simply can't overlook the fact that Lieutenant Colonel Mills completed his service in Southeast Asia by being awarded: three Silver Stars, four Distinguished Flying Crosses, two Bronze Stars for Service, one Bronze Star for Valor, three Purple Hearts, seventy-two Air Medals (six with V for valor), three Army Commendation Medals (all with V device), one Vietnam Service Medal, one Republic of Vietnam Campaign Medal (six battle stars). And from the Republic of Vietnam government: Republic of Vietnam Cross of Gallantry (with Silver Star and Palm), Republic of Vietnam Technical Service Honor Medal First Class, and Republic of Vietnam Civic Action Medal First Class.

There's another thing about Hugh Mills that can't be overlooked, and that's the pride he takes in his own work, and in all those who worked with him in Vietnam. The men of D Troop (Air), and especially the aeroscouts of the Big Red One's Outcasts platoon, hold to this day a very special place in Hugh Mills's heart. In Vietnam, the life of a Loach crewman was only as good as the other guy in the ship. They depended upon each other to stay alive—there was probably no closer military comradery than that between the aeroscout crew chief and his pilot.

Mills, in my observation, has never lost the spirit of that comradery even though his tours in Vietnam ended some 22 years ago. He still tracks those who survived and made it back home, and takes pride in knowing the whereabouts of his fellow Darkhorsemen:

Tom Chambers   A corporate pilot now living in Texas.
Bob Davis   Retired from the army as a CW-4, now a corporate pilot living in Ohio.
Al Farrar   Now lives and teaches school in his home state of Rhode Island.
Jon Gregory   Retired from the army, currently a civilian airplane pilot for the U.S. Army.

Stu Harrell Now lives in Arizona and works as an investment planner.

Bob Harris Went to flight school after his Vietnam tours, became a pilot, and now serves in the army in Texas as a lieutenant colonel.

Bill Hayes Now works as a police officer in Washington, D.C.

John Herchert Lives and works as a sales representative in Missouri.

Bob Holmes Retired from the army, now an airline pilot.

Larry Kauffman Lives in Texas and is a regional sales manager.

Chuck Koranda Currently serving as a CW-4 in the Wisconsin Army National Guard.

Tim McDivitt Now lives in Florida, where he is in business.

Major Charles Moore Lives in Tennessee, where he is a county executive.

Jim Parker Lives in Georgia, where he is a factory supervisor.

Dean Sinor Lives in Kentucky, where he is a corporate helicopter pilot.

Ken Stormer Currently living in Texas, where he is a rancher.

Doug Veitch Retired from the army, now an investment planner in Colorado.

Rod Willis Retired from the army as a lieutenant colonel, now a consultant for army programs in Kansas.

Mike Woods Retired from the army, now a plant manager in California.

My association with Hugh Mills began in August 1986, when *Low Level Hell* went from an abstract idea to a tangible effort. My work with him over these past five years has been a rich, fulfilling, and thoroughly enjoyable experience. I marvel at his vivid recall of those Vietnam days, at his sly sense of humor, at his heartfelt anguish in recounting the loss or injury of one of his fellow Outcasts.

My days of military service are long since behind me, and I still look forward to the day when sound political judgments can eliminate wars. But until then, I can only hope that our country continues to generate and be blessed with people like Hugh Mills, a man with whom I heartily agree when he appraises Vietnam's controversial aftermath by urging, "Blame the war, not the warrior!"

Robert A. Anderson

GLOSSARY

ACAV—armored cavalry assault vehicle

AK-47—Russian 7.62-caliber assault rifle

APC—armored personnel carrier M113

Arc Light—B-52 bomb strike

ARP—aerorifle platoon

ARVN—Army of the Republic of Vietnam

BDA—bomb damage assessment

C and C—command and control

CAR-15—carbine version of M-16 automatic rifle

Charlie Echo—crew chief

chicken plate—ballistic armor chest plate worn by aerial crew members

CHICOM—Chinese Communist

claymore—antipersonnel mine, directional in nature

Cobra (snake)—Bell AH-1G helicopter gunship with two crew members

CS grenade—riot control agent similar to tear gas

DEROS—date estimated to return from overseas

didi—Vietnamese slang for get out of here

Dustoff—call sign of medical evacuation helicopters

FAC—forward air controller, prop aircraft for tac air direction

fast mover—jet fighter or bomber

Firefly—UH-1H mounted with spotlights, night observation devices, miniguns, and a .50-caliber machine gun

fox mike—FM radio frequency

frag order—fragmentary order (change in mission)

FSB—fire support base, home to ground and artillery units

Guard—emergency frequency, 243.0 UHF and 121.5 VHF

gun—Cobra or snake AH-1G gunship

hootch—Vietnamese dwelling or American tropical hut

Huey—Bell UH-1H troop carrier with two pilots and two door gunners

hunter-killer team—one AH-1G and one OH-6A

ICU—intensive care unit

KBA—killed by air

KIA—killed in action

Kit Carson scout—former VC or NVA who has defected to the ARVN and scouted for U.S. troops

klick—military slang for kilometer

Loach—Hughes OH-6A light observation helicopter (LOH) with one pilot and one or two gunner-observers

LZ—landing zone

M16—Colt 5.56-caliber rifle, standard U.S. government issue

M48—M-48A3 main battle tank with 90mm main gun

M113—U.S. armored personnel carrier, basis for ACAV

M551—Sheridan armored airborne reconnaissance vehicle with 152mm main gun

minigun—General Electric 7.62-caliber electric Gatling gun, 2,000 to 4,000 rounds per minute

NDP—night defensive position for armored, mechanized units

Old Man—military slang for commander

OV-10—North American Bronco FAC aircraft with one or two crew members

PBR—patrol boat, riverine with two .50-caliber guns, one .30-caliber machine gun, and one 40mm grenade launcher

Pipe Smoke—UH-1s and CM-47s that recover downed aircraft

PSP—perforated steel plank construction material

push—frequency

R and R—rest and recuperation

red team—two AH-1G Cobra gunships

RESCAP—rescue combat air patrol

rocks—rockets

Rome plow—heavy bulldozer for clearing jungle

RPD—Chinese copy of Russian PK crew-served 8mm machine gun

RPG—rocket-propelled grenade

RTO—radio telephone operator

satchel charge—explosives charge

SGM—Russian .30-caliber crew-served medium machine gun

sitrep—situation report

slick—UH-1H, same as Huey

snake and nape—retarded speed bombs and napalm

Spooky/Spectre/Shadow—USAF fixed-wing gunships—AC-47, AC-130, and AC-119

squadron—unit containing four troops

tac air—tactical air, same as fast movers

TAOR—tactical area of operational responsibility

TOT—turbine outlet temperature

troop—armor or aviation unit, two hundred men, forty vehicles

Uniform—UHF radio frequency

USARV—U.S. Army Republic of Vietnam

VC—Viet Cong

Victor—VHF radio

VNAF—Vietnamese Air Force

VR—visual reconnaissance
white team—two OH-6A scouts
Willie Pete—white phosphorus
Zippo—flamethrower mounted on M-113 vehicle